I0752405

the High School

CRITICAL ISSUES IN SPORT AND SOCIETY

Michael A. Messner, Douglas Hartmann, and Jeffrey Montez de Oca, Series Editors

Critical Issues in Sport and Society features scholarly books that help expand our understanding of the new and myriad ways in which sport is intertwined with social life in the contemporary world. Using the tools of various scholarly disciplines, including sociology, anthropology, history, media studies and others, books in this series investigate the growing impact of sport and sports-related activities on various aspects of social life as well as key developments and changes in the sporting world and emerging sporting practices. Series authors produce groundbreaking research that brings empirical and applied work together with cultural critique and historical perspectives written in an engaging, accessible format.

For a complete list of titles in the series, please see the last page of the book.

ALSO BY MICHAEL A. MESSNER

AUTHOR

Unconventional Combat: Intersectional Action in the Veterans' Peace Movement
Guys Like Me: Five Wars, Five Veterans for Peace
No Slam Dunk: Gender, Sport, and the Unevenness of Social Change (with Cheryl Cooky)
Some Men: Feminist Allies and the Movement to End Violence against Women (with Max A. Greenberg and Tal Peretz)
King of the Wild Suburb: A Memoir of Fathers, Sons and Guns
Out of Play: Critical Essays on Gender and Sport
It's All for the Kids: Gender, Families and Youth Sports
Taking the Field: Women, Men, and Sports
Politics of Masculinities: Men in Movements
Sex, Violence and Power in Sports: Rethinking Masculinity (with Donald F. Sabo)
Power at Play: Sports and the Problem of Masculinity

EDITOR

Gender Reckonings: New Social Theory and Research (with James W. Messerschmidt, Patricia Yancey Martin, and Raewyn Connell)
Child's Play: Sport in Kids' Worlds (with Michela Musto)
Sport, Gender and Sexuality: Critical Concepts in Sports Studies
Men's Lives (with Michael S. Kimmel)
Gender Through the Prism of Difference (with Maxine Baca Zinn, Pierrette Hondagneu-Sotelo, Amy M. Denissen, and Stephanie J. Nawyn)
Paradoxes of Youth and Sport (with Margaret Gatz and Sandra J. Ball-Rokeach)
Masculinities, Gender Relations, and Sport (with Jim McKay and Don Sabo)
Sport, Men, and the Gender Order: Critical Feminist Perspectives (with Donald F. Sabo)

The High School

Sports, Spirit, and Citizens, 1903–2024

Michael A. Messner

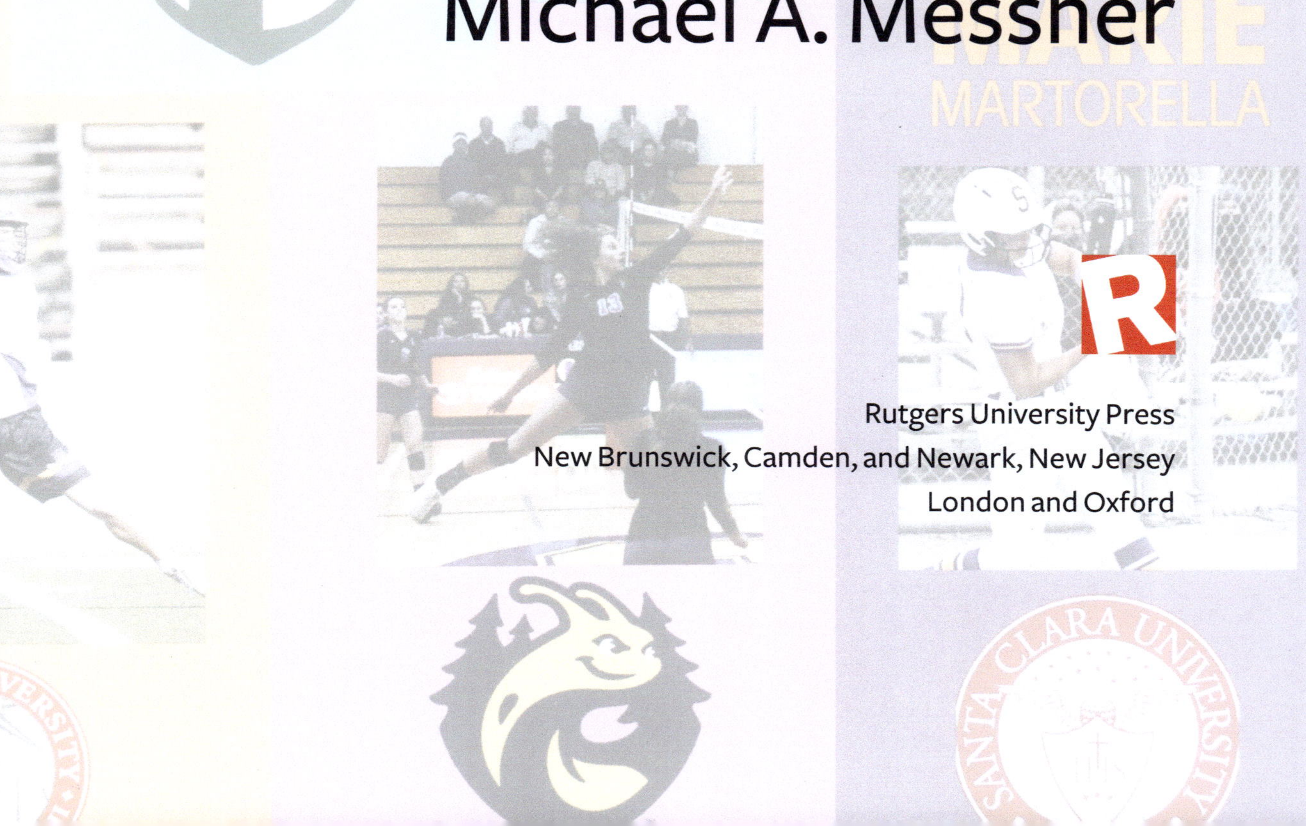

Rutgers University Press
New Brunswick, Camden, and Newark, New Jersey
London and Oxford

Rutgers University Press is a department of Rutgers, The State University of New Jersey, one of the leading public research universities in the nation. By publishing worldwide, it furthers the University's mission of dedication to excellence in teaching, scholarship, research, and clinical care.

Library of Congress Cataloging-in-Publication Data

Names: Messner, Michael A. author.
Title: The high school : sports, spirit, and citizens, 1903–2024 / Michael A. Messner.
Description: New Brunswick, New Jersey : Rutgers University Press, [2025] | Series: Critical issues in sports and society | Includes bibliographical references and index.
Identifiers: LCCN 2024027121 | ISBN 9781978839533 (hardcover ; acid-free paper) | ISBN 9781978839557 (epub) | ISBN 9781978839564 (pdf)
Subjects: LCSH: School sports—California—Monterey County—History. | School sports—Social aspects—California—Monterey County. | Male domination (Social structure) | Sex discrimination against women. | School sports for girls—Moral and ethical aspects. | United States. Education Amendments of 1972. Title IX. | Salinas High School (Salinas, Calif.)—Alumni and alumnae. | School yearbooks. | Collective memory. | Salinas River Valley (Calif.)—History.
Classification: LCC GV584.C2 M47 2025 | DDC 796.04/20979476—dc23/eng/20241121
LC record available at https://lccn.loc.gov/2024027121

A British Cataloging-in-Publication record for this book is available from the British Library.

rutgersuniversitypress.org

In loving memory of

Terry Messner (Salinas High School class of 1965),

Melinda Messner-Rios (SHS class of 1968),

Russ Messner (SHS coach, 1947–1977),

and Anita Messner-Voth (always far more than the coach's wife)

Contents

the High School

Introduction

EVERY SO OFTEN, MY COACH AT SALINAS HIGH SCHOOL would end basketball practice a few minutes early and direct his sweaty charges to sit on the floor in the center of the gym. There he would stand and deliver one of his speeches about "life." I found these moments excruciating because the coach was also my father. Tortured, I would pick at the rubber of my shoe, avoiding eye contact with my teammates as Coach Messner delivered lessons about honesty, hard work, making sacrifices for your teammates, and learning how to win and how to lose. He told us that how we conducted ourselves on and off the court as representatives of our school was preparation for the kinds of men we would later be—in our families, in our jobs, and as citizens. "Sports is life," he would routinely summarize.

The claim that young people learn things when they play sports is an idea infused into me since my childhood. Lessons learned through sports, I eventually realized, can be both fair and foul.[1] And later, as I became a sociologist, I noticed that many people think of "the sports world" as something separate from the rest of their lives, a less-than-serious place where they go to play, or to watch others play, as an escape from the routine worries, struggles, or drudgery of daily life. I came to see that the belief that sports is its own world, disconnected from the rest of social life, prevents us from clearly seeing the many ways that sports is intimately interconnected with families, the economy, politics, and the mass media. Sport also has a long history, especially in the United States, as a key part of high school life, helping to shape the ways we prepare youth for their future work and family lives. For over a century, high school sports has also been a powerful system through which schools and communities seek to build collective identity and group solidarity—more popularly thought of as "school spirit."[2]

Sometime around 2001 it occurred to me that looking systematically at high school yearbooks over a long period might open a fascinating window into the shifting meanings and organization of high school sports, cheerleading, and a range of other student activities. This idea likely came to me because I already owned about thirty copies of Salinas High School's *El Gabilan*—four of them my own books from when I was an SHS student from 1966 to 1970, and a nearly complete set of books from 1947 to 1976 that had belonged to my late father, Russ Messner, during his years as a teacher and coach at the school. Browsing through those books convinced me I was on to something. In 2003 I visited Salinas High School, and with the assistance of then-librarian Leslie Gruyer I accessed the school's archive of yearbooks and spent three days reading the books, taking notes and developing a template for a more systematic analysis. In subsequent years my attentions shifted to family life, administrative work at my university, teaching, and research on a range of subjects. For the next two decades, what I came to call "the yearbooks project" stayed on a very slow simmer on the back burner, though occasionally I would drag it forward and give it a quick stir. Meanwhile, I built my collection of yearbooks through a few donations from friends and family, an occasional find at a thrift store, and many targeted eBay buys.

In 2021 I could see some space opening in front of me and it felt like now or never, so I dove back into the yearbooks. By then I had gathered close to one hundred of the existing *El Gabilan* books for my personal collection. It was a thrill every time I acquired a copy, especially when I snared a very old one. I knew I would never possess the 1919 *El Gabilan*, however. Then-senior John Steinbeck makes several appearances in photos and print in this very rare book, the purchase price of which would be well beyond my means. I was able to view that book, and the other ones I do not own, during a trip to Salinas in the fall of 2023. I read each book from cover to cover, taking notes as I went, systematically counting pages devoted to one activity or another, tallying the numbers of students or faculty doing this or that, and deciding on pages to photograph for possible use in *The High School*. The research and the writing was a protracted and laborious grind, but it was in no way boring. I have never enjoyed a project so much.

Local Heroes and Towel Boys

Growing up in Salinas, California, in the 1950s and early 1960s, nearly everything I did with my friends revolved around sports. For adults, the seasons may have been fall, winter, spring, and summer; for us they were football, basketball, and baseball.

Figures I.1, I.2, and I.3. Tony Teresa, *El Gabilan*, 1951, 1952

The firmament above us was governed by larger-than-life heroes like Willie Mays of the San Francisco Giants, San Francisco Warriors center Wilt Chamberlain, and the balding but steely San Francisco 49ers quarterback Y. A. Tittle. We also grew up hearing the names of local sports legends, even ones whose heroics were before our time. Adults recounted the exploits of Tony Teresa, a Salinas High grad and three-sport star who decades later would be posthumously voted "Salinas Valley's Athlete of the Century" (Figures I.1, I.2, I.3).[3] While playing for Hartnell College in Salinas in 1952,

Figure I.4. My final year as towel boy, *El Gabilan*, 1966

Figures I.5 and I.6. *(opposite page) El Gabilan*, 1965

Teresa famously caught the winning touchdown pass in the Junior Rose Bowl with two broken wrists. He played for the Oakland Raiders and then returned to Salinas to become a successful football and baseball coach at Hartnell.

When I was a little kid, from around 1960 to 1966, I felt like the luckiest boy in town that I got to be the towel boy for my dad's basketball teams (Figure I.4). I relished walking through the Salinas High boys' locker room with my father late at night following the team's return from a road game in Monterey, Watsonville, or Santa Cruz. After the boys stashed their belongings in their lockers and left the building, my father would allow me to step into the suddenly still locker room to throw the breakers that shut off the lights. Just before doing so, I would glance at the wall far above, where the all-time records of Salinas High's track and field greats were chronicled. Eddie King, I could not help but notice, had set several of these records in the mid-1950s. Who was this Eddie King,[4] I wondered, and might my name one day replace his on that wall? (no, it most certainly did not). Tony Teresa and Eddie King were distant legends, but as my dad's towel boy in 1962, 1963, and 1964 I did get to witness Rusty Critchfield firsthand. Likely Salinas High's best basketball player ever, Critchfield was my boyhood hero. I practiced countless hours shooting hoops on our driveway, fashioning my outside shot after his, as I imagined replicating his greatness on the court

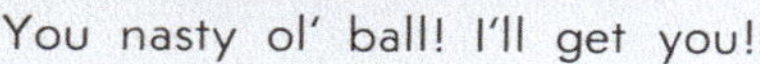

You nasty ol' ball! I'll get you!!

OK — NOW can I aim at the teacher?

(the reader need not skip forward to chapter 3 to discover that I also fell plenty short of this dream).

In retrospect, it stands out to me that my friends and I never questioned the fact that every one of these sports heroes, both distant and proximal, were all men. What I could not know at the time—and what readers of *The High School* will discover—is that the time during which I was growing up, the 1950s and 1960s, was a period when boys' high school sports were celebrated like never before. Meanwhile, girls' sports were at their nadir. Sports in my time, I can now see, was a powerful teacher of symbolic meanings about gender: boys and men excelled at sports; girls and women did not, perhaps could not. Even if a girl did have desire and potential to play sports—my sister Melinda, I believe, had such untapped ability—there was no avenue through which to develop skills and compete interscholastically. The *El Gabilan* yearbooks of that era starkly juxtaposed boys' sports in all their celebratory pageantry with a scant few pages of Girls Athletic Association (GAA) participants. At best, these brief spreads portrayed a random array of photos of unnamed girls playing sports in gym suits, often with no captions. At worst, the photos depicted girls in awkward positions, obviously failing to hit or catch a ball, with "humorous" captions that belittled their apparent athletic incompetence (Figures I.5, I.6).

Figure I.7. SUHS girls' baseball team, *El Gabilan*, 1920

These girls may have been terrific athletes, but who would know from the treatment they got in the yearbooks? The girls I did notice when I was young—and the ones on which the yearbooks lavished admiring attention—were the cheerleaders, popular girls (most of them white) whose job it was to root on and support the boys' football and basketball competitions. The messages about gender could not have been starker: boys take center stage; girls are on the sidelines providing supportive "spirit." This all seemed perfectly natural to me. Many decades later, as a sociologist, I learned that when social arrangements seem set in stone, as though reflecting the natural order of things, this shared belief becomes a powerful glue that holds together the status quo, however inequitable it may be.

Here is something else I had no clue of during my youth: a half century before my own high school years of 1966–70, the girls at Salinas High School enjoyed a vibrant interscholastic sports program, and their teams and games were treated respectfully in the annual yearbooks. Nor did I know that fifty or sixty years ago the cheerleaders were all boys, and they were called "yell leaders." I also never would have predicted that within a few years following my time in high school, many of the gender arrangements I had grown up believing were natural—including the fact that boys played sports and girls did not—would change dramatically. At first glance, *El Gabilan* photos of girls' teams in 1920 and 2020 (Figures I.7 and I.8) seem to show remarkable continuity over a century's time. But a closer look also reveals differences: Most obviously, the SHS girls in 1920 had a *baseball* team; in 2020 girls played *softball*. Why was this, I wondered? And looking only at these two snapshots in time erases another

Figure I.8. SHS girls softball team, *El Gabilan*, 2020

fact: for about a half century between those two moments, girls played neither interscholastic baseball *nor* softball. *The High School* chronicles the ways that sports, cheerleading, coaching, and student life in general have changed and how they have not, and how these changes and continuities are part of larger social contests over who counts as a fully enfranchised citizen.

This book reveals that there is nothing inevitable or linear about "progress." Rather, social change happens in fits and starts, moving forward, backward, and sideways. And when something that we might call historical progress does occur—the democratization of sports through the inclusion of girls and women, for instance—these changes do not happen by accident, or due to some benign "evolution." They happen because people organize, demand change, and crash through doors that had been previously locked to them. But doors, as we know, can swing both ways. Girls' and women's sports, a major focus of this book, are an excellent example of this. And yet many of our views of these matters seem frozen in time, mired in myth. Consider, for instance, a popular twenty-first century fable about gender and sports:

> *Once upon a time, girls were believed to be naturally unsuited for sports, and were not allowed to participate. Sports were set up exclusively by and for boys and men. But in the early 1970s, Billie Jean King beat Bobby Riggs in the Battle of the Sexes; girls sued Little League for the right to play baseball; and Title IX was passed, a national law that gave girls the legal right to equity in school sports. This opened the floodgates to girls' athletic participation. In the subsequent decades, tens of millions of U.S. girls and women*

have played community-based youth sports, school sports, and college sports. Today, though equity is not yet achieved, sport is no longer just for boys and men. Thanks to feminism and to Title IX, girls are free to choose to play sports, thus gaining access to the social and health benefits of athletic participation.

Most everybody knows this triumphant tale. Like any story that has legs, this one is based on some core truths. There is no doubt that girls' sport participation has skyrocketed in recent decades, and that high schools like Salinas High now accord more respect and devote more resources to girls' sports than in the past. And there is ample research that shows that parents tend to encourage their daughters to play sports, understanding that girls who play sports gain access to social and health benefits.[5] But we will see in this book that rather than reflecting some straightforward view of reality, the conventional story of girls' athletic progress outlined above distorts reality in three ways. First, it is a simplistic rendering of history, premised on a linear before-and-after view of progress. Readers of *The High School* may be surprised to learn that girls' interscholastic sports were thriving at Salinas Union High School, and nationally, during the first twenty-five years or so of the twentieth century, a full half century before the passage of Title IX. Second, the story narrates an undifferentiated view of girls and women, failing especially to account for the ways that class and race have differently constrained and enabled girls' and women's sports participation, in the past and in the present. We will see in this book that during the half century or so that preceded the 1972 passage of Title IX, girls' interscholastic sports were all but eliminated at Salinas High. But the girls who participated in the mostly intramural activities of the GAA during this time of doldrums for girls' sports were disproportionately girls of color. When girls' sports were revived in the 1970s and 1980s, white girls flowed enthusiastically into athletics. And third, while positioning twenty-first-century girls as fully empowered to choose sports, the story passively endorses the assumption that boys' relationships with sports are built into their nature, requiring no critical inquiry or explanation. This book challenges these commonsense understandings of the role of high school sports.

Salinas and Its High School

Situated roughly one hundred miles south of San Francisco and seventeen miles inland from Monterey, the city of Salinas, California, nestles near the head of the Salinas Valley, a rich agricultural floor walled in by the Santa Lucia Mountain range to the east and the Gabilan Mountains in the west. This latter range was described by John Steinbeck in his 1952 novel *East of Eden* as "light gay mountains full of sun and loveliness."[6] These mountains were also the source for the moniker chosen by Salinas High School for its annual yearbook, *El Gabilan*, which has been published every year between 1903 and 2024.[7] The 1905 *El Gabilan* was the first to include a

This Issue of EL GABILAN is Dedicated by

the Class of 1921

To the New High School,

Which is the Fulfillment of all Our Hopes

and Desires of the Last Four Years.

Figure I.9. *El Gabilan*, 1921

photograph of the graduating senior class. That all twenty of these students were apparently white reflected the demographics of the town that had been founded in the mid-nineteenth century mostly by settlers of European descent on land originally occupied by the Indigenous Ohlone people, and more recently by "mixed-race Mexican citizens known as *Californios*."[8] Salinas High School had first opened its doors in 1882 when the city's population was 1,884 people, about 5 percent of whom were Chinese, and nearly all the rest white (though people of Mexican origin were then classified as white).[9] In subsequent decades, the city's population grew steadily—3,304 people in 1900, 3,736 in 1910, 4,308 in 1920—and the high school outgrew its original campus on West Alisal Street.[10]

In 1920, Salinas Union High School celebrated its move to its current campus location. The building, situated in a position of prime visibility on North Main Street, was constructed in the Spanish colonial revival style so prevalent in California from the 1890s through the first two decades of the new century (Figure I.9).[11] Much has changed in the hundred-plus years since the new campus opened its doors to students: Salinas High School today employs more than a hundred teachers and scores of staff who serve roughly 2,500 students, 72.5 percent of whom identify as Hispanic or

Latino, 20 percent as white only, 2.1 percent as Asian, 1.7 percent as Filipino, 1.2 percent as Black or African American, and 2.5 percent as two races or more or "other." Two-thirds of the school's current students are categorized as "socio-economically disadvantaged," and 10 percent as "English learners."[12] Salinas High School's 93 percent graduation rate, and its 56 percent rate of graduates who meet the course requirements for admission to a California State University (CSU) or a University of California (UC) are a bit higher than those at the other four Salinas public high schools.[13] The size, diversity, and needs of the student population in 2024 are far cry from those of the school's early years. Salinas has grown to a city of more than 160,000 people, nearly 80 percent of whom identify as Latino or Hispanic, and a mere 12 percent as white only.[14] This dramatic demographic shift has been shaped by over a century of immigration, wars, booms and busts in the national and local economy, agricultural politics, and social movements for labor rights, racial justice, and gender equality—key elements of the story I tell in this book.

I title this book *The High School* for two reasons. First, until the private Catholic school Palma High opened its doors in 1951, and until North Salinas High became the town's second public high school in 1960, Salinas High School for three-quarters of a century was the only high school in town. Many of the school's buildings were demolished and rebuilt in the 1990s following the 1989 Loma Prieta earthquake, but designers wisely retained the original face of the lovely building, preserving the architectural gem of Main Street, images of which were frequently featured in the *El Gabilan* year after year. Though Salinas High School is no longer the only high school in town, it is still proudly referred to by many as "the high school."

The book's title also hints that *The High School* could be any public high school in the United States—especially those in small towns or suburban areas. The story I tell here probes how the local context of Salinas, California, especially the city's economic foundation in agriculture, has shaped the fluctuating demographics of the student population of Salinas High, as it is also the source of the school's mascot and public identity: the Salinas Cowboys. But it is also true that many of the high school activities I examine—sports, cheerleading, student government and clubs, and teen status systems—will be familiar to anyone who attended a high school in the United States, even though the meanings and dynamics of these activities vary with place and shift over time. I expect that many readers, in other words, will recognize aspects of "the high school" as their school.

High Schools, Democracy, Citizenship

As an American generic, "the high school" has long been a flash point for tensions in questions of citizenship, at the center of which are strains between the ideals of egalitarian democracy on the one hand, and on the other hand harsh exclusionary practices that reinforced hierarchies of gender, race, and class. A look at the early decades of Salinas High School offers a case study in how these tensions played out during a time of explosive growth of high schools across the United States in the late nineteenth and early twentieth centuries. The emergence of universal public education during that time was a response to strains generated by rapid industrialization and the expansion of wage labor, urbanization, bureaucratization, and changes in families. The political economy of the United States had long been structured by a fundamental contradiction. On the one hand, the ideal of political democracy was founded on the historically radical notion of equality for all citizens. On the other hand, from the nation's inception, a citizen was narrowly defined as a white property-owning man. Much of the history of the United States can be viewed as an ongoing effort—by working-class people, by women, by Black, Indigenous, and other people of color—to extend this ideal of political and legal equality to all.[15] Public schools have long been ground zero for these efforts.

Nineteenth-century reformers viewed public schools as an engine for producing democratic citizens. "The only pedestal on which Liberty can stand erect, forever firmly poised," asserted Philadelphia educator Thomas Dunlap in 1851, "is universal education." And the high school, Dunlap declared, "is the crowning stone in the arch [of the] noble structure of public education . . . It is the school of the Republic—it is emphatically the School of the People."[16] A half century later, school reformer John Dewey optimistically promoted universal public education as an institution that could make democracy possible in an economic system characterized by vast economic inequalities. In his 1915 book *Schools of To-morrow*, Dewey warned,

> It is fatal for a democracy to permit the formation of fixed classes. Differences of wealth, the existence of large masses of unskilled laborers, contempt for work with the hands, inability to secure the training which enables one to forge ahead in life, all operate to produce classes, and to widen the gulf between them. Statesmen and legislation can do something to combat these evil forces. Wise philanthropy can do something. But the only fundamental agency for good is the public school system.[17]

This was a heavy load of responsibility to place on the shoulders of public schools and their teachers. Indeed, subsequent critics argued that Dewey was overly optimistic about public education's ability to open avenues of upward mobility within a vastly unequal economic system. Economists Samuel Bowles and Herbert Gintis asserted in 1976 that "Education over the years has never been a potent force for economic equality . . . Schools justify and reproduce inequality rather than correct it."[18] And more recently, sociologist Thurston Domina collected data that show that schools function as "sorting machines" that actually *produce* inequalities, both within schools and in the greater society.[19]

For many, the bridge between the optimistic belief that education is an engine for equality and the pessimistic perspective that sees schools as largely reproducing

Future Homemakers of America

Seated are the officers of this organization and behind them are the members and advisors who have done a tremendous lot in helping the officers organize this club. Although this club is new, they have had several projects and plan for many more next year.

Figures I.10 and I.11. *El Gabilan*, 1959

social inequalities is the idea of *meritocracy*—the belief that individuals, no matter where they start in life, can use education as a ladder for upward mobility. To be sure, some individuals in every generation benefit from education in just that way—tugging themselves to higher levels of social status, income, and wealth than their parents had enjoyed. This reality is at the core of the American Dream. In my classrooms for over four decades, I saw this dream in action every day in the lives of first-generation college students for whom their poor, working-class, or immigrant parents had made huge sacrifices to make college attendance possible. But inspiring stories of individual success through education also exist alongside a grimmer reality, that stubborn structural factors in schools tend largely to *reproduce* existing group-based inequalities. The meritocratic ideal in schools has long been limited by the vast differences in the social class of students' families of origin, individual inequalities that are exacerbated by stubborn imbalances of support for schools across neighborhood and districts. Further, entrenched biases led to decades of disproportionate academic tracking of youth of color and students from poor or blue-collar families into vocational courses, while middle- and upper-class white students were channeled into college-preparatory tracks.[20]

Schools like Salinas High School also informally tracked students into extracurricular organizations and clubs—for instance, for several years during the mid-twentieth century the "Future Homemakers of America" club prepared girls for hearth, home, and motherhood while the "Future Farmers of America" readied Salinas High School's boys for their anticipated adult roles as leaders in local agriculture (Figures I.10, I.11).

Future Farmers of America

Officers: Dick Cota, Sentinal; Auston Faust, Reporter; Jim Violini, Vice President; Bruno Sala, President; Stanley Poncetta, Secretary; Lawerence Zediker, Treasurer; John Payne, Recreation Leader.

In *The High School* I show how these routine practices shaped campus life, and in the process reinforced beliefs and assumptions about gender and sometimes also about race and class.[21] But the 120-year scope of this book also invites us to see how, over this span, many once-routine customs and rituals—including the fact that Future Farmers of America was for boys only—were challenged, reformed, or even sometimes abandoned.

High School Sports and Citizens

For many decades, standard academic tracking coupled with shared assumptions about gender and race tended to exclude or marginalize girls and students of color at Salinas High School. The historian Carol Lynn McKibben observed that in the 1950s, "the Salinas schools . . . privileged whites (especially from elite agricultural families) and native English speakers. Salinas schools showed both class- and race-based bias in teaching and assessment of students."[22] By contrast, sports was viewed by many as a level playing field, a purely meritocratic site. Based entirely on their ability, hard work, and accomplishments, athletes make the team or they do not, earn playing time or they sit, are honored for their athletic accomplishments or not, win sports scholarships to college or they do not. Everett Alvarez, a 1955 Salinas High graduate and one of the school's most famous alums, seemed to take for granted that as a Mexican American boy from a poor family, he would face social divides and inequities.[23] But McKibben notes that Alvarez, for whom a high school in town would be named in

Figure I.12. Everett Alvarez, *El Gabilan*, 1955

1995 in honor of his service as a returning prisoner of war during the American war in Vietnam, "believed that sports served as a great equalizer for youth in Salinas: 'We were athletic. I became part of the guys that played football and ran track. We were pretty much integrated. We all played sports, basketball, clubs, I hung out with the kids who played sports. We are friends to this day'" (Figure I.12).[24]

Sports may have been a great equalizer across race and class lines for an athletically inclined Mexican American boy from "the other side of the tracks" like Everett Alvarez, and likely for others too. However, to adapt a satiric phrase from George Orwell's famous allegory *Animal Farm*, all kids at the high school may have been considered equal, but some were clearly more equal than others.[25] Sports was never a simple site of equal opportunity and meritocracy for all. During the era that Everett Alvarez enjoyed sports as a place for cross-ethnic camaraderie with other boys, the inclusion of boys of color on sports teams was spotty, and opportunities for girls to participate were nearly nonexistent. Instead, as I will show in this book, over time, sports has been a site of shifting inclusion and exclusion.

People have played games and sports around the world for centuries. But the organized, rules-based activities we now call organized sports were formed and institutionalized mostly during the late nineteenth and early twentieth centuries. Many of the same sports are today played in nations around the world, but there is something very particular about sports in the United States. I have noticed that scholars and students who are visiting the United States are frequently surprised to see the level of resources that U.S. high schools and universities devote to sports, and they are amazed to witness the prominence and centrality of athletics in campus life. The history of school sports tells a very American story about citizenship. The story I tell in *The High School* begins in 1903. But in the preceding decades of the mid- to late nineteenth century, sports were taking institutional shape across the nation. This was a time of disruptive social change, when modernization, urbanization, and an active women's movement were challenging conventional ideas and undermining the institutional foundations of work, families, and gender.

A powerful formative change of the nineteenth century in the United States was the perception that the conquest of the "frontier" was now complete. Conceptions of manhood among American men of European descent had long been shaped by a rugged individualism expressed through conquering nature—California, of course, being a final stop in the westward push of settler-colonists' "manifest destiny" in North America. With no more of the continent left to settle, with Indigenous peoples largely wiped out or subjugated,[26] frontier manhood eventually faded into myth. It was celebrated in literature and film and sometimes symbolically revived in politics (through Theodore Roosevelt in the first decade of the twentieth century and through Ronald Reagan in the 1980s famously linking frontier themes with militarism to revitalize a supposedly sagging American masculinity). The migration of families from farms and villages into urban areas separated men from activities such as hunting and fishing that had helped to define preindustrial manhood. Modernity had a particularly unsettling impact on middle-class men's lives, with the rise of bureaucratized work eroding the practical relevance of physical strength in everyday life. As boys were increasingly left in the care of women—with their mothers at home and women teachers in public schools—men also became uneasy about their sons' masculine development.[27] Prominent fiction of the mid-twentieth century—for instance, Arthur Miller's 1949 play *Death of a Salesman* and John Steinbeck's 1961 novel *The Winter of Our Discontent*—explored these themes of eroding manhood in modern society.[28]

All of these changes combined to kindle what historians have called widespread "fears of social feminization" among nineteenth- and early twentieth-century men.[29] In response, men flocked to an exploding number of fraternal organizations. American studies scholar John Ibson reveals that in the late nineteenth century, "When the nation's entire population was only around 75 million, lodges enrolled more than 5 million (between a quarter and a third of all adult males) in nearly six hundred different orders," including "the Masons, Odd Fellows, Knights of Pithias, Grand Army of the Republic, Modern Woodmen of America, and Improved Order of Red Men."[30] In these groups, bonds among men were cemented with practices roughly (often crudely) adapted from premodern, even tribal rituals that symbolically reconnected men with nature. Near the start of the twentieth century, U.S. men also imported a recent British creation, shaping the Boy Scouts of America as a way for urban men to remove boys (and themselves) from the supposedly feminizing influence of cities, schools, and women and instead reconnect them with nature and helping them develop traditional manly skills.[31]

U.S. colleges and universities were sites where nineteenth-century men—especially white middle-class men—organized informally to create fraternities and competitive sports as a kind of "revolt" against their supposedly feminized and "bookish" professors, thus forging ways to celebrate physical toughness and competition, and in the process countering fears of feminization in education and in their future professional careers. The creation of fraternities and sport as a closed world for elite white men helped to solidify their traditional power and privilege over poor and working-class men, men of color, and women. Universities first tried to suppress fraternities and sports, seeing them as uncivilized and unruly. Eventually, though, college administrators decided that frats and sports could be better regulated if institutionalized and integrated into campus life.[32] American high schools would not be far behind in similarly building in boys' sports as a central part of school life.

The nineteenth-century institutionalization of sports in schools and colleges managed to elevate the ideal of male bodily superiority in a context where opportunities to express male superiority were shrinking. But sports were also meaningful not simply as an expression of men's power. As I learned in a life-history study I conducted in the 1980s, middle-aged men who are former athletes do say that they miss the competition and sometimes also the respect and accolades they got from their visibility as jocks. But the main thing they miss is the connection and closeness with teammates that they enjoyed as young athletes. Sports offers boys and men the opportunity to experience a kind of bounded intimacy with each other, meeting a human need that is too often thwarted in modern society by cutthroat competition, homophobic fears, and lessons that boys learn from an early age about the importance of containing their more vulnerable emotions.[33]

The history of sports as a site first created by and for elite white men is in many ways the history of the United States in microcosm. Women and men of color—especially African Americans—struggled long and hard to compete in U.S. sports at the highest levels, as illustrated in the oft-told stories of baseball's Negro Leagues, Jackie Robinson's heroic struggles to gain inclusion and respect in previously white-dominated pro baseball, Althea Gibson's greatness in tennis, and Paul Robeson's breaking of college football's color line at Rutgers University.[34] The opening-up of sports across racial groups that continues today both reflects and helps to drive ideas and organizational practices that expand national ideals about who qualifies to be seen as a full-fledged citizen. This has been true of sports and gender as well. As we will see in chapter 1, the creation of school sports at the start of the twentieth century as an exclusive realm for boys and men did not blossom unchallenged. The late nineteenth- and early twentieth-century women's movement that pressed for the right to own property and vote was accompanied by a surge of women's claims to bodily strength and autonomy. Feminist celebrations of the rise of the "New Woman" included expansive physical activity and athleticism, a social movement clearly portrayed in the first two decades of Salinas High School yearbooks.[35]

Yearbooks, History, and Nostalgia

The High School is the result of my close reading and interpretation of the *El Gabilan*, Salinas High School's annual yearbook, from 1903 through 2024. I combed each yearbook cover to cover, paying special attention to changes and continuities in the meanings of sports and cheering at the school, while also exploring connections with other aspects of student life over the 120-year span. I read each book systematically, deciding along the way to reproduce certain photographs that illustrate important patterns and changes. My analysis sits on a foundation of my years of work in the academic fields of sport studies and the sociology of gender. But as much as this book is a product of the head, it is also a project of the heart, drawing inspiration from my deep connections with Salinas High School, my alma mater and also the school my sisters Terry and Melinda attended and where my father was a longtime coach.

Yearbook photos, with their captions and text, are a unique window into the ways that high schools in general, and sports in particular, have been key drivers of shifting gender, race, and class formations. Yearbooks, like all windows, can sometimes be clear, other times foggy. And windows are always bounded by frames that create vantage points that reveal some things while concealing others. One pitfall about which I was constantly aware, but likely managed still to fall into, was what cultural anthropologists have called "the big man bias," the tendency for researchers to fix their eyes on the most visible individuals who hold power and high status in a community while ignoring or giving short shrift to lower-status, less-visible members of the group. In her study of gender in elementary schools, sociologist Barrie Thorne noted that when she forced herself to look away from the high-status kids, the loudest kids at the center of activities on the playground, and instead focused on the quieter, perhaps lower-status and marginalized kids, she started to see and understand more about the routine ways that gender operated in kids' worlds.[36]

High school yearbooks, as it turns out, have their own built-in "big man bias." They routinely devote more space and more honor to higher-status students and their activities. Extending the metaphor of a high school yearbook as a "window," we might imagine how the large picture window of a house typically invites an outsider to gaze into some of the home's higher-status furniture and activities—the living room, perhaps the dining room, where everything looks good and tidy—but the shuttered smaller windows of the rest of the house might veil a messy kitchen, unkempt bedrooms, or a decrepit basement. So too, yearbooks are like large picture windows that typically focus the gaze of the reader on the most valued and honored features of a high school.[37] I tried as best I could to read outside this dominant frame that focused so consistently on the most loudly trumpeted kids and their activities, and instead to probe what the writer Tillie Olsen called "unnatural silences," the muting or suppression of the experiences and voices of those from marginalized and lower-status groups.[38] But in the end I was best able to focus my observations on the most evident themes in the yearbooks, doing my best to interpret the meanings of what was "inside the frame" and what was left to the margins or the shadows.

The Salinas High yearbooks from 1903 to 2024 are the primary source for the story I tell in *The High School*. The length, content, style, and template of the books changed gradually over the years (I discuss my strategies for meeting the challenges of analyzing the yearbooks in the Appendix). The body of *The High School* is divided into five chapters, each covering between twenty-one and twenty-seven years. The decision as to where to draw the line between eras—what historians call "periodization"—cannot help but seem a bit arbitrary. After all, was 1925 (my dividing line between chapter 1 and chapter 2) all that different from 1926? Most big social changes do tend to unfold gradually, so there was clearly no way for me to create neat divisions between my chapters. But my decisions were not entirely arbitrary: epochal events like the two world wars, bursts of feminist activism in the early twentieth century and in the 1960s and 1970s, and the local event of the rebuilding of the Salinas High campus in 1999–2000 were all jolts that accelerated social changes and were thus useful points of demarcation in my story.

My analysis of the yearbooks was deepened and broadened through my reading of works by scholars who have studied Salinas and California history, the history and sociology of sport and physical education, and race and gender inequalities in schools. In chapter 3, I draw on a few of my own memories to supplement my story, as this period of 1947–74 includes the quarter century during which my father was a coach at the school, and the four-year stretches when my sisters, Terry and Melinda, and I attended Salinas High. In chapters 4 and 5 I add some texture to my story with a small number of interviews with former and current teachers, coaches, students, and administrators at Salinas High.

Gazing back to our high school past cannot help but be an exercise in nostalgia. There is a veritable industry of popular film and music that fixes our gaze on a rose-tinted rearview mirror that recalls high school years as a time of innocent fun, young love, and adolescent hijinks, while also probing the trials, tribulations and challenges that many youth have faced in navigating their high school years.[39] Indeed, a stew of pleasure and pain permeates the history of popular film and music about high schools.[40] Many movies engage high school life—*Rebel Without a Cause* (1955), *The Breakfast Club* (1985), *Back to the Future* (1985), *Ferris Bueller's Day Off* (1986), *Election* (1999), *Mean Girls* (2004), *Hairspray* (2007), or *Ladybird* (2017)—with a complicated critical nostalgia that spotlights the cruelties of high school cliques and hierarchies, especially for kids who are outsiders to the school's status system. Popular music has routinely zeroed in on high schoolers' romantic yearnings, alongside their alienation and angst. The Beach Boys' 1963 rah-rah celebration of school spirit, "Be True to Your School," stands out as an anomaly. For the most part, much of the appeal of rock and roll of the 1950s to the 1970s—like Chuck Berry's 1957 "School Days," Alice Cooper's 1972 "School's Out," or Pink Floyd's 1979 "Another Brick in the Wall"—was pitching teen music as a means of escape and freedom from high school rules and drudgery. In subsequent decades, punk, metal, grunge, and hip-hop artists took up the banner of rebellion against the enforced conformity, sexual repression, jock-cheerleader-led status hierarchies, bullying, racism, or sexism that youths routinely bumped up against in high schools.

It is no doubt pleasurable to dive into this sort of nostalgic remembering, whether it be through film, music, or browsing old high school yearbooks. It is common for large pluralities of people to look back at an idealized past, remembering it as so much better than today. A Gallup poll found that 62 percent of Americans agreed that people were happier and more content a generation earlier, and Roper found more than half of polled people saying that young people had more common sense thirty years earlier. Those two polls were conducted in 1939 and 1949, respectively. Since then, national polls consistently show that a plurality of the population—especially middle-aged and older people—continue to look with fondness at "the good old days"—usually thirty or forty years ago—as a better time than today. In the closing decades of the twentieth century, the backward gaze was commonly toward the 1950s as an ideal time. We can see this in the Salinas High yearbooks of the 1980s, when students enjoyed 1950s dress-ups and dances that echoed popular films and television shows like *Happy Days* that idealized 1950s youth culture. More recently, people have started to look back fondly at the 1980s or 1990s.[41]

We should be wary of a ubiquitous nostalgia industry that plays on this inclination to look back on the "good old days" by tweaking the hope that if we simply buy this product, or cast a vote for that politician, we might return to an idealized past that, sanitized of its warts and moles, we imagine to be a time so smooth, so simple, and just plain better than our chaotic present.[42] That sort of one-dimensional nostalgia can be a myopic trap that, by ignoring the inequities or even the horrors of the past, locks us into a stagnant present. But stepping into nostalgia need not require also donning a set of historical blinders. Nostalgia, I believe, has gotten a bad rap. The philosopher Grafton Tanner says as much in his book on the politics of nostalgia, noting how the word's meaning has been paradoxical from the moment it was formed in 1688, when the Greek root *nostos* (yearning for home) was joined with *algea* (pain) to form the noun *nostalgia*.[43]

Reading, photographing, and analyzing 120 years of Salinas High School's *El Gabilan* yearbooks certainly steeped me in a paradoxical sense of nostalgia, my feelings oscillating between yearning and loss, joy and pain, laughter and criticism. My deep dives into the musty old books triggered sensory recall: the smells of the boys' locker room, the sounds of the creaky old wood gym floor under my feet as I drove for a layup, the embarrassment I can still feel from my awkwardness at school dances on that same gym floor. The yearbooks' images and comments on the school building itself—so visible from Main Street—is a recurring theme in the books, as students expressed a sense of pride in the beauty of the structure, despair as it was allowed to decline into disrepair, and eventually renewed pride as it was rebuilt. I shared these feelings as I read the books. The images of the old building conjured in me a yearning ache as I recalled the warm ring of the high school's bell tower chimes, the aural backdrop in my childhood home three blocks from the school to which, for three decades, my father would walk to teach every day, and where my sisters and I would traverse our own high school years. The heartfelt remembering sparked by these books also kindled, sometimes simultaneously, a painful sense of loss—of a time that can never be recaptured, of my father, mother, and two sisters now long dead—and sometimes a sense of outrage or shame from the yearbooks' portrayals of decades of inclusion of some students and exclusion of others, practices that were both routine and celebrated. In *The High School* I hope to mobilize for the reader a productive nostalgia that joins the pleasures of looking back with a critical analysis of what the books portray, and sometimes what they downplay or ignore.

EL GABILAN
June, 1904
Vol. I, No. 6

MERRY XMAS
EL GABILAN

EL GABILAN
1910

EL GABILAN

EL GABILAN
MAY
1915

EL GABILAN.
1916

EL GABILAN
1919

EL GABILAN
1920

EL GABILAN

JUNE 1924

Rack-a-tacka, rack-a-tacka, rack-a-lack rye;
Back-a-tacka, back-a-tacka, back-a-tack bye;
Rack-a-lacka, rack-a-lacka—Me, O my!
Purple and Gold! Salinas High!
Wow! Tiger! Wow!

—FOOTBALL YELL, *EL GABILAN*, 1904

Chapter 1

"All Prejudices Have Been Swept Away" 1903–1925

I THUMBED THROUGH THE 1919 *EL GABILAN*, eagerly scanning the photos of the boys' basketball and track teams, searching for the face of Salinas High School's most famous alum. Glancing over my shoulder, Lisa Josephs chuckled. "I can always tell it's John by the ears," she said. The helpful archivist at the National Steinbeck Center in Salinas was right. The tall, stern-faced boy was recognizable by his protruding ears, made even more prominent by his adherence to the shaved-at-the-temples haircut style of the day (Figure 1.2). In addition to being on those two sports teams, John Steinbeck was elected the 1919 senior class president, had a lead part in the class play, and was an associate editor for the yearbook (Figure 1.3). From all of this, I might have inferred that young John was a star among his classmates. "But this is misleading," Steinbeck's biographer Jackson J. Benson concluded. "Salinas High School had at that time only twenty-four graduating seniors. Nearly everybody was involved in some activity, and about half of the class appears to have been involved in everything that went on. Steinbeck," Jackson concludes, "was a failure as an athlete . . . Despite a willingness, he was heavy, slow, and not well-coordinated. He was also a bust in drama."[1]

Still, I surmised, because the yearbooks of the first two decades of the twentieth century were largely literary journals, chock-full of student-authored short stories and poems, surely the boy who would go on to win the 1962 Nobel Prize for Literature must have distinguished himself with a sterling piece of fiction or poetry. Not really,

SUMMARY

of Salinas vs. Monterey. Championship game. April 28 1921 at Salinas.

	AB	R	1B	PO	AV.
Humphries	6	2	2	2	.334
Bordges	6	4	3	1	.500
Shepherd	6	2	3	2	.500
Brum	6	3	4	2	.667
L. Nissen	6	4	4	2	.667
E. Koue	6	3	2	3	.334
H. Nissen	6	3	4	2	.667
A. Koue	6	0	3	4	.500
K. Gross	4	2	0	4	.000

Gilroy Girls forfeited the baseball game with Salinas because they would not play with a soft ball as the rules required, but had been practicing with regulation boys' ball and mitts.

SEASON'S AVERAGE G. C. C. A. L. GAMES

	G	AB	R	1B	PO	Av.
Humphries	3	20	9	10	8	.500
Bordges	4	20	9	10	8	.500
Brum	3	20	13	14	4	.700
L. Nissen	3	19	12	11	5	.579
A. Koue	3	19	5	4	12	.210
H. Nissen	3	16	8	9	6	.562
E. Koue	3	17	12	7	5	.412
K. Gross	3	15	8	7	9	.466
Rasmussen	1	4	1	1	3	.250
Shepherd	2	15	8	7	5	.466
*E. Bickmore	2	1	0	0	1	.000
*Thurlby	2	1	0	0	1	.000
*Worth'ton	2	1	0	0	1	.000
Total		169	86	79	63	.462

* Played only 2 innings.

Four games won; one forfeiture.

Figure 1.1. Champion Salinas Union High School baseball team, *El Gabilan*, 1921

it turns out. But Steinbeck did pen a page-long piece titled "How, When, and Where of the High School," the sarcastic tone of which struck a different chord from the usual earnest timbre of the student editorials of the era:

> Math is the science of getting the best mark from the least work. There is always a large class in Freshman algebra, the only conceivable reason being that the Freshmen are not given very much choice in the matter. After the first year, some are still fired with the zeal of an Archimedes (we don't know what that means but doesn't it sound grand?) but most of the students exhibit real intelligence and avoid math . . . The English room is the sanctuary of Shakespeare, the temple of Milton and Byron, and the terror of Freshmen. English is a kind of high brow idea of the American language. A hard job is made of nothing at all and nothing at all is made of a hard job. It is in this room and this room alone, that the English language is spoken. After taking English for four years we wish to advise Freshmen to use nothing but second hand books; they make the course much easier.[2]

Figure 1.2. (*left*) John Steinbeck (*center right*), *El Gabilan*, 1919

Figure 1.3. (*right*) *El Gabilan*, 1919

John Steinbeck left no mark in the literary sections of his school's annual yearbooks, but his three sisters did. Olive Esther Steinbeck was the "school notes" editor of the 1910 yearbook. During her junior year in 1911, Elizabeth Ann "Beth" Steinbeck's story, "Little Ysabel," appeared in the yearbook, and as a senior in 1912, Beth's "Sweet Briar," a poem about a rose, was published in the *El Gabilan*. As a sophomore in 1919, John's younger sister, Mary, published in the yearbook "Dismissed from the Service," a short story about a wartime aviator named Bugs. As a senior, Mary was the *El Gabilan*'s literary editor, and she saw two of her prize-winning pieces appear in the yearbook: "The Survival of the Fittest," an empathetic story about a high school boy who is shunned by his peers, as well as her poem "On a Mother's Birthday."

In microcosm, the Steinbeck siblings illustrate part of the story I will tell in this chapter about the earliest years of Salinas High School's annual yearbooks. The first decades of the twentieth century were times when girls and women, especially those who came from white, educated families, were breaking down barriers and claiming space in public life. Following decades of feminist activism, U.S. women finally won the vote in 1920, and for several years during the 1910s and early 1920s girls' and women's sports were flourishing. More young women were attending college. Beth Steinbeck went to Mills College in Oakland, and Mary Steinbeck attended Stanford University. But this time of expansion and ascent for girls and women was also a time of backlash, with limits being imposed just as girls were trying to push into new territory.

John Steinbeck quit Stanford University after a year or so, returned to Salinas, and worked off-and-on for nearby Spreckels Sugar—most productively at a night desk job that gave him time to sketch out story ideas. Over the next decade he muddled toward becoming one of the most celebrated authors of his time. Meanwhile, sister Esther became a teacher of domestic science in Watsonville, California. It is not clear to me whether Beth or Mary completed college degrees, though while at Stanford, Mary met and married a wealthy young businessman. These stories led me to recall Virginia Woolf's famous 1929 book, *A Room of One's Own*, which bemoaned how the lack of cultural and physical space constrained women from even imagining themselves as creators—even those who, like the Steinbeck sisters, had grown up immersed in the arts and literature.[3] As I read about them in the yearbooks, I wondered if Beth, or Mary, might have become famous writers under different historical conditions. Likewise, what might some of the girl athletes at Salinas High—for instance, those baseball champions shown in Figure 1.1—have accomplished had the ceiling not started to slam down on girls' sports in the mid-1920s?

The High School and Its Town

Salinas High School first opened its doors to students in 1882, temporarily housed in what was then called the West End School. In 1899, voters approved a $30,000 bond for a new high school building, which was subsequently built on West Alisal Street and first occupied in August 1900 (Figure 1.4).

My story begins with the school's first yearbook, issued in 1903. At least that is what I thought until I visited the school in 2023 and dove into the school's archive of early

Figure 1.4. *El Gabilan*, October 1907

Figure 1.5. Salinas High School graduating class, *El Gabilan*, 1905

yearbooks. There, I was surprised to find a single *El Gabilan* issued in 1896. In that fourteen-page journal the students announced their plan to publish four times a year henceforth. If that did actually happen, no other copies survived between then and 1903, when "principal L.E. Kilkenny urged students to revive the *El Gabilan*."[4] For the next decade the *El Gabilan* was published quarterly, its pages primarily filled with student-authored short stories, poems, humor pieces ("joshes"), editorials, a few hand drawings, an occasional photograph, and minimal focus on sports.[5] In 1913–14, the *El Gabilan* announced it would issue only twice, on Christmas and in June. The following year it became "the school annual," appearing as a single issue at the end of the academic year, some of its former journalistic and editorial functions having been subsumed by the school's new newspaper, *The Flashlight*.

The early issues of the *El Gabilan* were created primarily by and about the senior classes, so there was very little information about juniors, sophomores, or freshmen. The books do give us a clear idea as to who was graduating from Salinas High during the first decades of the twentieth century, and who wasn't. Many surnames of Salinas's early elite peppered these pages—Abbott, Hitchcock, Bardin, Adcock, Church, Hartnell, Davis, Tynan, Iverson, Sherwood—names that eventually would adorn city street signs, businesses, parks, and schools. The inaugural portrait of a graduating senior class appeared in the 1905 yearbook (Figure 1.5).[6] The fact that fourteen of that year's twenty graduates were girls was typical of the years up to 1911, during which girl graduates outnumbered boys two to one. Since 1894, school attendance for

California children aged eight to fourteen had been mandatory, in part as a means of reducing abusive child labor practices. But many Salinas boys over the age of fourteen were undoubtedly leaving high school before graduating—to work on family farms, to join the military, or to enter the workforce.

The 1905 graduating seniors appear all to have been white, a racial and ethnic homogeneity that continued at the high school for several years. Undoubtedly many boys and girls from poor families, and those from the growing Chinese community in town, were not attending high school at all. The Chinese Exclusion Acts of 1882, 1888, 1892, and 1902 had severely constrained the work and landowning rights of Chinese and other Asian-origin immigrants.[7] Chinese people were among the most important city-builders in early Salinas, but racist residency restrictions confined their families to a small area of town, and their children undoubtedly faced constraints on attending or completing school.

In 1915, the Salinas Union High School district was formed, broadening the reach of the high school beyond the Salinas city limits.[8] From 1912 to 1920, the number of graduating girls remained constant, at about fifteen per year, with the average number of boy graduates rising to twelve. There may have been some students of color enrolled at the school during those years—three dark-skinned boys, perhaps African American, appeared in the 1914 photo of the school orchestra—but for the most part the school's graduates were almost exclusively white. In 1916, Ulysses Cooper—a star pole vaulter and high jumper on the track team, and a member of the rugby team—seems likely to have been the first Black boy to graduate from Salinas Union High School (Figure 1.6).[9] The next year Leonard Cooper (probably Ulysses's brother) also graduated.

In 1900, only 6 percent of Americans graduated from high school.[10] By 1918, the United States had passed mandatory high school attendance laws. If schools were to become a foundation for building modern civilization, it was believed, then white boys needed to be educated to maintain their positions as leading citizens. "Middle-class white parents wanted their sons to remain in school to gain the credentials . . . for careers rather than dead-end jobs."[11] Nationally, enrollment in public high schools shot up from 519,000 in 1900 to 2,200,000 by 1920. Compulsory high school helped to create age-based youth peer groups, as it also cemented "adolescence" as a life-stage and "teenagers" as a cultural category that would blossom in the twentieth century.[12]

For Salinas Union High School, compulsory attendance, coupled with a gradual growth of the city's population from 3,500 in 1902 to 4,308 in 1920,[13] expanded the size of the student body and squared up the gender composition of the graduating classes, which averaged about 23 boys and 23 girls from 1921 through 1925. The student body continued mostly to be white during that time, despite the 350 Asians counted among the city's 1920 population.[14] There were no Chinese students to be

Figure 1.6. Salinas Union High School track team, *El Gabilan*, 1916

seen in the high school's graduating classes, but a few Japanese students began to appear during this time. Japanese laborers had begun to settle in the Salinas Valley in 1898, many of them young men who came to work in the recently opened Spreckels Sugar plant.[15] As more Japanese families settled in Salinas, their children began to attend public schools. George T. Yaminishi seems to have been the first Japanese student to graduate from Salinas High School, in 1918. Norio Urabe and Misao Takao graduated in 1921, Harry Y. Kita in 1922, Shigeto Onoye in 1923, Robert Fukunaga in 1924, and Sada Onoye in 1925. Foreshadowing the prominence of Japanese American athletes at the school in the pre–World War II years, several of these students were on sports teams, including Harry Kita, who played on the football, basketball, track and field, and baseball teams.

"Fight, Boys, Fight"

The start of the twentieth century was a time of considerable anxiety over the meanings of manhood in the United States, and this was especially true among white middle-class boys and young men. Just as they were spending many more years in high school (and sometimes college) than had their fathers, young men were learning from doctors that they were threatened by an emasculating modern disease: "Neurasthenia . . . was spreading throughout the middle class, due to the excessive brain work and

SALINAS CITY HIGH SCHOOL FOOTBALL TEAM

Figure 1.7. *El Gabilan*, 1904

nervous strain which professionals and businessmen endured. Civilization's demands on men's nerve force had left their bodies positively effeminate."[16] Turn-of-the-century educator G. Stanley Hall pointed to schools as a major culprit.[17] Hall believed, according to historian Gail Bederman, that "education . . . was ruining schoolboys' health in civilized countries. American teachers were neglecting boys' bodies, allowing them to 'atrophy, and chest, back, shoulders, hips, never to attain their fullest possible development.'" Instead, Hall advocated that "educators could 'inoculate' boys with the primitive strength they would need to avoid developing neurasthenia."[18] The proposed delivery system for this inoculation? Schools needed to counterbalance the feminizing impact of their intellectual endeavors by immersing boys in a "muscular education" that centered on vigorous team sports.[19]

As the twentieth century unfolded at Salinas High School, sports were growing in importance, and at first there seemed little question that school sports were by, for, and about boys. But it was not at all clear which sports would emerge as the most important ones; in fact, the first quarter of the twentieth century was a time of considerable turbulence in high school sports. Well before my story begins in 1903, the school had already been fielding a football team for some years.[20] The 1904 *El Gabilan* announced that "The Salinas High School Football Team has just completed a most brilliant season, winning seven victories out of seven games" (Figure 1.7). The yearbook editors insisted, "We justly consider the defeat of our sadly crippled team at Hollister" not to count as a loss, because it had been "necessary for us to use half of the men of our second team."[21]

Boys' sports were being rapidly institutionalized, both at the school and across the region. On February 6, 1904, a convention was held with faculty and student representatives from Salinas, Pacific Grove, Hollister, Gilroy, Watsonville, and Santa Cruz "for the purpose of organizing an Athletic League among the High Schools of the central-coast counties."[22] Later that spring, "The first field day of the Coast County Athletic League [CCAL] took place at the Salinas Race Track on May 14, 1904," with Salinas, Santa Cruz, and Hollister competing in running, jumping, hammer throw, and shot put. "Many white handkerchiefs were waived by gaily dressed co eds in the grand stand."[23] And the following year, under the cheer "Hot! Hotter! Hottest!! Heat! Salinas High School, can't be beat!" the *El Gabilan* applauded the football team's CCAL championship: "After several fierce struggles with the 'pigskin' we won it." That spring, the second annual Field Day was held at the Salinas Race Track on April 22, 1905, drawing five hundred spectators: "The grand stand was filled with the fair sex and the rooters, who were yelling for their respective schools."[24] Alas, Salinas High came in last place.

Just as it seemed that football was solidifying its place as the school's main autumn sport, with track and field dominating the spring, the 1907 *El Gabilan* hinted that not all was well: "Since there has been much dispute over football as it has been played, we are undecided whether we will play Rugby, or the old game under new rules."[25] Football did continue for the next three years, with Salinas High winning consecutive championships. "*El Gabilan* welcomes the opening of the football season with a Hip Hurrah!," the October 1908 yearbook declared. "Fight, boys, fight, not only for our honor but for the cup."[26] Track and field flourished. Alongside some action shots (somewhat blurry compared with the sharper, posed team photos), the 1909 yearbook noted that, "For the first time in the history of the C.C.A.L. the seven [schools] of which it is composed, were all represented. More than a thousand were congregated at the track to witness the events; public interest was never greater than this year, and was never more deserved. The spirit of good fellowship reigned supreme" (Figures 1.8, 1.9).[27] In 1910, Salinas won the meet for the fifth straight year.

Baseball came and went during the first decade of the century, resuming in 1908 after a three-year hiatus. Then, a 1911 *El Gabilan* editorial reported that the boys had held a meeting at the start of the school year "to discuss the football situation. After considering the two games, Rugby and the old American game we have been playing, a standing vote was taken, and Rugby was endorsed almost unanimously." It was noted that "high schools around the bay and in Los Angeles [were] adopting and making success out of Rugby." Stanford University and the University of California, Berkeley ("Cal") had adopted rugby four years earlier,[28] so "Rugby football must be better than the old American game." Besides, "a great many people are prejudiced against the old game, and will not let their children play it, though they would raise no objections to Rugby."[29] National debates about football had raged for several years, especially in universities, with critics decrying the professionalization of the college game, as well

C. C. A. L. Meet

STOLZ IN ACTION.

FELIZ VAULTING 9 FEET.

Figure 1.8. *El Gabilan*, 1909

as gambling, spectator violence, and the on-field violence, injuries, and deaths, which had spiked in 1909.[30] Starting in 1911 and for the next five years, Salinas High School would ditch "the old American game" of football, replacing it with rugby (Figure 1.10).

The SUHS rugby team thrived on the field, but in 1917 the game disappeared from the yearbook, with no comment from the book's editors. Stanford and Cal had revived gridiron football competition in 1919, but there would be no football of any sort at Salinas Union High School through 1921—neither rugby nor the old American game. Instead, baseball solidified its foothold—for a time holding its season in the autumn slot previously occupied by football—as track and field ascended as the undisputed king of sports on campus (Figure 1.11). The 1918 *El Gabilan* bemoaned the fact that the track team had lost the annual field meet, adding that "We had the right spirit, and we had the right grit, but three of our best men left us during the year to join the service, and sickness and consequent lack of practice had weakened some of our stars."[31] History had intruded: War had come, along with an influenza pandemic that would kill millions globally. And another change was in the air: It turned out that it was not just boys who wanted to play sports.

SALINAS HIGH SCHOOL TRACK TEAM, '09.

Figure 1.9. *El Gabilan*, 1909

Top Row, Left—F. Jacop, D. Keney, L. Hitchcock, P. Tavernetti, H. Wallace, F. Martin, P. Breschini. Middle Row, Left—K. Vanderhurst, L. Schneider, F. Barlow, M. Armstrong, E. Chappell, U. Cooper. Bottom Row, Left—C. Church, B. Church, J. Lapierre, A. Emery (captain), O. Fisher, M. Lapierre.

Figure 1.10. Rugby champions, *El Gabilan*, 1916

Figure 1.11. SUHS baseball team, *El Gabilan*, 1918

"Imagine the Girls with a Gymnasium"

The September 1905 *El Gabilan* editorial declared that "The spirit which has been so evident among the boys this year seems not to have escaped the girls, who, for the first time in the history of the High School, have entered athletics. Four basket ball teams have been organized and practice is going on with a vim . . . Good for the enterprising girls, who were the cause of it all. It is pleasant to see them running about playing Basket Ball."[32] It would be five more years before the yearbook mentioned another girls' sports team, but the question of women's rights had been in the air at Salinas High for some years. The 1896 *El Gabilan* included a cartoon depicting "our debaters on woman suffrage," an issue that was stirring the nation (Figure 1.12). And the 1903 *El Gabilan* reported that the school had faced off two girls against two boys to debate the desirability of coed schooling: "In the debate, 'Resolved, That coeducation is desirable,' the affirmative was taken by Misses Grace McIntyre and Nellie Bailey and the negative by Messrs. Harry Muller and Eldon Abbott. The decision was awarded to the affirmative."[33]

A national women's movement arose in the middle decades of the nineteenth century, spilling into the new century and pressing for equal education for girls, as well as voting, birth control, and property rights for women.[34] The twentieth century

Figure 1.12. Student debate on woman suffrage, *El Gabilan*, 1896

opened with "a wave of athletic feminism"—a push for bodily empowerment that included increased physical activity and competitive sports for girls and women.[35] In the United States and in other nations, women athletes were in the forefront of challenging Victorian limits on women's use of public space while disrupting widespread beliefs in female frailty.[36] At Salinas High School, girls' challenges to boys' monopoly on sports bubbled up gradually in the first decade of the century, eventually erupting in the mid-1910s and early 1920s. Following that first hint of girls' basketball at the school in 1905, there was no mention of girls' sports for the next five years. Then, a December 1910 *El Gabilan* editorial uttered "a hearty cheer for the girls who are working for the promotion of a basketball team."[37] On February 3, 1911, the girls played what appears to have been the school's first-ever interscholastic basketball game. "Santa Cruz showed their experience and defeated the S.H.S. girls by a large score."[38]

Top Row—Miss Peterson, Coach; Nissen, Irvine, Pesante, Binsacca, Rasmussen, H. Feliz, Vasquez. Middle Row—Green, Crawford, Moller, Johnson, Graves, R. Smith, Nelson, Christensen, Von Soosten. Bottom Row—Anderson, Brisbine, Black, M. Smith, Captain; N. Feliz, Hare, Winkle, Whisman.

Figure 1.13. SUHS basketball team, *El Gabilan*, 1915

For the next three years there was little mention of girls' sports in the yearbook, but the middle of the decade was a major takeoff point for basketball and eventually for other girls' sports. Accompanied by the first photo of a girls' team to appear in the yearbook, the 1915 *El Gabilan* announced that "Basket ball, after a lapse of four years, has been revived with more interest than ever" (Figure 1.13). The outdoor court the girls played on was in disrepair, but "with sleeves rolled up, skirts turned up, and each with a hoe, rake or broom in hand," the girls restored their playing court, including having to spread lime to create the lines on the court. "Now, all those girls had to do was play, and play they did," forming four teams that "enjoyed the fun for four months."[39]

For the next couple of years, and despite uneven support, girls' sports grew, driven by the students' enthusiasm and by the dedicated leadership of a string of women coaches. "For a long while athletics for girls have not been favorably regarded by our faculty and Board of Education," the 1917 *El Gabilan* noted, "but . . . when the Seniors of today were Sophomores, Miss Peterson came to this school fresh from college and—girls' athletics. She soon gathered about her girls who were interested in sports and basketball teams were again organized after a period of five years. But the teams were handicapped. They did not receive support from the faculty or the students and they had no suitable court. However, under miss Peterson as coach, they advanced and showed much skill." The report concluded with the most upbeat possible tone: "All prejudices have been swept away and the next season will enter a team in the CCAL. Rah! Rah! Rah! Basketball! Basketball! Zim! Boom! Ah!"

For a moment it seemed this optimism was well warranted. The yearbooks were treating the girls' teams with respect, reporting factually on their competitions with other schools. "For the first time the girls' basket ball team of the S.U.H.S. was allowed to take part in the C.C.A.L. basket ball games this year," the 1918 *El Gabilan* reported. "On the whole the games played showed that our girls had plenty of 'pep' and spirit . . . The first game played was at Pacific Grove December 17, 1917, which resulted with a score of 30 to 27 in favor of the Salinas girls." It was the team's only win of the three-game season. The yearbooks also often depicted the girls' and boys' teams in roughly symmetrical ways, though girls' teams were routinely gender-marked ("girls basket ball team"), while boys' teams were normally framed generically ("basket ball team") (Figure 1.14).[40]

The 1918 yearbook, however, tossed a bit of cold water on this optimism, pointing to some everyday struggles that girls and their coaches faced in having adequate athletic facilities, or even enough balls to play with:

> Imagine the girls with a gymnasium, a basket ball court, track and everything all of their own! Don't get excited girls, you know it is impossible. Can you remember a day over in that dirty gym when a bunch of boys, draped in (dirty) track suits does not appear and say—Oh! How familiar this is to the ears of any of the girls of the S.U.H.S., No.1: "Mr. Best says we can have the basket ball." (N.B. I think the Hi has about six balls, but, no, it must be the one we have.) No. 2: "Mr. Best says we can practice on the court." And so it goes. Of course, Miss Westerman, the dear, gives her opinion of men in general. (Sh!—which is some opinion, believe me.). She means well, but what can a poor woman do? The worst of it is we get all excited over our new prospects and someone always kills our joy.[41]

Still, girls' sports forged ahead. "Talk about pep," the 1920 *El Gabilan* gushed while noting the scores of girls' basketball games versus King City, Gilroy, and Watsonville, "well, the girls certainly know the true meaning of the word." The girls' baseball team also played two games versus Watsonville and King City—the latter beating Salinas in a football score, 47–36 (Figure 1.15). "Athletics of all kinds have been on a stronger basis than ever. The girls succeeded in getting a girls' manager and in this way the boys have very little to say about what the girls can do and what they can not do. A league is being formed on practically the same basis as the C.C.A.L., and, with this as a start, next year the girls hope to make girls' athletics as important as boys.'"[42]

The year 1921 was the inaugural one for the Girls' Coast Counties Athletic League (GCCAL). Salinas High's Irene Pauley was named president of the league, and the *El Gabilan* also noted that Pauley "entertained the girls' basketball team at a luncheon at the Jeffery Hotel on February 5, 1921 . . . toasts were responded to by Elita Rossi who spoke on 'Our Place in the High School'; Helen Nissen, who spoke on 'A Girl Officer of the Student Body'; Pearl Rasmussen, who spoke on 'Loyalty'; Phyllis

EL GABILAN

BASKET BALL TEAM

GIRLS BASKET BALL TEAM
65

Figure 1.14. *El Gabilan*, 1920

Rosendale, who spoke on 'Just a Girl Member of the Student Body.'"[43] Under the heading "SALINAS TAKES TRACK CUP," the yearbook celebrated the girls' and boys' track teams both having won their respective Field Days.

In retrospect, 1921 and 1922 were the high-water mark for girls' sports at Salinas High (at least until the years after Title IX, a half century later). If a girl had played on a team, her participation was listed below her senior portrait, just as with the boys (Figure 1.16). There was continuing enthusiasm among girls for competing in the Field Days (figure 1.17). But there were also signs that girls' interscholastic sports were

GIRLS BASE BALL TEAM

Figure 1.15. *El Gabilan*, 1920

eroding. Yes, the girls had a baseball team, but one can also see in the lower-left corner of Figure 1.1, which opens this chapter, the beginning of "adapted rules" for girls' sports (an issue I will discuss more at length in subsequent chapters). "The Gilroy girls," the caption informs us, "forfeited the baseball game with Salinas because they would not play with a soft ball, as rules required, but had been practicing with regulation boys' ball and mits [*sic*]."[44] And in 1922, despite having expanded basketball to two teams ("unlimited" and "limited") for each school, the GCCAL voted that henceforth, "No cups or trophies of any kind are given, the winners of each classification receiving only the name, 'Champion,'"[45] a gesture that signaled the erosion of interscholastic competition for girls.

Over the next three years the school would add a girls' volleyball team, and enthusiasm remained high for existing sports. "Girls' athletics opened this year with a bang!" the 1923 *El Gabilan* stated. "Over one hundred girls came out for basketball practice," it said, adding that "Much credit is due to Miss Knickrehm, who co-operated heartily with the girls in all sports."[46] Coach Marie M. Knickrehm, who appeared in several team photos from 1923 through 1925, seems almost singlehandedly to have coached, promoted, and supported girls' sports (Figure 1.18).

The tide was receding on girls' sports. Their teams continued to compete against other schools, but the institutional language and tone was shifting. "Field Day," a term used to describe boys' or girls' league-wide track and field meets, was now giving way to "Play Day" for the girls, which "in every sense of the word signifies a good time.

Figure 1.16. Graduating seniors, *El Gabilan*, 1921

The object is not for competition, but for friendly rivalry and pleasure."[47] Still, the 1924 "Athletics" section of the yearbook began with a roughly symmetrical collage of photos of girl and boy athletes. The editors crowed that "The senior class is famous for its athletes in both boys' and girls' athletics," and it went on to name seven girls and eight boys who had "starred" in sports. But the GCCAL governing body that year had shifted its focus "foremost [on] the regulation of athletics. That is, the girls' athletics this year have been placed in a sphere where good sportsmanship ability, and enthusiasm take the place of old competition which dominated every game."[48] With the exception of tennis, the plug was being pulled on interscholastic competition: "This year Salinas withdrew from the G.C.C.A.L. in basketball, and the playing of games was changed from inter-scholastic to intra-mural. Thus sixty girls were able to go out for basketball where hitherto only twenty-four tried for a place on the team . . .

Figure 1.17. Track team, *El Gabilan*, 1922

Figure 1.18. Coach Knickrehm and the volleyball team, *El Gabilan*, 1924

Figure 1.19. Kick-pin baseball team, *El Gabilan*, 1925

Because the Salinas girls desired to give every girl a chance to participate in athletics, they decided not to have baseball this spring."[49]

Girls' enthusiasm for sports was not waning. They continued to join teams in droves, and in the 1924 *El Gabilan* "senior horoscopes" page Lilian Lanini stated her desire to become a PE instructor, and Erma Smith said she hoped to be a gym teacher. But the organization of girls' sports was rapidly shifting, as was its underlying philosophy. The 1925 *El Gabilan* reported that "Because the C.C.A.L. has forfeited the idea of regular interscholastic games, 'play-days' were arranged." That year, the girls played a new game, "Kick-Pin Baseball" (later to be called kickball). Two things are notable in the 1925 photo of the Kick-Pin Baseball team (Figure 1.19). First, even though the school was starting to phase out interscholastic competition, the girls still wore SUHS team uniforms, a feature that would be eliminated in a few years. And second, though the athletes on girls' teams at the high school had been almost entirely white for the first quarter of the century, this team included two Japanese American girls, Dorothy Sugumoto and May Kubota. Japanese American girls—including a string of Kubotas—would become fixtures in SUHS girls' sports in the next two decades. The year 1925 also saw the introduction of "Nine-court basketball" for girls, an adapted form of the game that severely reduced running and jumping (as I will discuss more in the next chapter). At the girls' Field Day, the yearbook reported, there was "much friendly rivalry and enthusiasm—without the feeling of keen competition." In the afternoon, the Shenandoah Jazz Orchestra played and the girls "danced and ate when they pleased."[50]

If the dramatic early-century burst of girls' interscholastic sports competition had been driven by a national surge of women's rights activism, its regression in the mid-1920s was also precipitated by large social changes. The first tectonic shift—the waning of feminist activism in the wake of having won the vote for women, and the subsequent social backlash against vigorous physical activity and sport for girls and women—will be discussed in the next chapter. Here, I turn the spotlight on what was happening with boys and men, and this had much to do with the ways that war had compounded already-existing anxieties about masculinity.

"A Record to Be Proud Of"

"The first American Football game to be played in the Coast Counties since 1905 was played Saturday, October 9th, between Salinas and Watsonville," the 1921 *El Gabilan* announced.[51] The yearbook editors may have gotten their dates wrong here—by my reckoning, the school had played football through the 1910–11 school year, switched to rugby through 1917, and then played neither football nor rugby for the next three years. Dates aside, the message was clear: Football was back at Salinas Union High School, and it was something to be celebrated. Boys' basketball, baseball, and track received ample coverage in the 1921 yearbook, but in its first year back football seemed immediately to reclaim its place as the sporting centerpiece. The "Athletics" section of the book was introduced with a full-page etching of a football scene (Figure 1.20). The larger Salinas community also honored the return of the game. Under the

Figure 1.20. The return of football, *El Gabilan*, 1921

Figure 1.21. Student cadet drill, *El Gabilan*, 1920

Figure 1.22. *(opposite page)* Track team, *El Gabilan*, 1920

headline "FOOTBALL TEAM GIVEN BANQUET" it was reported that the gridders had been feted at the Jeffery Hotel. Hosted by Mr. Jeffery himself, and attended by the football coach, Mr. Rogers, Principal Van Dellen, as well as Mr. Melander and Mr. Corbaley, members of the business community, the football team was given a banquet and a celebration. "Mr. Jeffery then praised the team for their spirit they had shown, and urged them to always keep their word."[52]

What explains the sudden and celebratory return of football? The yearbooks gave only vague hints in answer to this question, but it is clear that it had much to do with the larger context of war and its aftermath. The United States had declared war on Germany in April 1917, and a year later the *El Gabilan* listed, beneath a red, white, and blue drawing of Old Glory, the names of ninety-seven Salinas High alums who were "Serving Under the Flag."[53] "S.U.H.S. has been wide awake this year, and has done her best to help Uncle Sam make it hot for the Kaiser," the yearbook editorialized, adding that the school's Junior Red Cross and War Clubs had raised funds to invest in $1,681.73 in War Saving Stamps, and the school had sent "Christmas Cheer . . . for our boys 'over there.'"[54]

Competitive sports in the spring of 1918 mostly gave way to war support and military training. "Physical culture was abolished for cadet drill . . . under the careful instruction of Sargent [*sic*] Richards."[55] In 1918–19, sixteen boys, among them John Steinbeck, served as military cadets, the high school equivalent of ROTC in colleges. The cadets drilled with uniforms and rifles, and in 1918 they were "drafted into the fields" and paid 35 cents an hour for farm work to make up for an "acute labor shortage during the war years."[56] The high school cadets tried to assist with the war effort, but the yearbook hinted that these boys—a bit too young to enlist or be drafted into the army—may have felt they had missed out on something.[57]

> Our soldiers come home filled with the seriousness of the symbolism of that uniform and what do they find? They find a bunch of half-drilled, half-grown, half-baked kids wearing the uniform for which they have offered their lives. It may be all right but it makes a High School Cadet or even a Boy Scout a little bit ashamed to meet a wounded soldier on the street and to have to endure a glance which says, "Who are you, and what did you do to be traveling around in uniform too?" Enough! . . . Let's get in there and dig, so that we will be able to face a soldier, wounded or otherwise with the idea that we have done something, that we are something. Let us be able to meet his questioning glance with one which says, "I am part of the machine of preparedness which will safeguard our country during peace and war in future years."[58]

By the next school year the war had ended, but the 1920 *El Gabilan* evidenced many ways that the militarization of school life had fused with sports. "Military training has become quite an important feature of the high school this year. Many of the boys, although not all, have taken up military drill instead of Physical Education. . . . On Saturday night of the encampment the cadets gave a program with consisted of boxing, singing and speeches on the value of military training by some of the prominent citizens of Salinas" (Figure 1.21).[59] Listed among the school's faculty that year was Mr. Niel O. Best, whose teaching field was listed as "Physical Education and Military." A discerning reader of this book may already have noticed the military uniform worn by the basketball coach in Figure 1.14. I assume this coach was Mr. Best, who also appears in the track team photo (Figure 1.22).

In the aftermath of the war, the schoolboys' masculinity had been challenged and destabilized. While other young men had done the actual work of war, these boys had worked in the fields and conducted military drills thousands of miles from combat zones. Might sports have provided refuge for boys to demonstrate their manliness? Well, girls were claiming equal status in the previously all-male world of interscholastic sports. A poem penned by F. L. Kellogg, the 1919 captain of the boys' basketball team, likely drew a laugh, but also may betray a hint of challenged masculinity. Bemoaning his team's loss to Santa Cruz, his poem ends with this: "But now we're glad it's over; And we will play no more; For now we sit around and watch; The girls run up the score."[60] It is in this early-1920s context that boys' football was revived, and a backlash against girls' sports soon began to stir.

The postwar militarization of physical education occurred because adults wanted high schools to be part of the nation's "preparedness" for future conflicts. Modernity, and especially the feminizing effect of public education, was said to be softening boys. This anxiety had deepened during the war, as the perceived "physical shortcomings of many military draftees raised concerns about the country's lack of vitality."[61] The late nineteenth- and early twentieth-century belief in the "spermatic economy," supported at the time by medical science, held that "the human male possessed a limited quantity of sperm, which could be invested in various enterprises, ranging from business through sport to copulation and procreation. In this context, the careful regulation of the body was the only path to the conservation of energy."[62] Masturbation was to be avoided, as it led to the dissipation of men's precious energies. Playing vigorous team sports, it was believed, would allow men to sublimate their libidinous energies, "to regenerate the male body and thus make efficient use of male energy."[63] The revival of high school football—joined at the hip with the militarization of physical education—can be seen as a response to these fears of feminization and sexual dissipation of male energy. Prewar arguments in favor of football were revived. National leaders "saw football as molding patriotic warriors, as did the military establishment."[64] Colonel Charles W. Larned of the U.S. Military Academy had argued that vigorous team sports were important because "They keep a man sexually clean and healthy, free from morbid emotions and a too highly developed subjectivity."[65]

But what of the physical dangers of playing such a violent game, a hot issue that had been partly responsible for doing away with football for several years? By the postwar years, the prewar words of educator Henry S. Curtis seemed to reverberate among policymakers and educators: "What does it matter if a leg is broken now and then? Broken legs are soon mended. It is worth a dozen broken legs, if you can teach a boy to be a hero and a patriot."[66] It was in this postwar context of militarized remasculinization of schools that the backlash against girls' interscholastic sports began to ferment at Salinas Union High School, at the same time that football—the manliest of sports—was making a triumphant return.

The football team was given star billing in the 1923 *El Gabilan*, with a team photo, individual portraits and short descriptions of each player, reports on games, and applause for team's having won "the third consecutive C.C.A.L championship, a record to be proud of."[67] That year also introduced something that would become more common in the next two decades: the elevation of the football coach as local hero. The two-page yearbook dedication included a full-page portrait of the coach (Figure 1.23), with the following inscription on the adjoining page: "To Frederick R. Rogers who, as coach of our athletic teams for the past three years has brought many championships to our school; Who, as coach, has developed a better spirit of true sportsmanship and fair play; We dedicate the 1923 *El Gabilan*."

Figure 1.23. Dedication page to coach Frederick R. Rogers, *El Gabilan*, 1923

Boys' baseball continued in the postwar years, and the school put two boys' basketball teams into league competition—"unlimited" (soon to be called heavyweight, and later, varsity) and "130 Lb" (eventually to be named lightweight) (Figure 1.24). Track and field remained popular too, but it seemed to be teetering on the precipice of boys' sports as football's status ascended (Figures 1.25, 1.26).

In 1925 the *El Gabilan* reported that "Forty ambitious young men" had turned out for football, and the coach trimmed the team to thirty. Aspirations to play the game were high among the boys, the public reputation of the football coach was growing, and the school was poised to make football the centerpiece of student life and school identity in the coming decades. But to accomplish this, another element would need to be grafted on to sports, a way to infuse the entire student body with the public "spirit" needed to support their team.

"We've Got the Rep for Lots of Pep"

From its origins in the late nineteenth century, high school sports were viewed not just as a way for boys (and for a time, also girls) to be physically active, but also as a means of creating a sense of group identity and belonging. Interscholastic sports competition can be especially effective in achieving this goal, as it creates sharp boundaries between "us" and "them," with a rules-based means of adjudicating whose team

Figure 1.24. Unlimited (*top*) and 130-pound basketball teams, *El Gabilan*, 1924

Figure 1.25. Track team, *El Gabilan*, 1924

Figure 1.26. SUHS football team, *El Gabilan*, 1924

(and perhaps by extension, whose school) is superior. But creating and sustaining a system through which "school spirit" can be mustered in support of a school's athletic teams did not happen naturally or easily. It took some prodding and coaxing. During its first two decades the *El Gabilan* routinely editorialized about the importance of students supporting their teams, its tone fluctuating between worry, praise, and scolding.

Boys, it was assumed from the start, were best suited to lead in pumping up the school spirit. The May 1907 *El Gabilan* noted that for that year's Field Day, "Edgar

McCollum and James Smith have been chosen to lead the rooters in yells." Girls were expected to show up in support, and were applauded when they did. "The girls made a great showing on Field Day with their new pennants . . . That's the spirit, girls!"[68] The March 1908 book again heaped praise on the girls for their efforts: "*El Gabilan* noticed the great amount of spirit which was shown by the girls during the football season. Think of the cup, girls, and keep the spirit up till spring. The track team is practicing and will need your encouragement."[69] That May the *El Gabilan* celebrated the Salinas victory in the CCAL Field Day held in Monterey, noting that "The rooting section of the S.H.S., under the leadership of Edgar McCollum, who is one of the best yell leaders we ever had, did some splendid rooting to cheer the boys on to victory."[70]

But an ebbing of rooter support for the school's teams created concern: "*El Gabilan* has noticed that there has been a very unusual lack of interest in regard to football," the editors worried in December 1909. "We still have a chance to win the cup, and no matter how well a team plays it can play better if it is backed by the school."[71] That spring, the editors noted hopefully, "We will have Charlie McCollum, the Freshman wonder, as yell leader for three more field days! Won't that help some though?"[72] Alas, a year later the editors again bemoaned the lack of student spirit and support for the track team, "*El Gabilan* suggests that a yell leader be elected next fall when the rest of the officers are selected, and that in future times the position of yell leader shall be regarded with greater distinction than it has been heretofore."[73] The following fall, in 1911, the editors implored their classmates, "Why can not those who are not actually on the field fighting for the 'purple and gold,' do their share by rooting and encouraging good work?"[74] Again in the spring of 1912, *El Gabilan* bemoaned the lack of spirit in support of the track team: "Why not get together, elect a 'live wire' yell leader, and show some spirit?" The editors added another practical suggestion (one that makes excellent sense when you consider the complicated 1904 yell that opens this chapter): "One of the chief difficulties last year was that the majority did not know the yells. Why not this year supply printed copies as was done several years ago? Here's to a winning track team. May S.H.S. carry the day."[75]

By 1915 the position of yell leader appeared finally to have become institutionalized, as the *El Gabilan* included a photo and a tribute to "Our Yell Leaders, Joy and Hare" (Figure 1.27). By 1917, the school had initiated some of the sports-related pageantry that would blossom in future decades. Led by yell leader "Louis Schneider, and his untiring lung capacity," on April 27 the students held a rally "to create a spirit of enthusiasm for that thrilling track meet which took place May 5th . . . Students serpentined down Main Street, giving school yells, blowing horns, and keeping in step with the brass band." At the athletic field, "a huge bonfire was in readiness for the throngs." The next year, a pre–Field Day rally began with a parade, complete with floats. "After the arrival at the athletic field, Bruce Church, the track Captain, gave the funeral oration over Santa Cruz's goat, which was afterwards placed on an immense funeral pyre and burned." Speeches were made by Salinas mayor Daugherty and others,

Figure 1.27. (*left*) *El Gabilan*, 1915

Figure 1.28. (*above*) Yell leaders, *El Gabilan*, 1917

and "after a few yells led by the yell leader, Louis Schneider, the meeting broke up."[76] It may have helped too that the yells were getting simpler and easier to remember, as with this snappy ditty that appeared in the 1917 yearbook:[77]

> Ice cream soda,
> Ginger-ale pop;
> Salinas High School
> Always on top!!!!

In subsequent years, the *El Gabilan* continued to feature photos of the school's yell leaders, all of them boys (Figure 1.28), sometimes accompanying the photos with the words of the official school yell and the school song (Figure 1.29).

If the students were going to sing "Rah! Salinas Hi!" at pregame rallies and at the games, it helped to have some accompaniment. The same year that it featured yell leaders John Berges and Mervyn Little, the 1922 *El Gabilan* crowed, "We certainly have a jazzy band this year . . . The band played at the Hollister Track Meet and helped us win. It also has played at rallies and programs given at assemblies" (Figure 1.30).[78] Perhaps buoyed by the revival of football at the school, the *El Gabilan* of the early 1920s

OUR YELL LEADERS: (Left) John Berges; (Right) Mervyn Little

Rah! Salinas Hi! Rah! Rah!
We're going to win this game or die! Rah! Rah!
We'll cheer every play! Rah! Rah!
Our husky team pulls off to-day, Rah! Rah!
We're going to beat you, Santa Cruz, Rah! Rah!
Make up your mind you're going to lose, Rah! Rah!
We've got the rep for lots of pep;
You'll never, never beat Salinas Hi! Rah! Rah!

WOW!! *Oski! Wow! Wow!*
Wiskee Wee! Wee!
Holy muckie-eye
Holy Salinas Hi!
Wow! Tiger! Wow!

Page Seventy

Figure 1.29. *El Gabilan*, 1922

applauded a growing panoply of the school's spirit-building apparatus, the efforts of which would expand in importance and scope in the following decades. What was at stake, we can see in retrospect, went far beyond simply elevating the school's sports teams; in many towns like Salinas across the country, rooting for and supporting the local high school's sport teams was becoming an important means of creating

Figure 1.30. Salinas High School band, *El Gabilan*, 1922

community solidarity and identity.[79] And despite the burst of girls' athletics (already eroding at its base by the mid-1920s), there was a clear gender divide developing: Boys composed the "jazzy band," and were the yell leaders who directed the rooters. Girls, members of "the fairer sex," were expected to show up in droves to the football games and track meets, prepared to "keep the spirit up" in support of the boys.

"A Place Where We Can Play"

The first quarter of the twentieth century had been time of growth and change at Salinas High School. The city of Salinas grew modestly during that time. But the student body of the high school grew at a faster rate, in large part due to the 1915 creation of the Salinas Union High School district that broadened the geographic reach of the high school beyond the city limits, and especially because of the institution of mandatory high school attendance in 1918. The compulsory high school attendance law retained more boys at the high school. By the start of the 1920s, the size of the faculty was also growing, and student extracurricular clubs were proliferating, including the Girls' Club, Hi-Y, Rifle Club, Glee Club, Mask and Mirror (theater), Orchestra, Campfire Girls, Fun and Funetics, and Junior Farm Center.

All of this growth put pressure on the physical plant of the high school building that had opened its doors in 1900 to serve a much smaller student body. That building was severely damaged in the April 18, 1906, earthquake that had leveled San Francisco. The next fall the *El Gabilan* noted, "We all regret that the last Senior Class, the 'Earthquake Class,' were unable to publish the commencement number, for which they worked so hard and faithfully."[80] It turns out (as we will see in chapter 4) these would not be the first Salinas High students displaced by an earthquake. But though the building was soon repaired, by 1912 the *El Gabilan* editorialized that "For the last five or six years the number of students has increased so rapidly that at present the building is too small to accommodate them . . . Up to the last two years there has been enough room inside, but never has there been any grounds outside, for either boy or girl sports." Finally, in the fall of 1920 the new campus on Main Street opened its doors. "Seniors take pride in realizing that they are the first class to be graduated from the new high school," the 1921 *El Gabilan* stated. "It is said to be the most beautiful building of its size in California . . . The freshman class of next year should be taught to love and respect their school as they do their country."[81]

The new campus not only included adequate space for classrooms, orchestra, and library resources. For the first time the school also had an expansive array of athletic fields and courts on which a flourishing sports program could develop. In the 1919 yearbook, girls had advocated for a new school, in part to expand their ability to play sports: "It is whispered about that we are to have a new High School within the next ten years, if nothing happens to the plans and if the good people of Salinas will vote on the bonds. And that's where we come in, girls. We all have parents who vote, so work to convince them that we absolutely need that new school—a place where we can play without being interrupted by Mr. Best's little angel boys."[82] In the first years of the 1920s, girls at the school may have hoped that the new facilities would expedite the further expansion of interscholastic sports. But as it turned out, "all prejudices" about girls' sports and physical activity had not "been swept away." By 1925, we can see in retrospect, boys' interscholastic sports were poised to explode in size and importance. Girls' sports were facing a very different future.

EL
GABILAN
1930

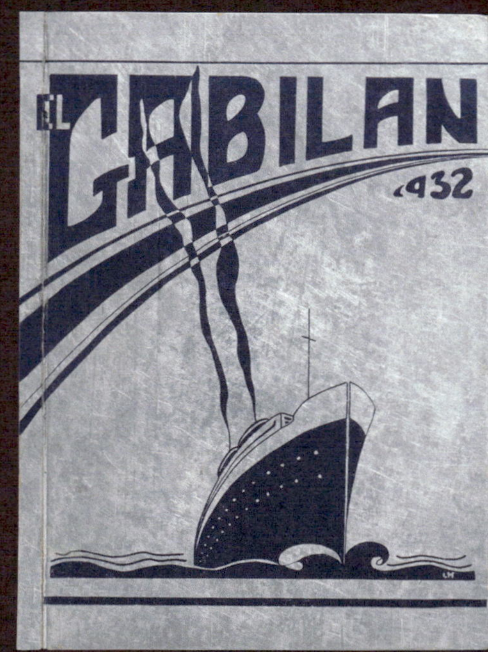
EL GABILAN
1932

EL
GABILAN
1933

EL GABILAN

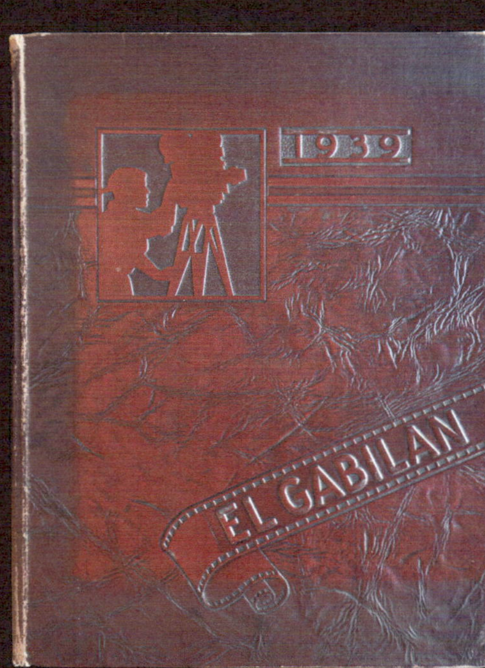
1939
EL GABILAN

EL GABILAN
1940

EL GABILAN
41

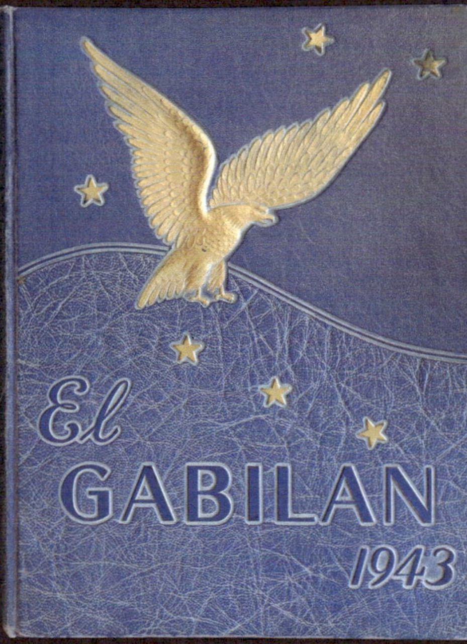
El
GABILAN
1943

1945
El Gabilan

You gotta be football hero
to get along with the beautiful girls;
You gotta be a touchdown getter, you bet
if you wanna get a baby to pet;
The fact that you are rich or handsome
won't get you anything in curls;
You gotta be a football hero
to get along with the beautiful girls.

—POPULAR SONG, LEWIS & SHERMAN, 1933

Chapter 2

Football Heroes and Girls with "Pep" 1926–1946

THE 1946 *EL GABILAN* OPENS WITH A LOVING DEDICATION to retiring teacher Mrs. Ruth Wing:

> *During the thirty-one years Mrs. Wing has been head of the Girls' Physical Education Department she has proved a friend to thousands of girls whose well being has always been close to her heart. As a teacher, she is tops. Her vitality and ever present wit bring to a game of hockey or baseball an excitement that would be lacking if she were not here. Besides teaching girls' sports, she stresses sportsmanship and health, which are often more important than the sport itself. In honor of you, Mrs. Wing, for the many years you have devoted to the girls of S.U.H.S., we dedicate this 1946* El Gabilan.[1]

This was the second time that the annual had been dedicated to Ruth Wing, though the first time, in 1928, she was known as Miss Ruth Rouse, who had arrived at Salinas Union High School in the fall of 1925 (Figures 2.2 and 2.3). The editors of the 1946 *El Gabilan* can be forgiven for their arithmetic error in adding a full decade to Wing's tenure at the high school. Taking together the range and depth of her contributions in anchoring girls' PE and supervising the activities of the Girls Athletic Association (GAA) for most of her twenty-one years at the school, it may just have *seemed* like three decades of labor. From her arrival in 1925 to her departure in 1946—the first seven years as Miss Rouse, the final fourteen as Mrs. Wing—she was routinely

Figure 2.1. Salinas High heavyweight football team, CCAL champs, *El Gabilan*, 1941

MRS. RUTH WING

Dedication

Figure 2.2. Dedication page, *El Gabilan*, 1946

DEDICATION

To Miss Ruth Rouse and Howard F. Ross, who have helped us to attain health of body and of mind, the Senior Class dedicates this 1928 issue of El Gabilan

Figure 2.3. Dedication page, *El Gabilan*, 1928

Figure 2.4. Mrs. Ruth Wing, *El Gabilan*, 1946

depicted in the yearbook as the GAA adviser, a position through which she organized a dizzying array of activities. She coached all of the usual sports—basketball, speedball, baseball, field hockey, soccer, tennis, volleyball—and also a range of other physical activities, often held outside normal school hours. The 1935 *El Gabilan* noted that Wing's GAA had been very active that year.

> On February 14, the old and present officers of G.A.A. had a lovely supper at the home of Mrs. Wing. Work for El Gab and Play Day was accomplished, but amidst the work the girls had loads of fun because valentines were exchanged . . . In addition to a "Roman Plunge" swim day, and a hayride to the hills, the G.A.A. joined about 600 girls for the annual Play Day in Santa Cruz on March 23 . . . the usual games were enjoyed during the morning, with the noon session devoted to eating and the presentation of the playlet, "Spring Fever."[2]

The girls were also introduced to tumbling that year, an elective activity that gathered "two nights a week, after school, for a period of six weeks . . . under the direction of Mrs. Wing."[3] The busy physical education instructor was also in charge of dance: "Girls who were especially talented and suited for extra chorus dances, were given special instruction by Mrs. Wing, and these dances were presented for the J.C. Jamboree, Christmas program, and operetta." Whatever was needed, it seemed Mrs. Wing was there to provide (Figure 2.4). In 1940, the annual GAA Christmas potluck saw "Mrs. Wing presiding in the role of Santa Claus."[4]

Ruth Wing witnessed tumult and change during her two decades at SUHS—the Great Depression, violent agricultural labor clashes in the Salinas Valley, a world war that included the removal and incarceration of the school's Japanese American students—and along the way experienced the steady growth of Salinas and its high school. When she started teaching at the high school in 1926, Salinas was undergoing an agriculture-driven boom that more than doubled the town's population during the decade, from 4,308 people in 1920 to 10,263 in 1930. During that decade, the historian Carol Lynn McKibben noted, "The production of lettuce pulled in new populations and made Salinas one of the most promising and wealthiest cities in the nation."[5] This local population explosion led inevitably to a growth spurt in the high school student body. When Ruth Rouse started working at SUHS in 1926, the graduating class consisted of 64 students; the senior class in 1946, the year of Ruth Wing's departure,[6] had ballooned to 250.

Sports were changing too. Interscholastic girls' sports had roared into the 1920s, riding the crest of the women's movement. But by the end of the decade, girls' sports had been squeezed down into spaces that restrained the physical movements of girls. Into the 1930s and through the 1940s, boys' sports ballooned in scope and importance, and their cultural centrality was increasingly celebrated in the annual yearbooks. The marginalization of girls' sports from the mid-1920s through the immediate postwar years, as we will see in this chapter, had the somewhat ironic effect of shrinking and containing girls' sporting activities and options, while simultaneously creating a space within which women physical educators controlled the action, nurtured sports programs based on what was asserted to be a female value system, and garnered what can be read in retrospect as a degree of grudging respect in the annual yearbook. The career of PE teacher Ruth (Rouse) Wing at Salinas Union High School bookended this era.

The Ascent of the Football Hero

The 1927 *El Gabilan* featured the first appearance of the Block "S" Society, described in the 1928 book as a club made up "of all boys who have won Block 'S's' in sports," and whose purpose was "to encourage high ideals of good sportsmanship among the boys."[7] The boys in the club proudly wore the "S" letter on the front of their school-colored sweaters, and, in later years, on leather-sleeved jackets (Figures 2.5, 2.6). Membership in the club (which would remain closed to girls until the mid-1970s) and the wearing of the Block "S" sweater or jacket would become a common public display of a boy's athletic accomplishments and his honored status in the school.

The annual yearbooks of the late 1920s to the mid-1930s devoted ample space to a range of boys' sports. Basketball—especially varsity, but also for a few years "midget basketball" for smaller boys—was routinely well covered, as were the annual standards track and field and baseball, along with expanding array of sports that for a time were dubbed "minor sports"—handball, tennis, wrestling, boxing, golf, archery, and tumbling (Figure 2.7). The yearbooks' treatment of boys' sports was consistently respectful and loaded with detail. Team photos—even for the so-called minor

Figure 2.5. (*top*) Block "S" Society, *El Gabilan*, 1928

Figure 2.6. Block "S" Society, *El Gabilan*, 1933

Figure 2.7. Coach Herbert Sykes and the boys' tumbling team, *El Gabilan*, 1930

sports—were routinely accompanied with win-loss records from interscholastic competition, scores and descriptions of big games, and praise for star players.

In the midst of this celebratory expansion of boys' sports, the game of football surged to the center as the most honored sport, a common development in American high schools and colleges in this era. During the teens and early twenties, track and field, basketball, and baseball had jockeyed for the high ground of the most celebrated sport on campus, but by the late twenties and early thirties, football was rising to the pinnacle. The yearbooks illustrate this fact: high achievement in football was becoming the central way through which a small number of boys were singled out for public honor. Football players in these years were occasionally referred to in the yearbooks as "men," an adult status rarely if ever bestowed upon other boys, much less on the girls who played sports.[8]

By the mid-1930s, references to "football heroes" became more routine. There is no way to trace the source of this honorific moniker with full confidence, but it's likely that the popular song "You gotta be a football hero, to get along with the beautiful girls," the lyrics of which introduce this chapter, both reflected and amplified a growing public adulation of gridiron stars. Written in 1933 by the songwriting team Al Lewis and Al Sherman, the song became wildly popular; it was first recorded in 1933 by Ben Bernie and All the Lads and later by many others. Even the gangly cartoon character Olive Oyl urged on her own hero with a rendition of this song in a 1935 *Popeye* episode.[9] As late as my 1950s childhood, I recall my father—a prewar college football player and then-current high school coach—marching around the house belting out this song.

The emergence of the football hero as a cultural ideal helped to usher in prep football as the primary anchor for the most honored expression of masculinity on high school campuses, a gender formation that would reach its apogee in the post–World War II era. If a boy's goal was to impress the "beautiful girls," and even possibly "get a baby to pet," well, gridiron glory was billed as the formula for success. Beyond the allotment of several pages for photos and text describing that year's football season, the *El Gabilan* books of the late 1920s and early 1930s regularly devoted a half page or even a full page to one or two football players posing with the gleaming trophies they had won as the year's Most Valuable Man or Most Inspirational Player (Figures 2.8, 2.9, 2.10). The first such photo, in 1928, is notable: The "Inspiration Cup," dubbed the Oyer Cup in honor of its first recipient, team captain and president of the Block "S" Society Frank Oyer, was donated by Roy Scracherd, "proprietor of Beebe's Drug Store."[10] The 1929 Oyer Cup winner, Clark Alsop, was lauded for being "the hardest fighter, the best loser, the finest winner, and a real sportsman."[11] The lovely Oyer Cup represented a public investiture from local businessmen for the school's football glory, a gesture that would be repeated in other ways in subsequent years.[12]

"A Builder of Men and Teams"

The mounting glory bestowed on football heroes in the late 1920s and early 1930s coincided with an escalating visibility of the football coach, a connection often linked in the yearbooks: between 1927 and 1936—during which the nation endured the Great Depression and California was jolted by fierce agricultural labor conflicts—year in and year out, the square-shouldered and ever-serious-looking Harry Shipkey can be seen towering over his charges in the heavyweight football and basketball team photos and in the group shots of the Block "S" Society (Figures 2.11, 2.12, 2.13). The 1934 photo of Shipkey, set between shots of that season's football heroes Ivan Pickens and Hugo Pia, offered a rare hint of a smile from the routinely stern coach, characteristically attired for photo shoots in V-neck sweater or buttoned jacket worn over a starched white shirt and tie.

During his decade-long tenure at SUHS, Harry Shipkey coached an array of varsity sports, including track and field, baseball, and basketball, a sport in which he won several CCAL championships. But it was his heavyweight football teams' annual triumphs that earned Shipkey the lion's share of his public adulation. The "Sports"

The Oyer Cup

Perhaps a great part of the enthusiasm for and interest in football this year was caused by the presentation of an "Inspiration Cup" by Mr. R. Scratchrd to the school. Each year on this cup is to be engraved the name of the most faithful and influential football player on the team. Frank Oyer, senior captain of the heavyweight squad, was selected as the most deserving player of this year's team. His name has been engraved on this trophy, and in honor of him it has been called the Oyer Cup. Our congratulations to Frank and our thanks to Mr. Scratchrd.

Figure 2.8. (*left*) Frank Oyer, Inspiration Cup winner, *El Gabilan*, 1928

Figure 2.9. (*right*) Clark Alsop, Inspiration Cup winner, *El Gabilan*, 1929

Figure 2.10. Hugo Pia, Inspiration Cup winner, and Herbert Smith, Most Valuable Man on the Team, *El Gabilan*, 1935

EL GABILAN

COACH SHIPKEY

COACH Harry Shipkey, who has just finished his fifth successful year as athletic mentor at Salinas high school. Coach Shipkey is one of the famous "Warner School" which has made for itself such a name in the athletic world. He was himself a great athlete of Stanford's heyday.

INSPIRATION CUP

This trophy was donated in 1927 by Roy Scatcherd. In that year Frank Oyer won the cup. The successive years saw it go to Clark Alsop, Bill Lingley, Elmer Machado, George Martella, and this year, Bryce Brown.

MOST VALUABLE MAN ON TEAM

This cup was donated in 1929 by Ray Deddy. The men who have been awarded this cup are Malcolm Fiese, Elmer Machado, and Ivan Pickens. Ivan Pickens has the distinction of having won this trophy for two successive years.

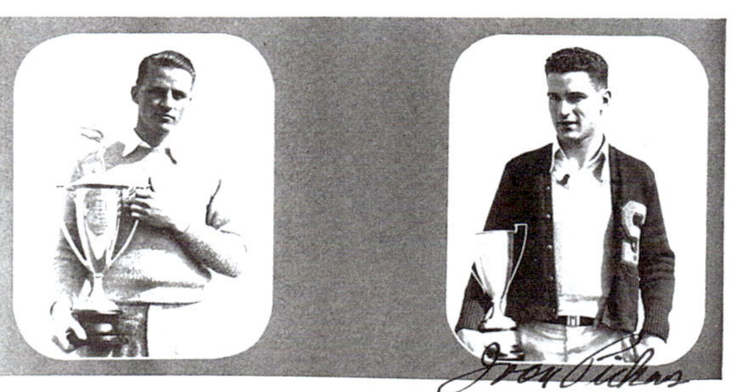

« 62 »

Figure 2.11 (*top*). CCAL heavyweight football champs and coach Harry Shipkey, *El Gabilan*, 1931

Figure 2.12. (*left*) Coach Harry Shipkey; Bryce Brown, Inspiration Cup winner; Ivan Pikens, Most Valuable Man on Team, *El Gabilan*, 1933

Figure 2.13. (*above, right*) Team captain Ivan Pickens, coach Harry Shipkey, captain-elect Hugo Pia, *El Gabilan*, 1934 section of the 1931 *El Gabilan* opened with a gush of praise for the football team's 9-1 record: "Every game was played cleanly, with true spirit, with undying fight; every player was a cog in a brilliant machine, and each man gave everything he had to the team . . . All tribute must be paid to coach Harry Shipkey."[13]

The 1932 *El Gabilan* was co-dedicated to Shipkey. By 1933, his fifth year at the high school, Shipkey was lionized for his continuing gridiron conquests, including another CCAL football championship. The "Sports" section of the book began with a lavish six-page spread on football, including a full page spotlighting the team's Inspiration Cup winner and Most Valuable Man on the Team, above whom looms "Coach Harry Shipkey, who has just finished his fifth successful year as athletic mentor at Salinas high school. Coach Shipkey is one of the famous 'Warner School' which has made for itself such a name in the athletic world. He was himself a great athlete of Stanford's heyday."[14]

The mention of Shipkey's grounding in "the famous 'Warner School'" references Pop Warner, the legendary college football coach who began a nine-year stint at Stanford University in 1924, following many years of coaching at other institutions. Unlike his equally famous counterpart Knute Rockne, who was known for his inspirational charisma, Pop Warner was a gruff tactician, credited with having innovated new blocking and tackling techniques and offensive sets such as the single-wing and double-wing formations. Warner's Stanford team won the national championship in 1926.[15] The 6-foot, 2-inch, 205-pound Harry Shipkey had earned All-America honors playing offensive line for Warner at Stanford in 1925. Following one season playing pro football (at that time a low-paid and low-status occupation), Shipkey turned to coaching, bringing Warner's successful offensive tactics, and apparently also his coach's stoic leadership style, to Salinas. In 1937 Shipkey would be lured back to Stanford to coach the freshmen football team. At the end of his final year at SUHS the 1936 *El Gabilan* bestowed one more burst of praise on Shipkey for his record as "a builder of men and teams."[16] That year's football team photo depicted Shipkey with his final crew of gridiron champions, posing like their coach—stern and sturdy with nary a smile—in their spanking-new stadium.[17] Perhaps it's not a stretch to think of Salinas High's football stadium, which decades later would be dubbed "The Pit," as, at least originally, The House that Shipkey Built (Figure 2.14).

"Carry Our Teams to Victory"

As boys' sports, especially football, was seizing the center of the prep status system, another position of masculine honor was emerging: the yell leader. Though they were not allotted a great deal of space in the yearbooks of the late 1920s and early 1930s—some years they did not appear in the books at all—when yell leaders were featured they were always boys, and they basked in the reflected glow of the masculine honor

Figure 2.14. CCAL champs with coach Shipkey in new SUHS football stadium, *El Gabilan*, 1936

that shined on football heroes. Sometimes they even shared credit for the team's victories. For two consecutive years—1930 and 1931—photos of the school's two yell leaders shared an *El Gabilan* page with the football players who had won that year's Inspiration Cup and Most Valuable Player award (Figures 2.15, 2.16). It was the job of the yell leaders, the 1931 book emphasized, to supply "spirit at the Games." The book lauded yell leaders Wesley McClure and Randy Smith, "whose ever-present 'pep' has done much toward carrying our teams to victory."[18]

In their history of cheerleading, Natalie Guice Adams and Pamela J. Bettis note that in U.S. high schools and colleges of the 1920 and 1930s, "Cheerleading began as an exclusively male activity and represented desirable masculinity. In fact, as recently as 1939 women were barred from being chosen for the [college] All-American Cheerleading squad that was chosen by sportswriters."[19] And as we shall see, the term "cheerleader" was not uttered in *El Gabilan* annuals until girls started doing the cheering. Boys were called "yell leaders"; apparently, boys did not "cheer."

Containing "the New Athletic Girl"

As Harry Shipkey was presiding over an expanding boys' sports program that was becoming more central to the school's status system, Ruth Rouse oversaw a girls' sports system that was contracting. The *El Gabilan* books of the early 1920s had tended to allot girls' sports nearly as many pages as they devoted to boys' sports (in 1926, it was

OLLIE LEE AND RANDOLPH SMITH

WILLIAM LINGLEY

Spirit at the games this year has been ably supplied by yell-leaders, Wesley McClure and Randy Smith, whose ever-present "pep" has done much toward carrying our teams to victory.

Elmer Machado, the smallest player in the heavyweight division of the entire league, received and deserved the honor of being voted by his teammates the Inspiration Cup for 1930. This trophy is donated by Roy Scatcherd.

Malcolm Fiese, for being the most valuable member of the team, was voted by all members of the school as deserving of the Duddy Fox-California Trophy.

Figure 2.15. (*left*) Yell leaders Ollie Lee and Randolph Smith, Inspiration Cup winner William Lingley, *El Gabilan*, 1930

Figure 2.16. (*right*) Yell leaders Wesley McClure and Randy Smith, Inspiration Cup winner Elmer Machado, Most Valuable Member of the Team Malcolm Fiese, *El Gabilan*, 1931

an even 12 pages for each), but the proportion of sports pages devoted to the girls began to shrink in the late 1920s (4 for girls, 11 for boys in 1928; 3.5 for girls, 11.5 for boys in 1929). By the mid-1930s, however, a pattern of devoting only slightly less space to girls' sports emerged (e.g., 6-to-8 girls-to-boys in 1935; 9-to-11 in 1936).

El Gabilan coverage of girls' sports had not evaporated, to be sure. What had changed is the sports themselves. By the mid-1920s, interscholastic sports competition for girls had been all but eliminated at Salinas High and around the nation. Near the end of the decade, girls posing with their sports teams were still wearing SUHS uniforms

(Figure 2.17). Within a few years the uniforms had become superfluous in the absence of competition with other schools (Figure 2.18). Nor could the yearbooks report scores, win-loss records, or championships, because these no longer existed. Instead, the girls posed in generic gym suits, sometimes divided into intramural "purples" and "golds," playing sports that had been adapted to reduce vigorous physical activity or bodily contact. Also, as we will see, dance ascended as a favored physical activity for girls.

The shift from girls' interscholastic competition that had been similar (though not identical) to the boys' sports activities, to a system of separate and very unequal forms of sport for girls and boys, happened rapidly. As we have seen, the pushback against "the new athletic girl" was well under way by the mid-1920s, fueled by anti-feminist backlash and post–World War I fears of the feminization of American boys and men.[20] As cultural conservatives and religious leaders raised fears that sport was creating "mannishness" in girls and women, medical experts raised alarms about the supposed dangers of vigorous physical activities for women's reproductive capacities.[21] The backlash was joined by a perhaps surprising professional group: "Tremendous pressure [was] exerted to limit competitive activities for girls from the women's physical education establishment."[22]

At Salinas Union High School, Ruth Rouse oversaw the containment of girls' sports into a separate and unequal sphere of physical activity, a system that would persist in roughly the same form until the early 1970s passage of Title IX. Rouse had arrived at the high school in 1926 with a degree from the University of California, Berkeley, where she most likely had been educated in the latest physical education philosophies and methods for girls. Between the 1920s and the 1940s, historian Martha H. Verbrugge observes, increasingly "anxious about femininity and sexuality," women physical educators sought to "personify virtue" through "codes of 'Phy Ed-iquette' [that] trained young women to be refined, intelligent, active ladies, free of masculine athleticism."[23] Driven in part by increasing fears of lesbianism, the aim of "Phy Ed-iquette" was "to bolster heterosexual femininity."[24]

In the two years before Rouse began, some girls' sports teams were still competing in a diminishing field of interscholastic contests, governed by the Girls' Coast Counties Athletic League (GCCAL). In 1926, Rouse and other leaders innovated a "telegraphic" form of interscholastic competition. The *El Gabilan* noted that under their new teacher, "Purple and Gold" intramural all-star teams played volleyball in the school gymnasium, and during the match, "the number of ace serves, returns, and faults made was counted in this game. These with the final scores were sent to the President of the G.C.C.A.L. at Monterey . . . The other schools were playing intramurally at the same time. They also sent their scores to the President, who decided up on which school had the best score. This was the first time a telegraphic volley ball meet has ever been held, and Salinas finished second."[25] This sort of virtual competition between schools was apparently not repeated in subsequent years, and was likely a one-off transition to what became the dominant form of girls' sports for

Soccer Team

Figure 2.17. *El Gabilan*, 1928

several decades: intramural adapted sports, punctuated by one or two interscholastic "Play Days" each year, all under the governance of the GAA. Similar shifts in girls' sports were taking place across the nation.

Repulsed by the supposed dangers for girls in conforming to a male model of competitive sports, the developing field of women's physical education carved out sport and physical activity that they believed would conform to the particular needs and supposed nature of girls' and women's bodies, emotions, and proper social standing.[26] The philosophy underlying the new physical education for girls and women was grounded largely in middle-class and predominantly white understandings of gender. "The moderate, wholesome athlete idealized by physical educators," historian Susan Cahn writes, "fused appropriate female athleticism with a middle-class concept of womanhood characterized by refinement, dignity, and self-control."[27]

By the mid- to late 1920s, girls' high school sports were being systematically restructured under the auspices of statewide organizations of the GAA. There were three dimensions of this restructuring, and each were reflected in the SUHS yearbooks. First, interscholastic competition was all but eliminated, replaced by intramural sports and occasional "Play Days" that gathered girls from different schools for physical activities. Second, the sports girls had played in the 1910s and early 1920s changed: some were eliminated; others persisted with adapted rules that limited vigorous play; and some new activities, like dance, were added. Third, the containment of girls' sports under the GAA created a space of relative autonomy governed by women, and driven by the ideal of popular participation for girls' physical activity. And for a time girls' sports were treated respectfully in the annual yearbooks.

Figure 2.18. *El Gabilan*, 1933

"A Team for Every Girl, a Girl for Every Team"

By the late 1920s, when schools did gather girls for physical activities, it was no longer to stage a competition to see which school's basketball or volleyball team would win out. Instead, it was to hold Play Days, conducted under the auspices of the GAA. The 1926 *El Gabilan* introduced the first Play Days with this description: "The idea of these play days is the social benefit which the girls get instead of mere competition between schools."[28] The girls did play basketball, volleyball, tennis, and soccer, but "it was not a

Figure 2.19. GAA, *El Gabilan*, 1929

contest of school versus school. There were no regular teams, but the girls were mixed, Salinas and Santa Cruz girls on each team." The 1927 *El Gabilan* sounded a sharper anticompetitive note: "As competition is no longer allowable between schools in girls' athletics, this play day was really more of a social gathering. The games that were played were basketball, volleyball, soccer and hockey. After all the games were completed, the girls went down to the Casino and had a very enjoyable swim."[29]

The GAA grew and thrived at Salinas High (Figures 2.19, 2.20). "The organization of G.A.A.," the 1930 *El Gabilan* declared, "was a step toward promoting the right kind of girls' athletics. It has offered a team for every girl." The new system rested on a democratized ideal of popular participation for girls, in contrast to the varsity competition model of boys' sports that restricted the number of athletes who could join teams. But the ascendant system also clearly subordinated girls' sports to boys' sports in the school's status hierarchy. The November 1930 GAA Play Day, held in Salinas with Watsonville and Santa Cruz high schools, was a prelude to the boys' football game: "The girls participated in hockey, speedball, soccer and tennis. After a picnic lunch, folk-dancing was enjoyed; all then went to the Salinas-Santa Cruz football game."[30]

The anti-competition ethos of the GAA may have achieved hegemony by the end of the 1920s, but there was apparently still some debate concerning what sport should look like for girls. The 1931 *El Gabilan* recognized this debate, while strongly affirming the GAA philosophy:

> The question uppermost in all Girls' Athletic Associations today is what type of inter-school competition will be developed—varsity competition or Play Day

Figure 2.20. GAA, *El Gabilan*, 1933

> administration, toward which latter the trend in girls' athletics seems very decidedly directed. A varsity program is narrow, and restricted to a few players, whereas in the Play Day, players for all the schools are intermingled at random on the same team. The proper amount of rivalry is present, as the players are divided into color groups . . . This impromptu mixing of strange players creates friendliness, courtesy, and sociability. Our G.A.A. has developed this method of organizing athletics. At our annual Play Day, the dances, entertainments, and luncheon offer the girls opportunity to form new acquaintances, as well as to promote our motto, "A team for every girl, a girl for every team."[31]

The social benefits and noncompetitive philosophy of the GAA were often trumpeted in these years, as in this *El Gabilan* description of the 1934 Play Day held in Santa Cruz, in which seven hundred girls participated: "The participants enjoyed a treasure hunt followed by an interclass meet. At the close of the event cookies and punch were served to everyone." But words on the very same page hinted that some athletic girls still reveled in vigorous competition, pushing up against the limits of the "refinement, dignity, and self-control" sought by the physical education establishment. The junior and senior girls who were competing intramurally to be on the field hockey all-star team, "were having a glorious time trying to injure and kill each other. Twenty-one girls fighting hard with feet, stick, and ball made the field a 'battle royal' . . . these poor benighted girls considered violence to be the best way of winning both the game and place on the All-Star eleven."[32]

Figure 2.21. *El Gabilan*, 1934

Figure 2.22. *El Gabilan*, 1936

The celebratory tone of *El Gabilan* descriptions of Play Days was rarely accompanied by photographs of Play Day events. Instead, most yearbook photos of girls' sports in these years were posed team shots, or staged photos of girls holding tennis racquets, readying themselves to shoot an arrow, forming a tumbling team pyramid, or poised with hockey sticks and ready to pounce (Figures 2.21, 2.22).

By 1940, the containment of girls' sports competition seemed nearly complete. That year, the *El Gabilan* noted that under the leadership of Mrs. Ruth Wing, "To safeguard the health of the girls, G.A.A. members voted to permit each girl to participate in only five sports during the year . . . Each member must have her health record checked and cleared by the school physician."[33] That same year, Ruth Wing gained a faculty colleague in girls' physical education. Trained at San Jose State College, Joan Hughes's teaching areas were listed in the book as girls' physical education and "hygiene," a field tethered closely to prewar pedagogies that emphasized the health benefits of limited and noncompetitive physical activities for girls.

Salinas Union High School was not alone in this transformation. All over the nation, local high school associations like the GCCAL that had organized interscholastic competition for girls were subsumed under the expanding umbrella of the GAA, which de-emphasized competition in favor of the health and social benefits of popular participation. Many girls may still have preferred rough-and-tumble team sports, but the reorganization of girls' high school sports made it more and more difficult to find an outlet for this level of vigorous competitive activity.

Adapted Sports and Dance

The game of basketball was the bull's-eye in physical educators' targeting of girls' and women's competitive team sports, especially those that regularly included bodily contact. Physical educators "suggested that individual games like golf and tennis made ideal replacements" for competitive team sports.[34] But girls continued to flock to basketball. "The girls showed a great deal of enthusiasm [for] basketball," the 1926 *El Gabilan* reported.[35] By the mid-1920s, attempts to modify the game were well under way, as this lively team sport that required frequent jumping and landing, running at breakneck speed, and routine bodily contact with opposing players was increasingly being viewed as dangerous and inappropriate for girls. Instead of outright eliminating what was "the most consistently popular sport among schoolgirls and young women since its invention in 1891," reformers engaged in "a concerted attack on the popular sport of basketball."[36] The modified game they settled on bore scant resemblance to the game that boys played: "The three-court, six-player 'girls' rules' . . . divided the floor into front-, center-, and backcourt regions, with players designated as forwards, centers, or guards correspondingly and confined to their section of the court. The rules allowed players to dribble the ball only one time (later, three bounces were allowed) and prohibited physical contact and any effort to hinder the shooter."[37]

Educators "pushed hard" for the three-court, six-player rules, but they "realized that many athletes preferred the more active, five-player, 'boys' rules.'" As a result, educators "compromised by inventing a third set of rules—a six-person, two court game that allowed more movement and active guarding."[38]

The Salinas High yearbooks of the early 1930s reflect this turbulence in girls' basketball rules (Figure 2.23). The 1934 *El Gabilan* noted that "the juniors and seniors played two-court basketball this year instead of the slower and less exciting three-court game."[39] This point was echoed in the 1935 yearbook: "Basketball is always the most exciting and popular game on the girls' sport program . . . While freshmen and sophomore girls played the three-court game, the junior and senior girls played two-court basketball."[40]

This more sedentary "girls' rules" basketball game was a manifestation of what sociologist Nancy Theberge called an "adapted model" of sports, institutionalized in the 1920s and 1930s, based on different rules from the sports that boys played.[41] Adapted sports ensured that girls engaged in less strenuous activity that required less movement, less bodily contact with others, and little if any aggression. Even the spaces designed for girls' sports reflected this bodily containment. The playing area of the girls' gymnasium at Salinas High was smaller and tighter than even the less-than-regulation-length boys' gym. With a wall perhaps two steps beyond the court's end line, the building itself placed a roadblock in front of any player who may have imagined scoring a layup at a full-speed run. Such smaller and tighter spaces created for girls' and women's sports were designed to contain and discipline women's bodies. "From the beginning," historian Patricia Vertinsky asserts, "the spaces of modern sports facilities such as gymnasia were sexed spaces involved in the construction of sexed bodies." The history of women's gymnasia in universities "reflected the paradox of women in sport and physical education."[42]

In addition to taming the female body through adapted sports in confining spaces, there was a second major change in the organization of girls' sports in the twenties and thirties: the expansion of noncompetitive physical activities like tumbling and dance. From the mid-1930s through the immediate postwar years, some of the most prominent photographic representations in the girls' sports section of the *El Gabilan* consisted of often highly stylized shots of girls posing in tumbling formations or dance routines (Figures 2.24, 2.25).

By the latter half of the 1930s, dance performances had been elevated at Salinas High as a celebrated alternative to competitive team sports. Below a posed photo of more than twenty girls in the 1937 *El Gabilan*, the following description highlighted the draw of dance as a performative arena of appropriately moving girls' bodies.

> Today, Modern Dancing is all the rage. Because movement of the body is not limited to a certain few people, but is part of everyone's life, dancing has a universal appeal that is common to no other art. The gym teachers praise it because it develops a

Figure 2.23. Girls' basketball, *El Gabilan*, 1934

> supple, well-coordinated body. The dancer loves it because it disregards the set formula and leaves her free for genuine, creative effort. Everyone loves watching it . . . In a whirl of colors, they appear again in March at the Salinas Gym, and in May at Santa Cruz Play-Day to present a sensational modern dance program."[43]

"Dancing Takes the Spotlight," ran the heading of a two-page photo spread in the 1942 *El Gabilan*. Indeed, by the prewar years, dance was firmly ensconced as perhaps the most highly honored of activities in the girls' sports section of the annual yearbook, which by 1940 was regularly devoting two full pages to dance (of six or seven total) in the section (Figures 2.26, 2.27).

The elevation of dance at Salinas High was hardly anomalous. Sparked by the development of progressive education in the 1920s and 1930s, modern dance was promoted as a central aspect of girls' and women's physical education. For a time, "the feminization of dance . . . empowered female teachers."[44] Through dance, reformers of girls' and women's sports hoped to counter fears of "mannish" women athletes. Coupled with the creation of adapted sports, the escalating importance of dance created two nonthreatening images of athletic womanhood, and "both incorporated athletic enjoyment and competence into notions of femininity. Yet neither fundamentally challenged the commonsense belief that rugged sports and physical activity were masculine in character." Thus, in the cultural imagination of prewar United States, "the unmodified 'athlete' remained a male figure."[45]

Relative Autonomy and Bounded Respect

The marginalization of girls' sports in the decades leading up to World War II severely limited the sorts of things girls could do as it contributed to the valorization of boys' sports. But girls' sports very containment also yielded some limited benefits, including helping them to sidestep the vicious counterpunch of patriarchal backlash. Girls' and women's sports became a relatively autonomous realm, mostly controlled by women, in an otherwise male-dominated social world.[46] The GAA also aimed to create a democratized field of universal participation in physical activity for girls, compared with the boys' sports system that restricted playing opportunities as it generated a few star athletes and a lot of spectators. "As an alternative to win-at-all-costs elite competition, women physical educators typically favored '*democracy in education*,' to allow everyone, regardless of sex or ability, to learn skills and play games."[47]

Girls' sporting accomplishments, by their marginalization and containment, were reduced in any threat they may have posed to boys' and men's supposed natural superiority. As a result, at least up until the war years, the treatment of girls' sports in the annual yearbooks was consistently couched in a positive, respectful tone. Gone were *El Gabilan* reports in the 1910s and early 1920s of interscholastic competition, nor were there team photos of girl athletes wearing SUHS uniforms. But the yearbooks

Figure 2.24. *El Gabilan*, 1935

consistently devoted several pages to "girls' sports" that included group and individual photos, sometimes captioned with the names of girls and accompanied with text that described the girls' activities with respect and even enthusiasm.

Within the generally democratized and anticompetitive realm of GAA-organized girls' athletics, some space was carved out for honoring the girls who were most devoted to sports, who perhaps consistently displayed the most "pep" and athletic accomplishment. In 1940 the *El Gabilan* started including a photo and some text to the honorific "G.A.A. Sweater Society." Somewhat akin to the boys' Block "S" Society, a white sweater emblazoned with an "S" was awarded to senior girls who had amassed at least three hundred points through their participation in GAA activities. The 1941 book noted that girls had the opportunity to choose from nineteen sports, joking that "Any girl who can't win an award now is simply 'nothin' but a nothin' as far as G.A.A. is

Figure 2.25. *El Gabilan*, 1939

Figure 2.26. *El Gabilan*, 1937

dancing takes the spotlight

Standing: Doris Snell, Olive Grainger, Mary Ann Bardin, Betty Anson, Anne Twisselman. *Laying down:* Esther Onoyue, Virginia Knude, Sachie Endo.

Figure 2.27. *El Gabilan*, 1942

concerned."[48] Regardless, the awarding of a sweater appears to have been a rare honor: only thirteen girls appear in the Sweater Society photo in 1940, and a mere eight in 1941.

Race and Class in the 1930s

The content of each annual high school yearbook seems to tell the story of a self-contained world insulated from—or even oblivious to—the historical shifts or public crises taking place outside the walls of the school, however tectonic they may have been. One needs to read between the lines of the early 1930s *El Gabilan* books, for instance, to see any hint of the Great Depression. The 1933 book noted glibly that the school newspaper, "*Flashlight* was slow in starting, because there seemed to be a depression,"[49] and the lower-quality paper used to print part of the 1934 book may be an indicator of reduced resources due to the Depression.[50]

Salinas was unusually insulated from the worst ravages of the Great Depression. Agricultural production fueled an early-1930s building boom in the city, and the Salinas Valley's lettuce industry was "green gold" for the area.[51] The Salinas chamber of commerce sought to draw tourists, especially touting its annual July "Big Week" and Salinas Rodeo. By the mid-1930s, "The bustling city of Salinas was known as the wealthiest community per capita in the United States."[52] Local economic prosperity fueled growth in the local schools, including the high school. But growth was uneven; a poor lettuce harvest in 1932 strained the local economy. In response, the city cut school taxes and slashed teachers' salaries. Quoting from a May 11, 1934, story in the *Salinas Index-Journal*, McKibben notes that "the school board decided 'not to employ any more married women teachers . . . [and] three teachers [presumably married women] now on a probationary basis would be released and no married women would be employed in the future as teachers, except those whose husbands are incapacitated from earning a living.'"[53] Mrs. Ruth Wing likely was protected from losing her job thanks to her successful decade-long tenure at the school. In the subsequent decade before leaving Salinas High in 1946, Wing would be joined by a few new girls' PE teachers, each one designated in the yearbooks as "Miss."

The High School and the Fields

If the Great Depression was barely mentioned in the annual yearbooks, the stormy agricultural labor conflicts in the fields and packing sheds of the 1930s Salinas Valley were even less visible. By the mid-1930s, big agriculture in California had consolidated its might in the Associated Farmers, which held a veritable stranglehold on state and local governments and law enforcement. When agricultural workers attempted to organize in California's Central Valley they were met, according to John Steinbeck, with "a system of terrorism that would be unusual in the fascist nations of the world."[54] The racist violence the Associated Farmers routinely visited upon workers throughout the state was less severe in Salinas, where pragmatic agricultural and city leaders modified the state's "racist ideology . . . to create a situational reality in which 'everyone had to get along with everyone.'"[55] But when push came to shove in Salinas, the velvet glove came off and the iron fist slammed down.

In a 1936 letter to friend George Albee, Steinbeck wrote that the labor strife was "so tense that . . . any reference to labor except as dirty dogs is not printed in the big press out here. There are riots in the streets of that dear little town in which I was born."[56] Steinbeck was referring to the growers' lockout of hundreds of lettuce packers in Salinas, the vast majority of them Filipinos who were joined by striking field workers. In his influential 1939 book *Factories in the Field*, Carey McWilliams described how the strike was finally ended:

> On September nineteenth, the Sheriff . . . ordered a general mobilization of all male residents of Salinas between the ages of eighteen and forty-five, and threatened with arrest any resident who failed to respond. In this manner, the celebrated "Citizens' Army" of Salinas was recruited . . . At the Armory, those of the volunteers who were not armed were given clubs which had been previously manufactured in the manual-arts department of the local high school. Two thousand five hundred men were mobilized, armed, and deputized in this manner.[57]

The strike was smashed, the Vegetable Packers Association was crushed, and the ex-strikers—many of them women—were blacklisted. In a series of 1936 journalistic pieces on migrant farm workers, published in *The San Francisco News*, Steinbeck lamented, "The history of California's importation and treatment of foreign labor is a disgraceful picture of greed and cruelty." Of the Filipinos who had been the main target of repression that year in Salinas, he concluded, "They were good workers, but like the earlier immigrants they committed the unforgivable sin [of] trying to organize for their own protection. Their organization brought on them the usual terrorism."[58]

The fact that some of the weapons deployed in this "usual terrorism" were created in the Salinas High manual-arts shop was of course not noted in that year's *El Gabilan*. But neither was the fact that eight hundred Salinas citizens calling themselves the Citizens Welfare League held "an impromptu meeting at Salinas High School condemning the violence and supporting the right to unionize and to strike . . . showing their collective disdain for those who were bullying the strikers."[59] The high school had been a locus for both supporting and attacking the Filipino lettuce workers. But the outcome was clear: The relatively kinder, gentler system of race relations in Salinas was still a regime in which "cultural inclusiveness of racially excluded people became a façade for actual inclusion . . . Salinas's apparent broad-mindedness in fact supported a system of white supremacy."[60]

From 1935 to 1939, between three hundred thousand and five hundred thousand Dust Bowl refugees—often dubbed "Okies"—arrived in California. Unlike the previously imported agricultural workers from China, Japan, Mexico, and the Philippines, these were American citizens, most of them white. Eventually their descendants became assimilated into Salinas, their children attending the town's public schools. But at first Californians did not treat them well. In 1938, Steinbeck complained to his editor and friend Elizabeth Otis how a "fascist group of utilities, banks and growers" were "sabotaging" efforts to provide relief for roughly five thousand families in the Central Valley who were "starving to death . . . But the crops in any part of this state could not be harvested without these outsiders. I'm pretty mad about it."[61] The Associated Farmers vilified Steinbeck, labelling him a "red" in hopes of discrediting him. Steinbeck was not a communist; rather, he was a dedicated New Deal liberal.[62] He expressed disdain for communist labor organizers in his 1936 novel *In Dubious Battle*, and he clearly understood how the Associated Farmers used red-baiting as a strategy to undermine farmworkers' quest for fairness.[63] When a worker in Steinbeck's landmark novel *The Grapes of Wrath* asks a grower what a "red" is, his boss replies, "A red is any son-of-a-bitch that wants thirty cents an hour when we're payin' twenty-five."[64]

"Into the American Melting Pot"

The *El Gabilan* shed no light on these clashes of race and class in Salinas during the 1930s, nor on the controversial writings of the school's most famous alum, relegating these issues to the shadows. Perhaps this is because high schools were often viewed as sheltered spaces where young people were insulated from the troubles or debates of the outside world—a tendency likely enhanced by the realities of who went to high school, and who did not. Taken together, the yearbooks of the first decades of the twentieth century unselfconsciously chronicle a racial order dominated by white people. Viewing the books in retrospect, it's striking how the SUHS faculty, year after year, decade after decade, was entirely white. But for a notable and growing population of Japanese students, and a smattering of Chinese and Filipino youth, the student body too was mostly white in these years. By my count, the school's senior classes between 1926 and the early 1940s ranged between 80 and 85 percent white.

The hegemony of whiteness in the annual books was occasionally punctuated by the casual appearance of what today would be considered overtly racist depictions of Black people, of whom there were almost zero at the high school during the two-plus decades covered by this chapter.[65] Most striking are the occasions when white students appeared in blackface for school performances (Figures 2.28, 2.29). These included a cartoon drawing, noting the school's production of *Showboat*, of "Cullid people with rhythm in their feet and music on their lips" in the 1934 *El Gabilan*, a 1939 stage shot of the cast of *You Can't Take it With You* that included two actors in blackface, and a photo of four freshman members of the Girls' League putting on a "Minstrel Skit" in the 1945 book.

December 8—During the production of Show Boat, the annual J. C. Jamobree, one couldn't be sure of recognizing his best friend. It might be any of a number of cullid people with rhythm in their feet and music on their lips.

Figure 2.28. *El Gabilan*, 1934

Figure 2.29. Freshmen girls' minstrel skit, *El Gabilan*, 1945

In his analysis of college yearbooks from the state of Virginia between 1890 and 1930, sociologist Stephen C. Poulson viewed routine racist depictions of Black people in the yearbooks of white colleges as windows into the ways that "these institutions acted as more than just sieves that sorted people and helped maintain social distinctions; they also, at times, incubated destructive normative beliefs associated with race that were then disseminated by students throughout society."[66] No doubt this was also true of high school yearbooks like the *El Gabilan*, but compared with the Southern yearbooks Poulson examined, Salinas High School yearbooks rarely expressed overt racism. Instead, depictions of racial or ethnic groups in the 1930s and 1940s yearbooks tended to echo an ethic of coexistence and assimilation, such as the 1940 "Into The American Melting Pot" GAA ethnic dance program that celebrated "Immigration to the United States of people from European countries, Mexico, the British Isles and Japan" (Figure 2.30).

A surface reading of the annual yearbooks of this era does depict a sort of "melting-in" of students of Asian and Pacific Islands descent into the majority-white student body. Chinese, Japanese, and Filipino/a students appear in *El Gabilan* books as participants in most extracurricular activities—a great exception being student government, which in those years remained a domain of white students (the student body president was a white *male* year after year).[67] This sort of integration of the children of immigrants in local public schools is a clear sign that a group has settled into a community. Chinese families increasingly put down roots in Salinas during the first two decades of the twentieth century. Legally constrained by the Chinese Exclusion Acts of the late nineteenth and early twentieth centuries, some found in the small agricultural town of Salinas "a reprieve from the worst assaults and discrimination . . . and virulent anti-Chinese violence" they had experienced in San Francisco and Los Angeles.[68] Segregated in Salinas by local residency restrictions, some Chinese settled in the then-unincorporated Alisal district outside of Salinas, while others built a vibrant Chinatown community in town, centered on Soledad Street. Periodically, white citizens displayed "open hostility toward the Chinese population, with recurring fires destroying Chinatown."[69] However, "Chinese people were needed and wanted as workers, retailers and horticulturalists," and they made deep and lasting contributions to building the city.[70]

Given their foundational contributions and their early settlement in Salinas, it is puzzling how very few Chinese students appear in the Salinas High yearbooks of the 1920s, 1930s, and into the mid-1940s. Two Chinese members of a graduating senior class appeared in the 1933 yearbook, and between that year and 1946 there were on average about four Chinese students in each graduating senior class, just under 2 percent of all graduates.[71] The number of Filipino/a students at the high school during these years was similar, constituting about 1.5 percent of the graduating seniors.[72] Their senior photos were mixed in with those of their classmates, but racial prejudice prevented these students from fully "melting in" with the white majority.

TAP DANCES

HIGH HOP: M. Riggin, J. St. Clair, M. Lew, M. Yee, P. Cline, J. Cline, K. Kobara, A. Parsons, M. Deguchi

CHATTER BOX -- GOSSIP: J. Simas, P. Easton, M. Silk, V. Sargenti

Dance Program

Quaint patterns and traditional music of folk dancing; the rollicking spirit of tap dancing; and the rhythmic grace and symbolism of modern dancing—combined—the result was the Annual Dance Program of February 28.

Immigration to the United States of people from European countries, Mexico, the British Isles, and Japan was expressed by the freshman girls in their folk-dancing numbers. The first of their two groups of dances was entitled "Into the American Melting Pot" and included numbers such as "La Cucaracha", "Sword Dance", and "Aizenun Katsura". The second group, "To Become Americans All," included typical American dances—"The Virginia Reel", "Star by the Right", and "Eight Hands Over."

"Salinas High School Life", as portrayed by sophomore tap dancers,

• PAGE 108

FOLK DANCES

P. Iverson, A. Twisselman, O. Grainger, C. Hall, D. Palmer, N. Mitchell.

A. Kunde, E. Moranda, L. Friere, E. Coroniotis, L. Williamson, H. McLeod

Figure 2.30. GAA folk dances, *El Gabilan*, 1940

McKibben notes that "Interracial dating and marriage were red lines in Salinas that prompted many acts of violence against Filipino American men in California and in the Salinas Valley."[73] These pressures and others likely contributed to students, despite their modest numbers, forming a Filipino Students' Club, which appeared in the *El Gabilan* in 1932, 1934, and 1935 (Figure 2.31).

By contrast, the number of Japanese American students at the high school was expanding. Drawn initially to work in the nearby sugar plant opened in 1898 by Claus

Figure 2.31. Salinas Filipino Students' Club, *El Gabilan*, 1931

Figure 2.32. Japanese Students' Club, *El Gabilan*, 1941

Spreckels, many single Japanese men came to Salinas after the turn of the century. "Horticulturalists at heart, deeply connected to the land,"[74] Japanese families began settling in the Salinas Valley. During the 1920s, each senior class at the high school included one or two Japanese students, and their numbers ballooned in the next decade. Between 1932 and 1942, Japanese students constituted between 12 and 16 percent of each SUHS graduating class. A Japanese Students Club was formed in 1931, and was pictured in each *El Gabilan* for the next decade (Figure 2.32). The club's activities—including celebrations of traditional Japanese music, dance, and food—were a clear expression of what historian Lon Kurishige identified as Nisei

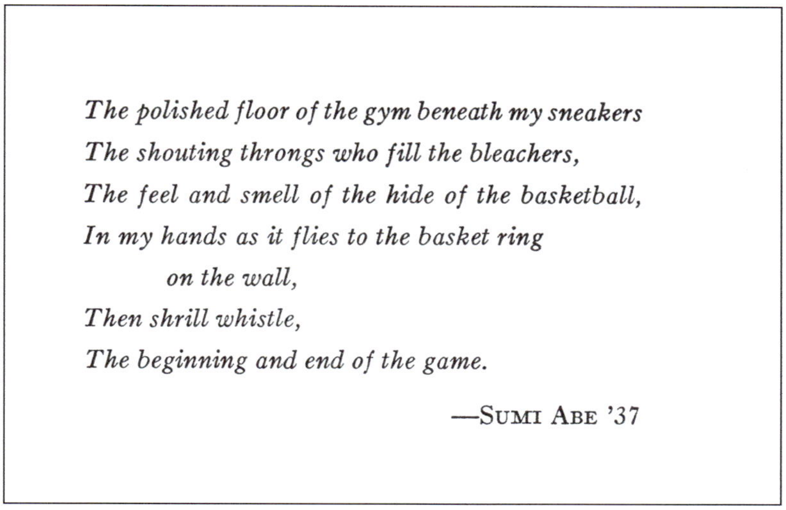

The polished floor of the gym beneath my sneakers
The shouting throngs who fill the bleachers,
The feel and smell of the hide of the basketball,
In my hands as it flies to the basket ring
on the wall,
Then shrill whistle,
The beginning and end of the game.

—SUMI ABE '37

Figure 2.33. (*left*) *El Gabilan*, 1936

Figure 2.34. (*right*) Sumi Abe, *El Gabilan*, 1937

(second-generation Japanese Americans) attempts to navigate increasingly unstable relations between Japan and the United States, as well as tensions within Japanese American communities in the 1930s and early 1940s. Many California Nisei forged a "biculturalism" through which they hoped to fuse assimilationists who were committed to Americanization with those still connected with nationalist pride in the Japanese homeland.[75] This biculturalism is evident in the growing Japanese Students Club at Salinas High. The 1940 *El Gabilan* shows 81 members in the club, and notes that the club had hosted the Northern California Japanese Students' Convention in Salinas, April 27–28, with 500 students attending.[76] The 1941 yearbook pictures 102 students in the Japanese Club, many of whom were engaged in a wide range of student activities, from music to the Scholarship Society to sports—especially sports.

That Japanese American students were well represented in sports should not be too surprising, especially when it comes to the game of basketball. As sociologist Nicole Willms has documented, Japanese American communities all along the West Coast of the United States have long been passionate about the game of basketball, organizing leagues for boys and girls and men and women of all ages for more than a century.[77] This West Coast passion for basketball was echoed at Salinas High School. As a junior poet at SUHS, Sumi Abe penned a veritable love letter to the game for the 1936 *El Gabilan* (Figures 2.33, 2.34).

The 1939 *El Gabilan* praised Japanese guard Lloyd Onoye, "who played wide-awake ball" for the boys' varsity basketball team, and the photo of the lightweight team depicted six Japanese boys on a squad of sixteen (Figure 2.35). Credited as "the undisputable champs of the C.C.A.L.," the Cowbabes' stars included "'Mouse'

GROUP I, VARSITY—*Back*: Coach Regli, H. Iverson, W. Gipe, R. Taylor, J. Heer, J. Abeloe, J. Condon, C. Patterson. *Front*: P. McIntosh, B. Fulle, L. Onoye, B. Gruber, D. James, W. Fleming, J. Hicks.
GROUP II, LIGHTWEIGHTS—*Back*: Coach Hall, B. Kruger, S. Takeshita, J. Prader, S. Gadsby, T. Sakasagawa, T. Stephens. T. Hirozawa, J. Hayes, H. Brummitt, S. Colburn. *Front*: B. Smith, B. Pierson, J. Fujino, H. Sgheiza, P. Yamamoto, D. Kasavan, G. Hanamura.

Figure 2.35. Boys' varsity and lightweight basketball teams, *El Gabilan*, 1939.

Fujino—guard, excellent ball handler, fastest man on the squad," and "Schiro Takeshita—forward. From the corners, tip-ins, everything went in for him."[78]

If anything, the sports participation of Japanese American girls was even more striking than that of the boys. Through the 1930s and into the 1940s, Japanese American girls were frequently included in GAA photos. Even given the GAA disdain for competition and sports stars, it's easy to see that during these years several Japanese American girls were standout athletes. This seems especially true if your last name was Kubota. The 1928 *El Gabilan* recognized Mae Kubota as a member of the school's all-star soccer, basketball, volleyball, and baseball teams (Figures 2.36, 2.37). Not to be outdone, after serving as the school's GAA president in 1934, Alice Kubota was listed in the 1935 yearbook as GAA vice president and an all-star for speedball, volleyball, hockey, basketball, and baseball. Manifesting the mid-1930s GAA eschewing of both team competition and individual honors for girls, however, neither the 1934 nor the 1935 yearbooks included team photos or action shots that identified Alice Kubota.

Reflecting both their love of sports and their high skill levels, Japanese American athletes were also disproportionately represented among the girls in the honorific GAA sweater society. Two of the five sweater-winners shown in the 1942 book—Esther Onoye and Emi Tsukamoto—were Japanese girls, as were two of the four listed as "not in picture"—Mitsuko Miyanaga and Alice Kita. By the time that book was released in the spring of 1942, these four girls had been removed from the campus and from the Salinas community.

Basketball Team

Girls who won sweaters: Esther Onoye, Mary Davies, Jenny Panziera, Phyllis Easton, Emi Tsukamoto.
Not in picture: Barbara Lamb, Violet Sargenti, Mitsuko Miyanaga, Alice Kita.

Figure 2.36. (*top*) Mae Kubota (*far right*), *El Gabilan*, 1928

Figure 2.37. (*left*) GAA Sweater Society, *El Gabilan*, 1942

War and Its Aftermath

The 1942 *El Gabilan* opens with "a tribute . . . to over 350 former Salinas Union High School students now serving in the armed forces of the United States."[79] If the yearbooks of the 1930s had mostly left big events like the Great Depression and agricultural labor disputes outside the frame, World War II was a different matter. That opening tribute in the 1942 *El Gabilan* was the only mention of the war in that book, but half of that school year had passed before the December 7, 1941, Japanese attack on Pearl Harbor and the subsequent U.S. declarations of war against Japan, Germany, and Italy. By the time the 1942 yearbook was disseminated in the spring, the nation was fully engaged in war. The war effort permeated the 1943 *El Gabilan,* which was themed "Things Worth Fighting For." Its leather cover patriotically embossed with a gold eagle and six gold stars set against a blue background, the book was dedicated to the boys "who have now left the campus of Salinas High to fight for our fundamental

Part of the Field Army

Figures 2.38 and 2.39. Students supporting the war effort, *El Gabilan*, 1943

rights and privileges."[80] Noting that boys' interscholastic competition had been eliminated for the year, the "Sports" section of the *El Gabilan* opened by proclaiming that it had been necessary to "transplant many of the players from the athletic field to the battlefield, but the spirit that brings students out for sports, that exalted feeling of a hard-fought battle, and the sense of justice and fair play—these things can never die."[81]

For the girls, GAA activities continued during the war years, sometimes with a decidedly militarized bent: "Under the guidance of Lieutenant Hurt," it was reported in the 1943 *El Gabilan*, "a large number of the girls have become proficient in close-order drill. It has become a fairly common sight to see a squad of the fairer sex marching about the back campus to the commands of 'to the rear march' and 'columns left.'"[82] Several pages of the 1943 book were also devoted to photos of students working in the fields, as during World War I, "to aid in farm labor shortages," practicing for air raids, and "doing our bit Toward Victory" by promoting war bond sales or engaging in weekly military drills with rifles or machine guns at the local armory (Figures 2.38, 2.39).

The size of the high school's 1943 graduating class had plunged from the 1942 count of 320 seniors. "Starting out the year with an enrollment of 278 seniors," the 1943 book pointed out, "the class gradually dwindled to about 216. At the time of this writing 35 boys had left for the armed forces." A second reason for the shrinkage of the student body was due to the removal of all Japanese American students, then the school's largest nonwhite group. The senior class photos in the 1942 *El Gabilan* included forty-five Japanese American students, 12.5 percent of the graduating class. These students, along with Japanese American members of the junior, sophomore, and freshman classes, appeared in a full range of photos in the 1942 book. But President Franklin Delano Roosevelt had issued Executive Order 9066 on February 19, 1942, ordering the internment of all people of Japanese descent, including those who were American citizens. By April, well before the school year ended, the rounding-up of Japanese Americans was underway. Local Japanese residents were first held for sixty-nine days at the Salinas Assembly Center at the Rodeo Grounds before being incarcerated with roughly seventeen thousand others for the three-year duration of the war, mostly in Poston, Arizona.[83]

Suddenly amplified by wartime fears, the region's long-simmering racist views of Japanese people resulted in very few voices speaking out against the internment. Carey McWilliams's 1944 book *Prejudice: Japanese-Americans, Symbol of Racial Intolerance* struck a rare note of critical dissent.[84] In Salinas, "the silence was deafening" from the local press "when thousands of Salinas residents, citizens and noncitizens alike, were rounded up . . . and forcibly incarcerated."[85] The lack of support from most of their neighbors likely came as a shock to many of those who were being rounded up, especially since the Japanese community in Salinas had largely sided with the white agricultural establishment during the previous decade's crackdowns against Filipino agricultural workers.[86]

There are few silver linings to this otherwise shameful moment in American history. When the seniors of Salinas High graduated on June 5, 1942, the forty-six Japanese American members of the senior class were allowed a separate graduation ceremony at the Rodeo Grounds, where they received their diplomas and yearbooks. That this happened at all was largely due to the school's dean of girls, Gertrude Waterman (Figure 2.40). McKibben quotes a friend of Waterman's who recalled that "She was very determined that the Japanese children graduated in 1942. They were all out at the Rodeo grounds, so she got all the caps and gowns and diplomas and handed them out. It was very important . . . You don't often use the term 'noble' with respect to a woman, but I thought Gertrude Waterman was noble."[87]

This "noble" act by Waterman—a beloved dean, counselor, and eventual vice principal to whom the 1932 *El Gabilan* had been co-dedicated (along with coach Harry Shipkey), and for whom, following her retirement, a student scholarship would be awarded for decades in her name—was no doubt appreciated by students and their families.[88] But surely Waterman's gesture barely dented the harm and humiliation Salinas's Japanese population absorbed as a result of their forced removal and roughly

Figure 2.40. Dedication to Miss Gertrude Waterman, *El Gabilan*, 1932

three years of incarceration. The editors of the 1943 *El Gabilan* made no mention of their missing Japanese classmates. What McKibben observed about Salinas in general seems true of its high school as well: "It was as though the Japanese people in Salinas evaporated in plain sight."[89] Instead, the 1943 yearbook centered on patriotic unity, pointing to the creation of new organizations like "The Victory Corps," which aimed "to unite students who want to help the war effort."[90]

The tone of the 1944 *El Gabilan* was grim, as the local impact of another year of war settled in (Figure 2.41). The book opened with a two-page dedication to the 108 Salinas men who fought in the Pacific as part of the 194th Tank Battalion. Many of these men would die in the infamous Bataan Death March. In April 1942 the Japanese army had brutally force-marched sixty-six thousand captured Filipinos and ten thousand Americans sixty-six miles with little or no food. Along the way, several thousand prisoners perished, among them sixty-one Salinas-area men. News of the Death March did not reach the United States until after the war had ended, but when it did, "it only intensified residents' collective scorn for all people of Japanese descent and opposition to their return to the Salinas community after the war."[91]

194th TANK BATTALION

DEDICATION

To those brave men of Bataan we pay sincere and never ending tribute. The entire nation is proud of the Salinas Tank Battalion, but Salinas Union High school is especially proud of these boys. A few short years ago they were one of us—studying the same books we are now studying—having the same fun and good times we are now enjoying. They are no longer here—some will never be here. May we never forget them nor the sacrifices they have made for us. To the memory of these heroes of Bataan we dedicate this 1944 *El Gabilan*.

Figure 2.41. *El Gabilan*, 1944

Welcome Home!

The *El Gabilan* books of the immediate postwar years exuded a sense of relief and a much-anticipated return to normal. The 1946 yearbook featured a celebratory "WELCOME HOME!" school assembly that included a "pre-assembly bullsession between happy servicemen and awed students" and a moment at the gathering when "former students in armed forces rise for recognition."[92] Mostly though, the yearbooks of the immediate postwar years gazed forward rather than looking back. They

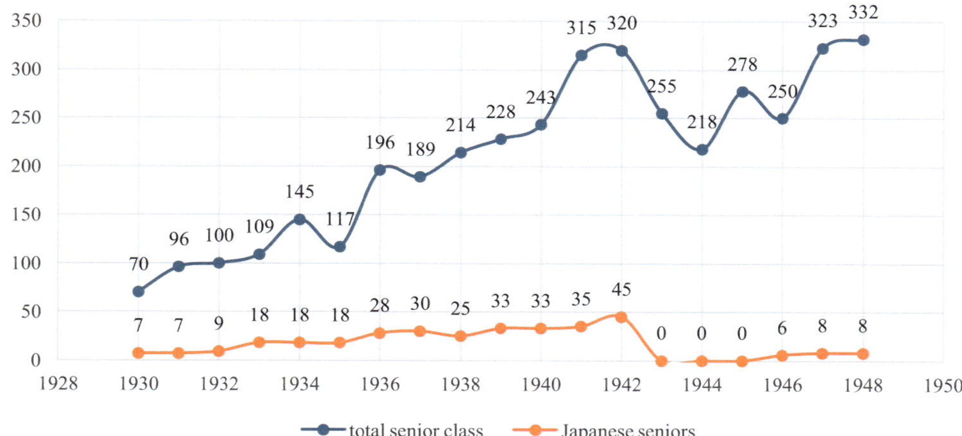

Figure 2.42. Japanese students in SUHS graduating senior classes, 1930–48

also hinted at changes that would blossom in the 1950s and 1960s. One such change would be the demographic mix of Salinas High students. Following their wartime internment, some Japanese American people returned to Salinas, including six who appeared among the graduating seniors of 1946 (Figure 2.42). But the proportion of Salinas High students of Japanese descent never approached their prewar numbers. In her book on the nearby town of Seaside, California, McKibben noted that many former residents of Salinas, when they were released from the internment camps, had lost their property and found Salinas to be unwelcoming after the war. Instead they settled in Seaside, a multiracial town whose growth and diverse demographics had been shaped by the adjacent Fort Ord army base.[93] For a short time, the depletion of what had been its largest minority group made the student body at Salinas High even whiter than it had been before the war. But by the late 1940s and early 1950s the numbers of students with Spanish surnames would start to tick up.

The 1946 *El Gabilan* was also the first to include graduating seniors posing for local businesses' advertisements that appeared in the final section of each book. Ads proliferated of youth posing for local dealerships next to gleaming new cars—"Look into the future with a new 1946 Buick," urged the ad for Johnson's garages. Smiling students posed in ads that anticipated themes that would become familiar in future years—hanging out in stores that sold radios, phonographs, and records, enjoying a cold Coca-Cola or a milkshake in a local creamery—making for a celebratory introduction to an expanding postwar commercialized youth culture.

Three things had begun to shift in the yearbooks' coverage of school sports during the war and in the immediate postwar years. First, through the 1930s, *El Gabilan*'s treatment of athletics was almost always entirely contained within the "Sports" section of the book. By the early to mid-1940s, boys' sports photos started leaking into other parts of the book. This seepage, we will see, opened the gates for a flood of

Figures 2.43 and 2.44. Expanding sports spirit complex, *El Gabilan*, 1942

Figure 2.45. *El Gabilan*, 1941

Figure 2.46. *El Gabilan*, 1945

boys' sports images that would permeate the yearbook pages of the 1950s and 1960s. Second, what I call the "sports spirit complex" was starting to form at the school. A school marching band and organized baton twirlers now joined the yell leaders in the foreground of an expanding pageantry of school spirit swirling around boys' interscholastic sports, especially football games (Figures 2.43, 2.44).

The gender composition of yell leader groups, previously exclusively boys, also began to shift. As more mixed squads began to appear in the yearbooks, the words used to describe this activity were disrupted. This started in 1940, with "Songleader" Gloria Silva joining yell leaders Dick Cava and Johnny Dovolis. The next year, the rooters

Figure 2.47. *El Gabilan*, 1944

Figure 2.48. *El Gabilan*, 1944

of Salinas High were led by "Johnny Dovolis and the three Glorias—Brink, Silva, Stevens." In 1942, the first time the term "cheer leader" appeared in an *El Gabilan*, all three "active pepsters" were girls. For the next four years, the term "yell leader" was used exclusively in describing mixed squads of girls and boys (Figures 2.45, 2.46).

Sparking what would become a mid-century boom, interscholastic boys' sports competition fully revived in the postwar years. For the girls, GAA Play Days resumed in 1946—the year that would be physical education teacher Ruth Wing's final one on the faculty. The *El Gabilan* had covered girls' sports with a tone of bounded respect up until the war years. But the mid-1940s saw the first hints of ambivalent framings of girls' sports, including photo captions that were nonsensical, that pointed to girls' supposed lack of sports knowledge and skills, or that highlighted their feminine attractiveness rather than their athletic abilities or accomplishments. In the following decades, this ambivalence would devolve into full-on trivialization and disrespect for girls who played sports.[94]

Humorous and mildly scolding captions, for instance, accompanied the 1944 shots of girls doing calisthenics—"Up and down! Up and down!" Dance was celebrated as a site of girls' "Grace . . . poise . . . and beauty," benefits that apparently didn't automatically accrue, just from girls simply showing up: "1 . . . 2 . . . 3 . . . 4 . . . Joan! Rhythm, rhythm!" the dancing girls were scolded in the accompanying text. "Please try and dance more smoothly, Roberta . . . This is a dancing class, Beverly, not a gymnastic course." The ultimate purpose of all this vigorous bodily movement was made abundantly clear: "Amid groans and wails, the girls went through their exercises knowing that soon bulging hips and not-too-thin waistlines would be banished"[95] (Figures 2.47, 2.48).

Like their counterparts across a nation that imagined itself moving into a long era of peace and prosperity, the students at Salinas High were resuming their studies and pouring their time and energy into social activities and sports in the postwar years. But they would do so within a drastically shifting social order.

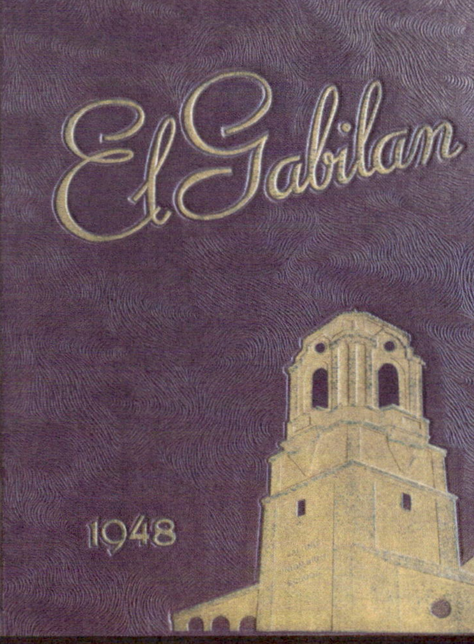
El Gabilan
1948
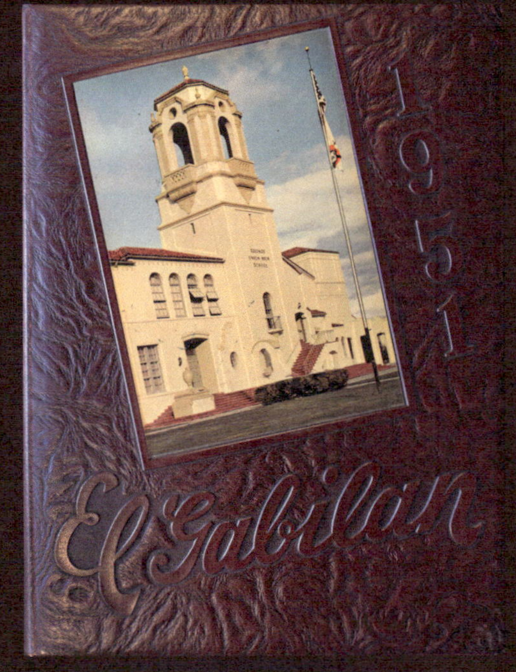
1951
El Gabilan

1955 El Gabilan
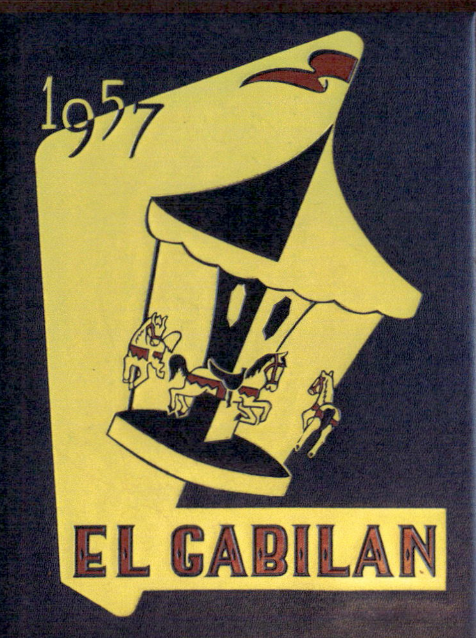
1957
EL GABILAN
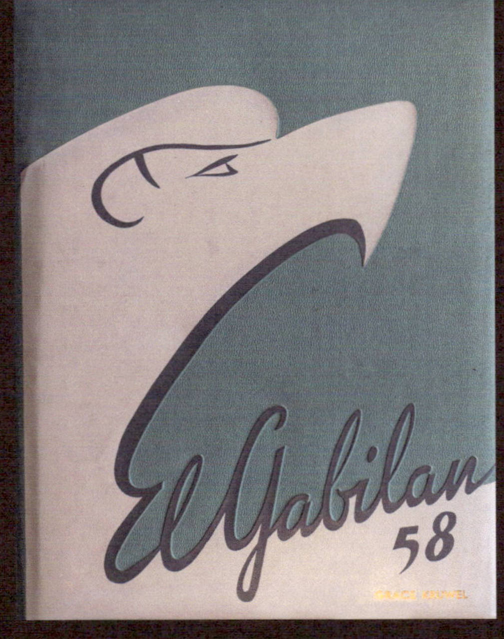
El Gabilan
58

nineteen sixty El Gabilan

EL GABILAN
64

1967

El Gabilan
'71

Do it! Do it!
Alright . . .
Do it! Do it!
Alright . . .

—SALINAS HIGH CHEERLEADERS URGING ON THE BOYS' TEAMS, 1969

Chapter 3

Pageants of Gender 1947–1974

FROM THE MOMENT I HAD LEARNED to dribble a basketball I had fantasized performing in the high school gym in front of a packed crowd. But this? This was certainly not the scene I had imagined. Sure, the stands were packed with my peers, and if they were not exactly cheering, they sure were hooting. I scuffled across the familiar wood floor of the gymnasium not in my white Adidas but sporting fringed leather moccasins and knee-high red tights. Most everything I wore belonged to my sister Linda: a long "fall" of brunette hair draping my shoulders; a beige sleeveless blouse over a bra stuffed with Kleenex; a red plaid skirt, its hem just above the knee. The 1968 *El Gabilan* dubbed us "Go-Go girls," who were rocking an all-school assembly to live music (Figure 3.2). I had known for some time that I would have to endure this moment of public humiliation as a necessary initiation into the Block "S" Society, but this knowledge barely muted the embarrassment I felt in the moment. As I shuffled forward, I tried to deploy a basketball player's strategy, "turning a deaf ear to the crowd," but I could not help but notice that my fellow jocks in front of me seemed to be having fun with this, camping it up with an exaggerated sashay. Hoping to fit in, I suppose, I tugged up my skirt, revealing a bit more thigh.

Images of boy athletes parading in front of a student assembly, exaggerating the extremes of feminine dress and comportment, were barely hinted at in the 1950s yearbooks. By the 1960s, they were routine events built in to the annual rituals of student life. These public performances were part of an expanding postwar pageantry of

Figure 3.1. Salinas High football team explodes into stadium, flanked by cheerleaders, *El Gabilan*, 1968

Figure 3.2. Block "S" initiation (*author at far left*), *El Gabilan*, 1968

gender that promoted and celebrated the supposedly natural differences between boys and girls. High school sports were at the center of these pageants: boys' sports, from the postwar years through the start of the 1970s, were elevated to near-mythical status, while girls' sports descended to their historical apogee—shrunken, mostly ignored, and, when noticed in the yearbooks, routinely disparaged.

From the immediate postwar years through the early 1970s a sports-based pageantry of gender was expressed in the annual yearbooks in three ways. First, more and more pages of the *El Gabilan* were devoted to celebrating boys' sports, which were expanding in both size and stature. Second, in support of boys' sports, the school's rosters of cheerleaders and pom pon girls, along with those of the marching band, majorettes, drill teams, and rooters' clubs—collectively constituting what I call the *sports spirit complex*—exploded in size and prominence in the annual yearbooks. And third, in the postwar decades, the yearbooks devoted more and more pages to depictions of theatrical gender performances, such as the Block "S" initiation described above. These performances were not confined to the "Sports" section of the book. The permeation of images of sports pageantry across all sections of the yearbooks is the hallmark of how sports surged to the center of mid-twentieth-century student life, and in so doing helped to create and celebrate a world that was divided unequally between boys and girls—"opposite sexes" assumed to be separated by nature into two categorically distinct worlds. These shifts in the organization and meanings of sports and gender, of course, were not unique to Salinas High School. Rather, they reflected broader social processes, both local and national.

Figure 3.3. *El Gabilan*, 1949

Postwar Salinas and Its High School

Through the 1950s, Salinas Union High School—the town's only high school—was still accurately (and proudly) referred to as "The High School." Annual volumes of *El Gabilan* routinely featured photos of the lovely exterior of the Spanish colonial revival–style gem on Main Street (Figure 3.3).

The 1951 launch of Palma High School, an initially tiny Catholic school, barely dented the growing size of the Salinas High student body. The high school campus strained to keep up with the growing size of the city of Salinas. In the decades following World War II, according to historian Carol Lynn McKibben, the city inaugurated "a new era of breathtaking expansion and development," constructing new shopping centers, a state-of-the-art hospital, and a public library. The city planners sought to "ensure that Salinas was the urban center of the entire Central Coast region."[1] Annexations in the 1940s, along with postwar immigration, nudged the city's 1950 population to 13,917. Over the next decade, Salinas's population more than doubled, reaching 28,957 residents in 1960.

The booming growth within the city limits was far from racially diverse. In 1960, Salinas was about 90 percent white. Only twenty-five of Salinas's three hundred Japanese American families who had been incarcerated during the war had chosen to return to the town.[2] Though some neighbors and the local Japanese Presbyterian church sought to welcome them back, a postwar survey of the town's residents conducted by the Salinas chamber of commerce revealed many citizens' hostility toward their former neighbors. In the widely publicized survey, Louis R. Jenkins, an official in the plumbers and steamfitters' union, asserted that it was "a pleasure seeing no Japanese faces amongst our children" in the recent Salinas High yearbook. "I sincerely hope that Japanese faces will never appear again." Hotel owner W. L. Young put an even sharper point on it: "The only loyal Jap is a dead one."[3] Conversely, Salinas High alum John Steinbeck and his friend Ed Ricketts joined others in publicly advocating "for the return of Japanese Americans to the Monterey Peninsula in the name of 'democratic values.'"[4] But having endured insults small and large, including death threats, Steinbeck himself was not long for the area he had grown up in. In the spring of 1945 Steinbeck wrote to his friend Pascal Covici, "there is no home coming nor any welcome. What there is is jealousy and hatred and the knife in the back . . . And the town and the region—that is the people of it—just pure poison . . . I hate a feeling of persecution but I am just not welcome here . . . This isn't my country anymore. And it won't be until I am dead. It makes me very sad."[5] By the end of 1945, Steinbeck had moved to the East Coast, where he resided for most of the rest of his life.

Filipino/a and Chinese American communities in Salinas remained vibrant in the postwar years, but relatively small. Meanwhile, as the number of Mexican immigrants settling in the area steadily grew, economic barriers and racially restrictive housing practices forced most to reside outside the Salinas city limits, in the unincorporated area of Alisal. That changed in 1963. After three failed tries, voters decided to annex Alisal. In one fell swoop, Salinas added over 16,000 residents.[6] By 1968, Salinas had boomed in size to 57,000, in the process becoming more racially diverse.

While the postwar numbers of Asian American and Black students at Salinas High School remained low, the 1950s saw a steady increase of Hispanic students, mostly of Mexican descent, with names like Garcia, Guzman, Gutierrez, Flores, Jaramillo, Lopez, Martinez, Morales, Robles, and Rodriguez. From 1951 to 1960 Spanish-surnamed youth constituted the largest nonwhite group in the school, averaging about 8.3 percent of the graduating classes. These kids did not always find it easy to fit in. Mexican American student Alex Zermino told historian Lori A. Flores that "When he arrived at Salinas High School in 1953 there was noticeable class and racial tension. 'I got a bit of wetback jokes and stuff like that,' he said."[7] By 1961, the Spanish-surnamed proportion of the senior class had grown to double digits, peaking in 1965 at 15.6 percent. By the start of the 1960s, Salinas High School was nearly bursting at the seams. While the size of the school's senior classes between 1947 and 1957 averaged about 380 students, the senior class surged to over 500 in 1958 and 1959. In anticipation of the opening of a second public high school in town, the school board in 1958 officially changed the name of Salinas Union High School to Salinas High School. In 1960, North Salinas High School opened its doors.[8] In 1966, the opening of Alisal High School—located in an area where Mexican Americans were concentrated—arrested the growth of racial and ethnic diversity at Salinas High, at least for a time.

Opening Up and Clamping Down

It is common for people to look back on the post–World War II years with a glowing nostalgia, viewing them as The Good Old Days.[9] In some ways, and for many Americans, they were just that. Postwar optimism grounded in collective hope for a peaceful world, the GI Bill's support of returning veterans, the baby boom, steady economic growth, expansion of public investments in schools, highways, civil service, and public sector jobs—all created a sense of progress, possibility, and hope for the future.[10] The Salinas High yearbooks reflected this shared sense of an expanding, wide-open future for youth. The 1948 *El Gabilan* was flush with photos of students with cars, cars, and more cars, signaling postwar teens' immersion in an expanding consumer culture, with automobiles as symbols of teen fun and freedom (Figure 3.4).

Figure 3.4. *El Gabilan*, 1948

The 1949 *El Gabilan* expressed hopefulness of a different sort, dedicating the volume to the theme of peace. Under a growing shadow of an escalating arms race and brewing Cold War, the book's cover featured a dove of peace, and its editors wrote hopefully, "There are those who believe that war is inevitable . . . but there are others who still hope for a peaceful world . . . We, the *El Gabilan* Staff, believe in that dream. We dedicate this book to that ideal—everlasting PEACE."[11] Bucking stubborn historical headwinds, the staff of the 1950 *El Gabilan* doubled down, dedicating the book "to the ideal of Universal peace, in the hope that it will soon become a reality, a reality to be observed and protected by future generations."[12] The Korean War would explode shortly thereafter in June 1950, with much of the worst fighting occurring in the first several months.

In addition to the dwindling of hope for a lasting peace, domestic postwar optimism was experienced very unevenly. By the early fifties, the economy was growing and public education was expanding, but the extent to which one could benefit during these boom times depended on who you were. If you were white, and if you were a man, the postwar years were more likely to feel like truly expansive times. But many people experienced the postwar period as a time of contracting possibilities. Black and brown veterans of the war returned to a discriminatory Jim Crow racial order.[13] The postwar era was also time of fear—of nuclear war with the Soviet Union, and of a mostly drummed-up cabal of domestic communists and homosexuals bent on destroying The American Way. The 1951–52 Korean War and the McCarthyite "red scare" clampdown on domestic dissent were government attempts to contain perceived threats—militarily from outside, and repressively from within.

Women were central targets for containment in the postwar years. During World War II, the nation had celebrated the contributions of millions of "Rosie the Riveters," women who had surged into all levels of the labor force to aid in the war effort.[14] As men returned from war, the government, employers, and labor unions squeezed women out of higher-paying jobs; meanwhile, medical experts, leaders in education, and a flood of images in popular culture claimed a natural basis for a clear separation between men and women in social life. Rational, goal-oriented, strong men were naturally suited, it was believed, for paid labor, family breadwinning, and public leadership. Women's supposed physical frailties and emotional nature meant that they were better suited for domestic life, especially caring for children. All this reactionary clamping-down had implications for sports—especially girls' sports—both nationally and at Salinas High School.

Disappearing Girls' Sports

"That's all folks." So read the caption below a small photo of two girls, apparently retreating from a badminton court, on the final page of the girls' sports section of the

1962 *El Gabilan* (Figure 3.5). The caption—undoubtedly intended as a wink and a nod to the popular "Looney Tunes" animated shorts that this generation of kids had grown up seeing in movie theaters and on TV, each episode ending with Porky Pig waving goodbye and uttering "That's all folks" with an exaggerated stutter—was likely intended as a humorous way to close the girls' sports section of the yearbook. But in retrospect, we can also read the caption as an accurate description of the quality and quantity of coverage of girls' sports in the yearbooks of this era. Placed on the last page of a scant four devoted to girls' sports that year (boys' sports received twenty-two pages), the page layout consisted of two thumbnail photos, placed in the upper left and lower right corners of the page. Rough sketches of a basketball dropping into a hoop, and a bow, arrows, and quiver filled the otherwise empty space in the center of the page. That's all folks. The editors of the 1963 book deployed a similar form of humor to close the four-page girls' sports section. About eight girls in gym suits face each other in a circle, on hands and knees, perhaps struggling with push-ups; one girl's rear end is prominently foregrounded in the photo. The caption, "The end," gave at least one high school boy the opportunity to enhance the joke with his own comment and signature (Figure 3.6).

The 1947 *El Gabilan* noted that this had been a year of transition for girls' sports, as the now-retired physical education teacher Ruth Wing was replaced by Miss Isabel MacKay. In short order, Miss MacKay would be joined by Miss Jean Madison and Miss Anna Davis (Figure 3.7). A few others would come and go, but these three would form the nucleus of the girls' physical education program for the next three decades.[15] Nationally, the work of women physical educators between 1950 and 1970 became increasingly "arduous"; as their noninstructional tasks expanded, their salaries typically lagged behind those of their male counterparts.[16] Moreover, "homophobia remained physical education's unspoken prejudice, and many gay and lesbian teachers stayed securely in the closet."[17] The mood of sexual stigma and fear that hovered like a dark cloud over physical educators like MacKay, Madison, and Davis spilled onto girls, undoubtedly repelling many of them from sports participation.

The PE staff at Salinas High School was not the only thing changing. The organization of girls' sports was shifting, and their representation in the annual yearbooks was shrinking in size and declining in quality. From 1947 to 1960, the *El Gabilan* devoted an average of 8.4 pages to girls' sports, during a time when boys' sports were annually receiving an average of 22.5 pages. Because there were no interscholastic girls' sports to cover in these years, perhaps this was an understandable allotment. But coverage of girls' sports was even more limited than the numbers might suggest. The grudgingly small space allotted to girls' sports was permeated with editorial choices in photos and captions that reflected the evaporation of the bounded respect that had been afforded to girls' sports in the decades preceding the war. Instead, the tone of the text and captions on these pages expressed three intersecting themes: dry description,

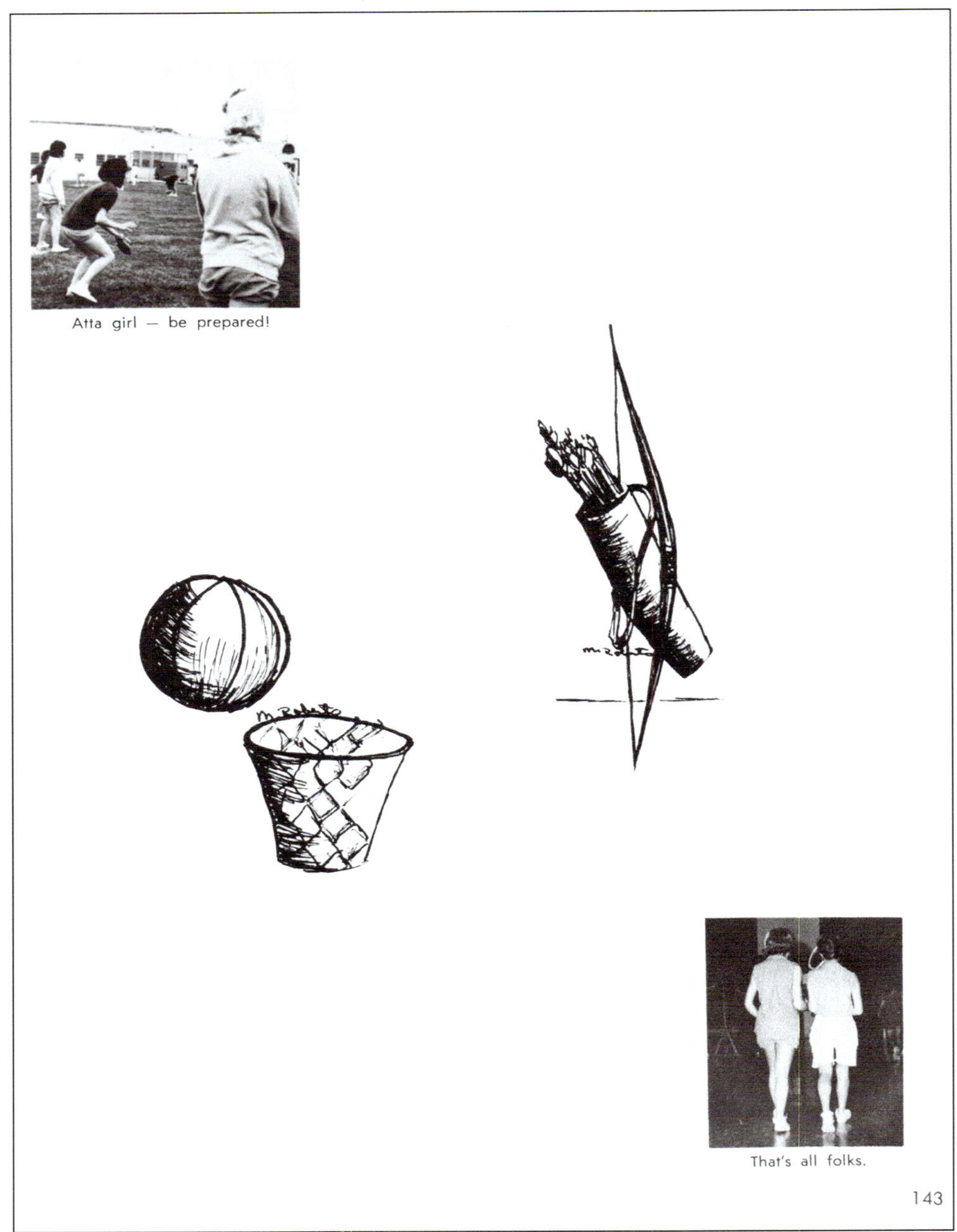

Figure 3.5. *El Gabilan*, 1962

scolding condescension, or humorous comments on the attractiveness of girls' bodies.

Descriptive photo captions, though not overtly insulting, were usually delivered with dry prose. Some, such as the 1958 caption that accompanied a shot of girls playing speedball, deployed the passive voice to inform viewers what they were seeing: "A field sport which is very fast and strenuous is speedball, a combination of soccer and football."[18] A few pages later, readers were reminded that girls' basketball is

Figure 3.6. *El Gabilan*, 1963

different from the game that boys play: "The girls play this sport very effectively and have a lot of fun in spite of the limited dribble and the stricter set of rules than the boys' version."[19] A second common practice in these years was to arrange a scatter of photos of girls playing various sports—sometimes in awkward, off-balance moments, or in goofy staged poses—captioned with condescending comments on the girls' lack of athletic ability, or scolding commands on how to do it right. Even, for instance, when a 1951 photo appeared to show a girl correctly diving into a swimming pool, the caption—"Belly Flop?"—suggested a laughable failure (Figures 3.8, 3.9).

The girls' sports section of the 1957 book led off with a two-page cartoony drawing of a carnival sideshow: an amused man and a boy laugh as they view a male barker on stage, showcasing "Snake Lady," "The Fat Lady," and what appears to be a mermaid and a pygmy (Figure 3.10). This girls'-sports-as-freak-show frame contrasted sharply with the opening of the boys' sports section, presumably drawn by the same artist, that depicted a weightlifter, a juggler, and a sword swallower (Figure 3.11). Both drawings were surely efforts at humorous caricature, but the boys' side was clearly about men performing amazing athletic feats, while the girls' was plainly not.

A third theme deployed photos of girls in action with captions that were likely intended as humorous comments on the relative attractiveness of their bodies. The 1949 book opened the girls' sports section by featuring that year's "new uniforms" (Figure 3.12), and the collage of over twenty photos on the next page included several captions that celebrated what these new outfits revealed: "Legs! Legs! Legs!";

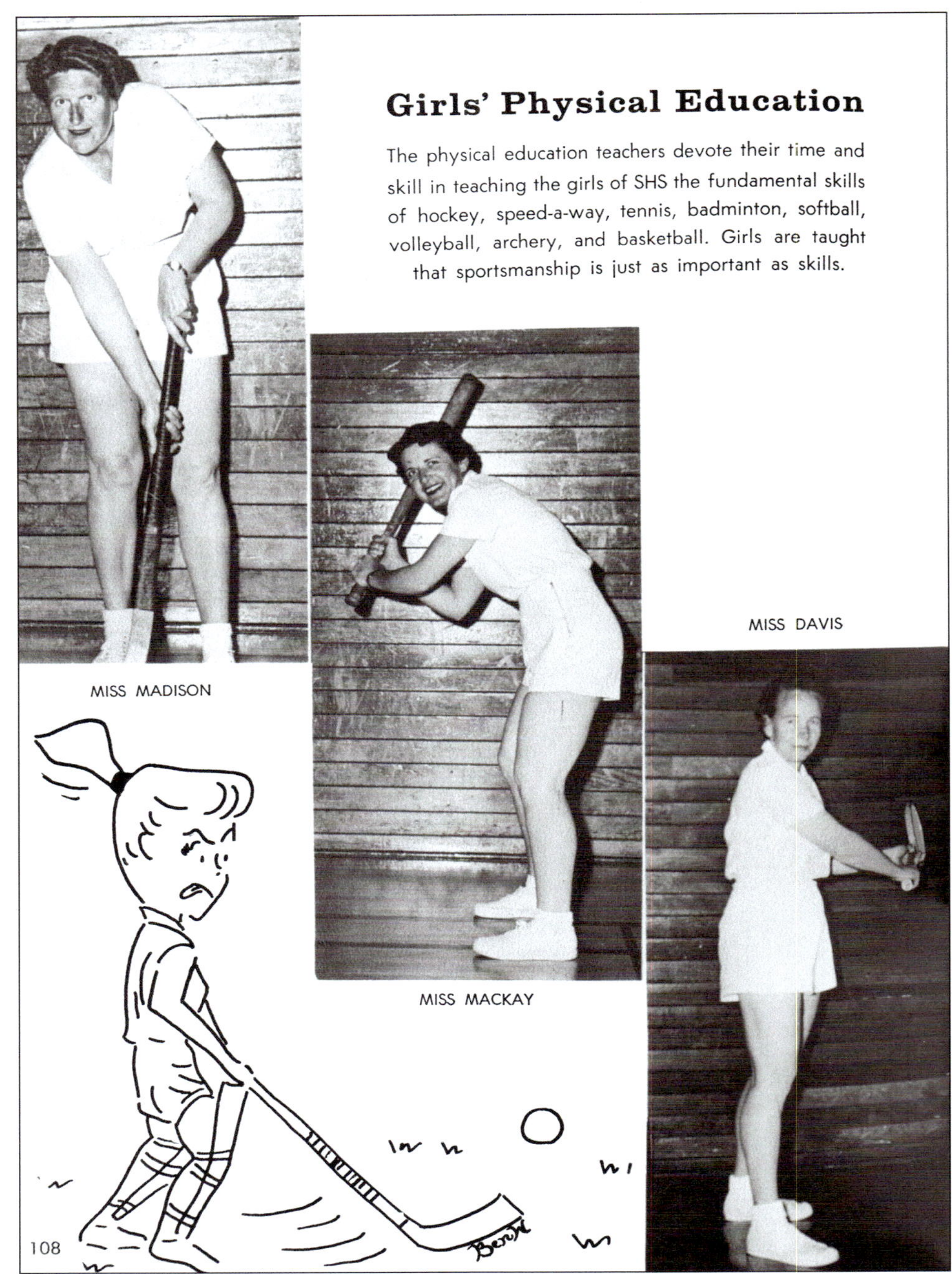

Figure 3.7. *El Gabilan*, 1960

"Shocking Shorts!"; "Bevy of beauties"; "Your shorts!" The allure of girls' bared legs was a common theme during these years. A page in the 1956 *El Gabilan* featured three photos of girls at the nearby YMCA pool, the site of the high school's swim instruction. A shot of diving girls was captioned "The Green Bikinis"; a second shot of girls exiting the pool suggested an embarrassing swimsuit disaster: "Rip——!"; the third, of girls practicing synchronized swimming noted, "Look at Those Purty Legs!" (Figure 3.13).

Modern dance, such a big part of girls' physical education in the 1930s and 1940s, faded in importance in the 1950s. This decline of dance at Salinas High reflected much broader shifts taking place in girls' physical education, nationally and internationally. Historian Sheila Fletcher observed that as women physical educators began to lose their grip on the field in the postwar years, dance and gymnastics were de-emphasized in favor of growing emphases on fitness and games.[20] When the *El Gabilan* did feature modern dance in the postwar years, the more respectful tone of earlier decades was gone, replaced by the generally more trivializing comments that tended to frame girls' sports in era. The "Dancing" page in the 1955 book, for instance, captioned three photos, "ring around the rosy," "heel toe," and accompanying a shot of girls dancing in couples, "Who needs boys." Still, the caption of a 1959 photo of girls dancing in the gym echoed earlier descriptions of dance as a school for shaping desired ideals of femininity: "The purpose of modern dance is to help girls become more graceful and poised."

If sports had any purpose for girls beyond making them objects of derision, the yearbooks seemed to declare, it was to become "more graceful and poised," so as to become more attractive to boys. The two-page cartoon drawing that opened the 1953 girls' sports section of *El Gabilan* hammered home this lesson. Four girls riding in a convertible jalopy with "GAA" written on the driver's door carry a tennis racquet and a hockey stick, but one in the back seat is engrossed in a book titled "How To Date," and the driver has apparently stopped the car so the girl in the front passenger seat can welcome a hitchhiking U.S. Navy sailor into the ride (Figure 3.14). This apparent tension between women's athleticism and their heterosexual attractiveness was a focus of national debate. "In 1960 a *New York Times Magazine* headline asked, 'Do men make passes at athletic lasses?' Columnist William Furlong answered no for most activities, concluding that except for a few 'yes' sports like swimming, women athletes 'surrendered' their sex."[21]

The 1950s were not a good time for girls' sports, but they were not the low point. In the 1960s it would get even worse, as girls' sports nearly disappeared from the annual yearbooks. From 1961 to 1969, *El Gabilan* devoted a scant 4.4 pages, on average, to girls' sports. In this same span, the average length of the boys' sports section of the books swelled to more than 28 pages. With a mere 2 pages, the girls' sports section of the yearbook hit its nadir in 1965, a year when the boys' sports section expanded to 34 pages. The scant photos of girls' sports in the 1960s, routinely coupled with trivial and insulting captions, resulted in the absolute containment of the girls' sports sections of the yearbooks at a time when boys' sports were spilling across the pages of the books (Figures 3.15, 3.16).

The rare moments of praise for a girl athlete in the 1950s and 1960s yearbooks—such as a softball photo in the 1959 yearbook, captioned "Catcher Wanda Oliver proves

Figure 3.8. *El Gabilan*, 1951

that girls play a rugged game of softball as she forces an out at home plate"—stand out as stubborn assertions that ran against the grain of the normal narrative.[22] It would have come as common sense to readers of these books that girls' high school sports were surely not serious activities, nor were they, like boys' sports, a source of collective pride and school spirit. If dance and gymnastics had once been havens for shaping and displaying a culturally celebrated form of femininity, their postwar decline

SPEEDBALL

Ballet?

It went that-a-way

BASKETBALL

Don't just stand there!

Good game, girls?

61

Figure 3.9. *El Gabilan*, 1952

coincided with many girls—especially higher-status white girls—fleeing from the increasingly polluting imagery of sports. At worst, sports sections of the yearbooks were sites of scorn over girls' humiliating lack of athletic knowledge, and mocking derision for their physical incompetence; at best, they offered the viewer a source of voyeuristic pleasure in the grace, poise, and beauty of girls' bodies in motion.

Figure 3.10. *El Gabilan*, 1957

Figure 3.11. *El Gabilan*, 1957

But not all girls fled sports. Across the nation, girls and women in the 1950s and 1960s—especially those from working-class families and from communities of color—continued to participate in sports.[23] Such was the case at Salinas High School, where girls ranging in number from thirty-five to more than one hundred appeared annually in the GAA yearbook photo. At a time when the high school's senior classes were roughly 85 percent white, it is striking how girls of color appeared in disproportionate numbers in GAA photos (Figures 3.17, 3.18, 3.19). Filipina American, Chinese American, several of the school's few remaining Japanese American girls, a few Black girls by the late 1950s and early 1960s, and a growing number of Spanish-surnamed girls appeared prominently as members, and frequently as officers, of the honorary Girls' Sweater Society.

The members of the Girls' Sweater Society were surely the elite athletes of their era. But their accomplishments on the playing courts and fields were rendered mostly invisible in the yearbooks of the 1960s. These girls were rarely identified by name, and they were almost never publicly celebrated for their athletic exploits in the yearbooks. One photo of five girls sprinting hard on the track in the 1967 *El Gabilan* stands out as anomalous (Figure 3.20). The caption names the five runners and notes that they "show their vitality as they practice for the coming Hartnell Turkey Trot race."[24] Denied any formal opportunity to run for their school interscholastically, the girls saw the annual Thanksgiving Day community-based Turkey Trot as a rare opportunity to compete publicly. I learned from an interview with one of these runners, Jo Ann (Langenhovel) Curtis, that these girls had formed an informal track team. They trained with the boys, wearing their blue PE suits. "We ran laps, stadium steps, and miles to and from Hartnell."[25] Curtis recalls that one teammate, Jil Spiegel, took second place in the race, but "They wouldn't acknowledge her because we weren't 'official'—we weren't recognized." This 1967 photo offers a very rare window into a phenomenon that was likely bubbling below the surface in the years before the passage of Title IX, but was mostly kept outside the frame of the annual yearbooks: Girls were denied the opportunity represent their school in interscholastic sports competition, but some of them were pushing up against those constraints. It is not hard to see how these girls' determination, so visible in this photo, situated them as precursors to an explosion of girls' athleticism a decade later.

"We're No. 1!"

As a veil of silence obscured the efforts of girl athletes, the boys' sports section of the *El Gabilan* ballooned in size in the 1950s and 1960s. Each year, the school's four football teams led off the boys' sports section of the book, and took the largest share of pages, with basketball allotted the second-most pages.[26] The 1963 *El Gabilan* was typical in this regard: of twenty-four total pages devoted to the boys' sports section of the book, the first ten were devoted to football, basketball received seven, two pages

Figure 3.12. *El Gabilan*, 1949

each were allotted to track and to swimming, one each to baseball and wrestling, and one half page each to golf and tennis. The teams did not need to be winners to receive their page allotments, but when they did win championships, the books showered the victors in glory (Figures 3.21, 3.22, 3.23).

As the yearbooks of the fifties and sixties celebrated successful boys' teams, they also highlighted individual boys who were star athletes. There were very few Black students at Salinas High in the 1950s, but several members of the Boutte family were standout athletes in boys' and girls' sports during the decade.[27] Harold Boutte appears to have been the first Black male multisport star at the high school since Ulysses Cooper in 1916. Boutte was co-captain of the 1954 champion varsity basketball team, and the *El Gabilan* lauded him as an "outstanding" player on the football team (Figure 3.24). Joe Kapp, a Mexican American sophomore, was a reserve on the 1953 varsity basketball team alongside Boutte. Though he is likely the most successful football player to come out of Salinas High, Kapp never played varsity football for the school. Kapp's family moved from Salinas after his sophomore year, and he would eventually star at Cal, quarterback the Minnesota Vikings in the 1970 Super Bowl, and later return to coach the Cal football team. The 1955 yearbook accompanied an action shot of track star Eddie King with a caption praising him as the "top quarter miler in the nation, finishing a 440 in 48.4" (Figure 3.25). King's school records in the 440-, 220-, and 100-yard events, inscribed high on the wall of the boys' locker room, went unbroken for many years. Perhaps the best boys' basketball player ever to come out of Salinas High was Russ Critchfield, who in 1964 as MVP of the newly formed Monterey Bay

Figure 3.13. *El Gabilan*, 1956

League (MBL) led the team to its first championship since 1956 (Figure 3.26).[28] Rail-thin and only five feet, ten inches, Critchfield used his speed and uncanny outside shooting touch to become the (then) career scoring leader at Cal. He would play for the Oakland Oaks of the American Basketball Association before coaching college teams for several decades.

The bright spotlight of the *El Gabilan* illuminated the star boy athletes of the era. These were the Big Men on Campus, and their ascent was part of larger social

Figure 3.14. *El Gabilan*, 1953

She's just pretending; she really doesn't know how to play tennis.

Have mercy! No more exercises!

Figure 3.15. (*above*) *El Gabilan*, 1964

Figure 3.16. (*right*) *El Gabilan*, 1965

Here it comes — duh, now what!?

transformations taking place around them. Resurgent postwar patriarchy obviously benefited men, especially in the ways it cemented and celebrated their domination of sport and other aspects of public life. But it had its downside for boys and men as well. In his examination of the rise of mid-century football in the United States, sociologist Jeffrey Montez de Oca illustrates how, in the context of growing fears about communism and homosexuality, Cold War–era anxieties about America's growing softness, projected mostly onto boys, fueled a "muscle race" that paralleled the U.S.-Soviet nuclear arms race. "Fear of a depleted masculinity just as the U.S. was taking leadership of the free world 'greatly concerned' President Eisenhower and quickly took on a Cold War coloring."[29] As the 1960s commenced, President John F. Kennedy appointed University of Oklahoma football coach Bud Wilkinson to direct a national youth physical fitness program, a central goal of which was to counter American boys' feared descent into flabby femininity. By the mid-1960s, physical fitness programs, along with rigorous testing and ranking of boys' successes or failures in doing pullups, sit-ups, push-ups, and sprints, were institutionalized in the nation's junior highs and high schools.

Physical fitness training and testing sought to harden the bodies of all boys. Organized sports had a less democratic role, helping to create and publicly celebrate an athletic elite among boys and men. Cold War fears of the feminization of boys, coupled with the rise of television, fueled the explosive popularity of college and professional football.[30] Athletes, especially football players, became public exemplars of masculinity on high school and college campuses. Homophobia, as we have seen, cast a dark shadow over mid-century girls' and women's sports, and it affected boys' and men's sports too, but in the opposite way. If sport participation enveloped athletic girls with sexual and gender suspicion, for boys it affirmed their heterosexual masculinity.[31] This was especially true for boys who played football. The escalating status of football players created an honored place for a few boys atop a school's status hierarchy. Basketball was a not-too-distant second, followed by boys who played lower-status sports. For non-athletic boys, their very lack of sports participation tended to press them lower in the status system, perhaps sometimes rendering them more vulnerable to homophobic abuse from other boys.

For all boys—athletic or not—Cold War–era fears and anxieties admonished them to constrain public expressions of vulnerability, weakness, or actions that risked generating even a whiff of femininity. In his book *The Mourning After,* historian John Ibson argues that postwar constraints on women were joined with a severely homophobic closure of intimacy among men. "Fear was the fundamental emotion of the era," driven by the cultural hysteria surrounding the "monstrous conjoined twin" of communism and homosexuality. As a result, "the fear of being, or being thought, homosexual . . . [became] such an integral part of boy culture that the very nature of relationships among young males was altered."[32] Fathers were deployed to the front

Girls' Athletic Association

President
Evelyn Aledo

Secretary
Pat Kita

Vice President
Diane Laporte

Treasurer
Doris Kitamura

Publicity
Myrleen Fisher

Year started off with initiation of new members with plenty of fun and refreshments and jinxs . . . Class representatives chosen . . . Girls coming out for sports to earn blocks . . . Weiner roast and swimming party held . . . Girls attended annual Girls' Coast Counties Athletic League and Play Day, held in Hollister . . . Activities ended with election and installation of new officers at award dinner . . . All made possible by leadership of Prexy Evelyn Aledo and Advisor Miss MacKay.

First row—D. Kitamura, C. Olivette, A. Alverez, S. Lim, C. Galicia, M. Oka, D. Garcia, D. Ybarra, P. Hamblen. Second row—B. Watson, B. Munoz, P. Kita, C. Vance, B. Pepper, D. Pepper, B. Sing, B. Watson, E. Aledo. Third row—G. Koller, J. Fanoe, K. Walker, M. Livingston, C. Parra, K. Godsey, N. Herman, C. Herrera, V. Reyes, J. Anderson. Fourth row—B. Kelly, S. Hennigan, J. Horsley, D. LaPorte, M. Fisher, L. Mason, C. Adams, G. Fisk.

83

Figure 3.17. GAA, *El Gabilan*, 1954

lines to fight against the "national concern over sissy sons." These adult men in the 1950s likely inflicted "their own increased restraint and anxieties on their sons."[33]

Echoing the years following World War I, organized sports were tasked after the Second World War with inoculating American boys against the feared diseases of softness, femininity, and homosexuality. Fathers were expected to toughen their sons up, and it was left to sports coaches—many, like my father, military veterans fresh from the war—to inject boys with the masculinity booster. Mid-twentieth-century

Left to right: Miriam Kataji, President; Pat Bandalan, Carmen Ramirez, Jessie Ann Montano.

Figure 3.18. Girls' Sweater Society, *El Gabilan*, 1967

football had become a kind of "school for masculinity" where boys learned from football coaches to submit to male authority, endure and dish out pain, retain emotional self-control, and avoid any and all "feminine activities and values."[34] At Salinas High School, at the same time that MacKay, Davis, and Madison were taking over girls' physical education, a new cohort of boys' PE coaches was arriving. Russ Messner and Bill Kearney both started at the high school in 1947. Two years later they would be joined by Gene Frassetto. Messner and Frassetto had both played football at UC Berkeley—Messner before the war, Frassetto as captain of Cal's 1948 Rose Bowl team. Before long, Kearney became the main coach for track and field. In various combinations, Messner and Frassetto shared coaching varsity football for the next few years (Figure 3.27).

Figure 3.19. GAA, *El Gabilan*, 1966

Turkey-trot runners Melissa Babcock, Cathy Cacas, Anita Villarte, Jil Spiegl, and Jo Langenhovel show their vitality as they practice for the coming Hartnell Turkey-trot race.

Figure 3.20. *El Gabilan*, 1967

1954-55 CCAL Champs

COACH MESSNER

Salinas' coach Russ Messner can always be counted on to floor a good, dependable team. After losing eight boys out of the first ten, seven via graduation and one, Rody Conway, to West Point midterm, it was not expected to do much this year.

But Salinas' pre-season showings left some of the fans gasping as they handed favorites like Campbell, San Jose High, James Lick and Monterey defeats. The Cowboys had a good season losing only four games--two of these to college frosh teams. The high-spirited Cowboys made the powerful San Jose frosh team work for their 48-43 victory.

The free-wheeling Cowboys went to the Tournament of Champions for the 2nd consecutive year. Even though they finished on the bottom, they showed good sportsmanship and desire.

Messner again faces the loss of graduation, losing starters co-captain Ron Critchfield, co-captain Jim Langley, Gus Andersen and transfer Bob Howard. Critchfield and Howard sparkplugged the Cowboys. Langley and Andersen aided in the rebound and scoring departments. Critchfield exhibited some of the best floor shows seen on the C.C.A.L. courts in years.

Mike Storm, Larry Hitchcock and Norm Steinbach will be a vital asset in Salinas' attack next year. Steinbach, who led the team in scoring with a 17 point average, will be the only 1st stringer back. Norm hit for a tremendous 56.6 percentage.

We	Varsity	They
62	James Lick	51
41	Pacific Grove	40
57	San Jose Tech	39
49	Campbell	56
40	Palma	25
53	San Jose High	46
42	Stanford Frosh	80
57	James Lick	47
46	Gilroy	28
75	Campbell	65

Ron Critchfield
CO-CAPTAIN

Jim Langley
CO-CAPTAIN

Figure 3.21. (*above*) Varsity basketball champs, *El Gabilan*, 1955

Figure 3.22. (*left*) Lightweight basketball champs, *El Gabilan*, 1965

WE'RE NO. 1!

Figure 3.23. Varsity football champs, *El Gabilan*, 1970

Figure 3.24. (*left*) Harold Boutte, *El Gabilan*, 1954

Figure 3.25. (*center*) Eddie King, *El Gabilan*, 1955

Figure 3.26. (*right*) Russ Critchfield, *El Gabilan*, 1964

Figure 3.27. Coaches Russ Messner and Gene Frassetto, *El Gabilan*, 1957

Football's position at the pinnacle of the sports hierarchy had its downside for coaches, even those who came to the job with reputations as former college stars. The community expected the football team to win, and for the most part the Salinas High gridders fell on hard times under Frassetto and Messner. The 1950 *El Gabilan* jabbed Messner's varsity football team for being the league's "undisputed cellar dweller." And the 1957 yearbook noted that Frassetto and Messner had guided the varsity football team to just one win that year. My father told me years later that the toughest part of the job had been dealing with the town's "Monday morning quarterbacks" who thought they knew better than the coaches how to win football games. "Even the milkman," he recalled with a laugh and a shrug, "left me notes of advice on what we should have done differently on Friday night." By 1958, Arvin Smith was appointed head football coach. He immediately turned the team around, winning the CCAL championship the next year, "the first since 1941," according to that year's *El Gabilan*. Smith would go on to become a successful coach at Hartnell College in Salinas. Frassetto would settle in as head wrestling coach and longtime boys' athletic director. Messner would remain as the varsity basketball coach for a quarter century, winning several championships. Often referred to as "The Dean of Basketball" in the region, several of Messner's players would go on to become successful coaches in the town: Ron Critchfield at Palma High School, Bob Steinbeck at North Salinas High, and Joe Chappell, who would succeed Messner at Salinas High.

Inflating the Sports Spirit Complex

The swelling size of the boys' sports section of the 1950s and 1960s *El Gabilan* all but eclipsed the evaporating girls' sports pages, but this was not the most dramatic shift

Figure 3.28. *El Gabilan*, 1948

The Varsity C.C.A.L. Champs are "The Conquerors"
in their league because they drink

GOLDEN STATE

214 Abbott Street • Phone 7326

Figure 3.29. *El Gabilan*, 1954

in the yearbooks of the postwar decades. In the late 1940s and through the 1950s, images of boys' sports started to leak out of the previously contained boys' sports section of the book, spilling into other parts of the yearbook. Shots of boys bedecked in their Block "S" sweaters bubbled up all over the books, infusing boys' athletic honor into non-sports realms of student life (Figure 3.28). By contrast, yearbooks of this era

Figure 3.30. *El Gabilan*, 1957

never depicted girls wearing their white letter sweaters, except in the single photo annually designated for the Girls' Sweater Society.[35] Meanwhile boy athletes and their winning teams also began to appear in the final "Advertisements" section of the book, for instance posing for a local milk company, or for a sporting goods store (Figures 3.29, 3.30). By the 1960s the leakage became a deluge, with images of boys' sports fully permeating the non-sports sections of the book. The "Activities" section of each *El Gabilan* tended to include a few photos of student dances or theatrical or music performances, but pictures of boys' sports—especially football and basketball action shots—appeared with such regularity that a core truth could not be missed: boys' sports had staked a claim as the undisputed centerpiece of student life.

But it was not just shots of boys playing sports that permeated the yearbook pages. In the previous chapter, I noted that the yearbooks of the 1940s introduced images of a budding *sports spirit complex*—an array of groups and organized activities set up explicitly to celebrate and support boys' sports, especially football and basketball. Driving the mid-century high school sports spectacle was the cheerleader, surrounded by an expanding array of others: pom pon girls, baton twirlers, rooters' clubs, marching bands, drill teams, and majorettes. In addition, playful pageants with ritualized displays of gender inversion became the theatrical centerpiece of Block "S" initiations, and spirit-building for game-day football or basketball rallies. Girls' sports sat entirely outside this celebratory pageantry. As a result, the expanding sports spirit complex and its entertaining rituals were not simply building school spirit, they were also creating and publicly celebrating separate activities for boys and girls (Figure 3.31).

From Yell Leaders to Cheerleaders to Icons of Femininity

In the 1940s the gender composition of Salinas High yell leader squads had begun to shift from previously all-male to mixed groups. Between 1947 and 1958, there were five years when one or two boys joined three or four girls on the squad. In all but one of these mixed groups, a boy (often the lone boy) was named "head yell leader" (Figure 3.32). During this time there were seven years when all the yell leaders were girls, usually four or five of them (Figure 3.33). Over this dozen years, regardless of the composition of the group, they were referred to as "yell leaders" (though the term "cheer leader" was used once in the 1954 book).

Starting in 1959 and for every year hence (but for a single exception that I will discuss later), every SHS cheer squad was made up entirely of girls. By 1960, the term "yell leader" was for the most part abandoned in favor of "cheerleader," a linguistic shift that accompanied the move to all-girls' squads. About the same time—1958, to be exact—pom pon girls[36] were added to the school's expanding spirit complex. Cheerleaders and pom pon girls were praised in the 1963 *El Gabilan* for together supplying "never-ending pep and vitality" for boys' sports contests. But their jobs were different. The new group's gender-marked name, "pom pon *girls*," designated this as a space

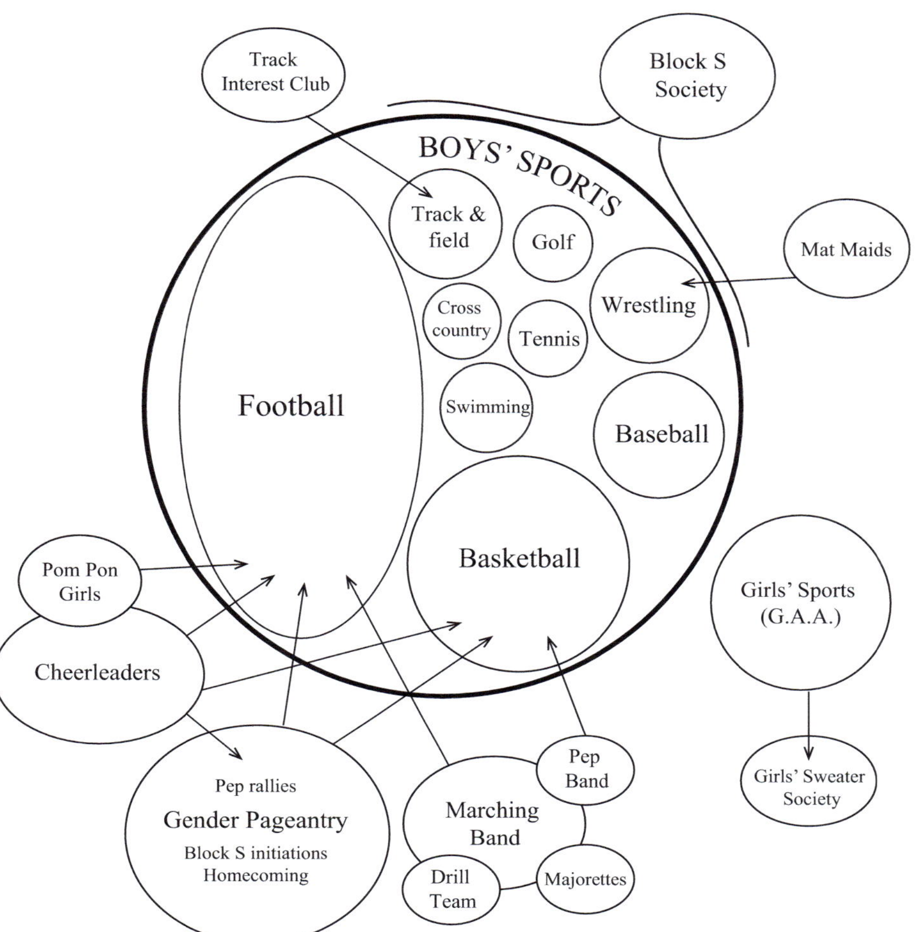

Figure 3.31. Sports Spirit Complex

Yell Leaders, Boots York, Dorothy Evans, Virginia Wade
Standing—Bob Cava, Bob Peavy

Head Yell Leader,
Bob Cava

Figure 3.32. *El Gabilan*, 1949

Figure 3.33. *El Gabilan*, 1955

cordoned off from boys (Figure 3.34). What is more, the primary duty of pom pon girls at boys' games was dancing (rather than leading cheers), clearly marking their niche in the spirit complex as one of feminine performance. By contrast, cheerleaders were tasked with directing their student peers on how and when to clap, cheer, and chant for the boys' sports teams—the word *leader* is part of the name, after all. As such, the gender composition of cheerleader squads remained contested, at least through 1965. I will draw from memory to show how this transitional year illuminated tensions in the school's mid-1960s gender divide.

My sister Terry Messner was elected as one of the school's five cheerleaders for her senior year in 1964–65. The previous spring Terry had run for vice president, and when she lost to a boy she was angry. "Everybody knows," I recall her saying, "that president belongs to a boy, so a girl should get to be vice president." Then, when Chris Smith, a muscular blond boy with a surfer tan, was elected cheerleader with Terry and three other girls, Terry once again cried foul. She liked Chris, she said, but cheerleading and pom pon were *girls'* positions. They had been, exclusively, since 1959. So when some folks assumed that Chris, being the only boy on the squad, would just naturally

Cheer-leaders

Working hard for more school spirit this year were the cheerleaders Marlene Lawrence, Charlotte Morris, Reanie Barker — Head Cheerleader, Gail Johnston, and Diane Bolz.

Pom-Pon Girls

Keeping up a lively routine at our games were pom-pon girls Jonni Nucci, Cheryl Monteiro, Susan Foster, Linda Cooper — Head Pom-Pon Girl, Jaci Walz, and Pat Smith. Serving earlier also was Sara Turner.

100

Figure 3.34. *El Gabilan*, 1962

be named head cheerleader, Terry bristled and campaigned among the other girls for the position. She won, but even in the *El Gabilan* photo of the squad, Chris Smith occupied a central position as he elevated two of the girls and supported them on his thighs; meanwhile, Terry, the head cheerleader, squatted in the left margin of the photo (Figure 3.35). This sort of juxtaposition is not unusual in mixed-gender cheer squads. Sociologist Laurel Davis observed that when boys cheer with girls, they tend to wear

Figure 3.35. *El Gabilan*, 1965

different cheer uniforms, deploy distinctly masculine body postures and movements (including adopting a more serious, even grim facial demeanor), and perform different roles (such as lifting girls into the air) in group stunts, all of which accentuate gender differences between the boys and the girls.[37]

In the 1960s, the boundaries that separated the high school's boys and girls were hardening. Girls like my sister who aspired to positions of public leadership and honor had come to assume that there was some justice in institutionalized set-asides for girls, even when they were consolations for not having access to the highest-status positions. In student leadership, boys would always assume the top offices; for decades, the student body president had always been a boy, and it appears that all of them were white boys. It only seemed fair to my sister that a girl should be second in command. In sports, boys would be on the receiving end of the cheers as heroes on the gridiron, courts, and fields; girls, however, should expect to be able to *lead* the cheers. But the gender boundaries were not so impermeable; when a boy wanted to cross into a high-status field that seemed to be set aside for girls, well, he sometimes could and would. From 1947 to 1974, for instance, the position of yearbook editor was usually occupied by a girl, but for eight of those twenty-seven years a boy held that position. And if a boy wanted to run for vice president, or if he sought to cross over into cheerleading, it appeared he could do so. It is likely that girls' routine experiences of second-class citizenship in the mid-1960s—from the glass ceiling that blocked access to the pinnacle of student leadership, to the recurrent affronts experienced by girl athletes, to the channeling of high-status girls into acceptably feminine positions of support for boys' sports—kindled their feminist awakenings during the next decade.

By the latter half of the 1960s and into the 1970s, cheerleading at Salinas High had become a realm designated for girls and only girls, and this reflected a national

Figure 3.36. *El Gabilan*, 1970

pattern.[38] In 1967, Salinas High cheerleader squads expanded in size, from five or six girls to eleven. They also became more visible in the annual yearbooks. Just as images of boy athletes (especially football and basketball players) spilled out of the boys' sports section, so too did images of cheerleaders burst from the "cheerleaders" page and sprouted all over the book. Images of cheerleaders on the sidelines at boys' games, leading all-school rallies in the football stadium, or performing at game-day rallies in the school's inner court permeated the pages of the yearbooks (Figure 3.36).

Action shots of cheerleaders—most of them white and conventionally pretty—were scattered liberally throughout the yearbooks. Just as football players had come to symbolize the dominant expression of mid-century masculinity in the school, cheerleaders (and somewhat less so, pom pon girls) represented the most honored form of femininity on campus.

If cheerleaders and pom pon girls exemplified white femininity in the school's race and gender order, other developments in the growing spirit complex were more diverse. The marching band routinely included both boys and girls. And by the 1950s cheerleaders and pom pon girls were joined with other, lower-profile groups of girls who performed at football games, and sometimes at basketball games. Four or five girls—mostly white girls until the start of the 1960s—joined the marching band as "majorettes." In the next decade, the majorettes expanded in number, and they were joined in performing at football games with the drill team. In subsequent years, a posed photo of the majorettes and of the drill team became regular features in the annual yearbooks (Figures 3.37, 3.38). These groups became a platform of public performance that included girls of color, but they did not receive near the amount of public exposure, much less the respect and admiration that was showered upon the cheerleaders.

Majorettes

Judy Silva, DiAnne Mahler, Carla Damerell, and Pam de Franco, SHS majorettes, add color to the performances of the Salinas High marching band.

Figure 3.37. *El Gabilan*, 1961

SHS DRILL TEAM

STANDING: June Morris, secretary; Terri Whitford, sgt.-at-arms; Kari Peterson, Helen Singley, co-lt.; Leslie Bryggman, Jackie Shook, co-lt.; Marla Driskell. SITTING: Terri Estrella, Mary Berglin, Liz Estrella, Nancy Lampkin, Lyn Arnold.

Figure 3.38. *El Gabilan*, 1971

The school's gender hierarchy was most symbolically evident when the cheerleaders and football players were theatrically juxtaposed at games and at rallies. In her study of her own high school class of 1958, anthropologist Sherry Ortner concludes that "Jocks and cheerleaders . . . seek to be admired, even envied."[39] The Salinas High yearbooks of this era delivered amply on the admiration. Make no mistake, cheerleaders were at the pinnacle of the school's status hierarchy. They tended to be the most popular girls on campus; they were elected, after all. They were also *leaders* who served in some ways as the public face of the school. But their

Figure 3.39. *El Gabilan*, 1966

official roles were defined always as *in support of* boys' athletic competitions with other schools. They *stood behind* their boys, promoting their names and cheering their athletic exploits (Figure 3.39). Several *El Gabilan* yearbooks of the era depicted very similar versions of what I came to think of as "the tunnel photo": The cheerleaders—smiling, leaping in the air, cheering—are placed on either side of the tunnel that opened into the football stadium, gripping the sides of a paper banner that the football team dramatically ripped through, as they burst into the stadium to do battle (Figures 3.1, 3.40).

The tunnel photo captures the moment: Boys were the sports heroes, placed literally and symbolically at the center of postwar high school culture. Cheerleaders were there to spotlight, celebrate, and support the boys' heroic actions. In so doing, "Cheerleaders came to symbolize the All-American girl."[40] In the 1940s or 1950s, attired in long, flowing skirts and sporting omnipresent smiles, the cheerleaders would pump their arms as they led their charges in chanting what in retrospect seem like innocent cheers of school spirit:

> *Well,* who's *got the bestest team in the league?*
> *Well,* we've *got the bestest team in league!*
> *We got the T-E-A-M,*
> *It's on the B-E-A-M,*
> *We got the team, it's on the beam*
> *It's really hep to the jive.*
> *Come-on' Cowboys, skin 'em alive!*

Figure 3.40. *El Gabilan*, 1967

By the late 1960s and early 1970s, cheerleaders' dress, movements, and cheers became more sexually suggestive. Reflecting national fashion trends, cheerleaders' hemlines had risen well above the knee. By the start of the 1970s the sexualization of cheerleading became increasingly overt. Still smiling ubiquitously, the Salinas High cheerleaders performed now with more sway in their hips, their cheers conveying hints of the sexual revolution of the times. The girls introduced two such cheers at the end of the 1960s, each culminating with a sexy sigh:

Go-go get 'em get 'em
Ooooh! Aaaaah!
Go-go get 'em get 'em
Ooooh! Aaaaah!

And,

Do it, do it!
Alright. . . .
Do it, do it!
Alright. . . .

The mid-century idealization of the cheerleader as the epitome of the wholesome, All-American girl continued, now tinted more overtly with the sexual meanings of the times. The cheerleader had come to represent "in one package the ultimate male fantasy: a woman who is both a virgin and a vamp."[41] The symbolic bond between the school's dominant form of masculinity—the football player—and most honored expression of femininity—the cheerleader—was thus cemented with heterosexual meanings.

Sports, with its supporting spirit complex, was the most visible arena of gender division in the yearbooks of the era, but not the only one. Most academic classes were mixed, of course, as were many extracurricular activities. But the fifties and sixties also saw a proliferation of same-sex clubs. The Future Farmers of America (FFA) was a perennial favorite for many boys in this agricultural town. Juxtaposed with the FFA on the facing page of the 1949 *El Gabilan* was a new club, Future Homemakers of America (FHA), a group that aimed to help girls learn "to live better today to better their lives and those of their families tomorrow."[42] The yearbook's juxtaposition of FFA and FHA symbolically marked the postwar belief in a natural division between men's public world of paid labor and industry and women's domestic world of homemaking. This division was not merely symbolic: There were real skills boys were learning in FFA that would prepare them as farmers and ranchers of the future. Likewise, girls in FHA were learning real skills, including cooking, sewing, knitting, and embroidery, that prepared them to be more effective homemakers.[43] This is a classic example of what sociologists call "anticipatory socialization," where schools channel boys and girls into different activities that prepare them for their future expected roles in society.

Not all girls, though, were destined exclusively for hearth and home. The 1962 *El Gabilan* juxtaposed a photo of 28 boys in that year's FFA with a page depicting the 18 members, all girls, of the Future Nurses Club. The following year the Future Teachers club appeared in the yearbook, with 29 members, all girls. In subsequent years, these occupational clubs continued to appear in the yearbooks, and by the mid-1960s, Future Nurses was disproportionately girls of color (Figure 3.41). Future Teachers grew to 108 girls by 1969, and though the club was predictably all girls every year, in 1965 a sole boy joined; Jim McGuffin was named that year's club president.[44]

Pageants of Gender

In John Ibson's fascinating book *Picturing Men*, the author analyzes the shifting meanings of scores of photographs of American men posing together, from the dawn of photography through the post–World War II years. Through the late nineteenth century, men routinely posed for photos with relaxed intimacy—holding hands, sitting on each other's laps, heads touching. "Those photographs," Ibson laments, "captured a world of feeling between men that eventually would largely disappear from view."[45] This ease of men's intimate touch was disrupted in the early decades of the twentieth century by social changes in gender, especially a mounting stigma against

Future Nurses

Information regarding nursing and nursing education in the form of films, speakers, and field trips are provided to the members of the Future Nurses Club. Important events of the year were the annual field trip to a hospital, attending student career day conference in Palo Alto, and selling Christmas candy.

Figure 3.41. *El Gabilan*, 1964

effeminacy and its supposed links with homosexuality. Suddenly, intimacy between men—emotional closeness, vulnerability, gentle touch—became suspect. An awkward distance emerged—space between men—when they posed for photographs. As a response to this awkwardness, men developed a bevy of posing rituals, "distinctive performances for the camera." Shots of men lighting each other's cigars proliferated, as did photos of men pouring and drinking out of booze bottles, wielding pistols or rifles, mock fist-fighting, posing with dead animals, perhaps garbed in "cowboy and Indian" costume. Ibson called these performances "pageants of masculinity" and argued that they functioned as "efforts by the subjects to affirm something about themselves that may have acutely seemed in need of affirmation."[46]

As I read through the *El Gabilan* books of the 1950s and 1960s I could not help but think of what I was seeing as "pageants," not simply of masculinity, but of mid-century gender relations. As we have seen, the postwar years comprised an era of containing women, containing homosexuality, and celebrating an emotionally contained ideal of manhood. The shrinkage and debasement of girls' sports, the expansive celebration of boys' sports across the pages of the yearbooks, the sports heroes symbolically linked with cheerleaders as icons of femininity—all helped to create and affirm gender boundaries. But a deeper ritualization of boundaries, a rich pageantry of gender performance, bubbled up in the 1950s and exploded all over the yearbooks in the 1960s. There are two expressions of this pageantry I will touch on here: public rituals that directly affirmed gender differences, and public gender reversals performed by boy athletes and girls, usually the cheerleaders.

Fuzzerino Kings and Homecoming Queens

Two new elements of the expanding sports spirit complex, introduced in the late 1950s and the early 1960s, can be seen as rituals that affirmed and celebrated gender difference. The 1958 *El Gabilan* was the first to depict images of the "Fuzzerino," a contest where boys competed to grow the longest, thickest beards. "Fuzzerino season," the 1961 *El Gabilan* joked, "separates the men from the boys."[47] The theatrical public finale of the contest also clearly separated the men from the girls.[48] Culminating during the halftime of the big rivalry basketball game between Salinas High and North Salinas High, the SHS cheerleaders and pom pon girls playfully inspected, measured, and pondered the relative merits of the contestants' facial hair, finally bestowing awards to the longest, thickest, or best "All-Around Beard" (Figure 3.42).

The 1961 *El Gabilan* introduced another ritual that would persist far longer than the short-lived Fuzzerino. Likely echoing an established tradition in universities, Salinas High celebrated its football homecoming game by electing its first-ever homecoming queen. "This event will mark the beginning of a tradition for Salinas High School," read the caption accompanying photos of queen Diann Mahler riding into the stadium in a convertible, and members of her court being escorted through a gauntlet of football players (Figure 3.43). Indeed, the naming of a track queen in 1961 and a basketball queen in 1963 were short-lived events, but the election and celebratory crowning of football queens—"nominated by the football teams and elected by the Block 'S'," according to the 1970 *El Gabilan*[49]—would persist for years to come, marking yet another important symbolic moment of sport's role in the ritual affirmation of the gender boundaries of the era.

"Roles Are Reversed"

The meanings of another performance by male athletes in this era might not seem so straightforwardly masculine, at least initially. In an era of rigid gender boundaries, what are we to make of boy athletes "cross-dressing" as girls in public performances? First hinted at in the 1950s—for instance, a photo in the 1950 *El Gabilan* captioned "Three queens" of (apparently) a girl cheerleader speaking into a microphone at a rally, alongside two boys in grinning blackface, wearing skirts and

The Fuzzerino Contest finals took place at the Cowboys vs. Vikings game. Cowboy Steve Davidson was our All-Around Beard winner!

Figure 3.42. *El Gabilan*, 1965

HOMECOMING

Our queen and her court were in their glory on November 5. This event will mark the beginning of a tradition for Salinas High School.

Excitement mounts as Queen DiAnn enters the stadium to be crowned.

Gary Plumlee escorts Attendant Pam de Franco down the aisle before the crowning of the queen.

QUEEN AND HER COURT
Pam de Franco, Jane Taylor, Queen DiAnn Mahler, Jan Wilson, Lynn Blair

Figure 3.43. *El Gabilan*, 1961

wigs—these sorts of performances (sans blackface) became wildly popular at the high school during the 1960s. Echoing a photo in the 1963 *El Gabilan*, the 1964 yearbook depicted an image of the stars of the school's champion varsity basketball team performing as cheerleaders at a noon rally, dressed in gunnysacks tailored to simulate girls' dresses (Figure 3.44). In 1965 the football team got in on the act, with the high-kicking, dress-wearing jocks dancing the can-can in the school's inner court at a noon football rally.

Figure 3.44. *El Gabilan*, 1964

It was not long before the Block "S" society found a ritual use for these cross-dressing performances. By the early 1960s, it was no longer enough simply to play a sport to gain membership into the Block "S" society. To become a full-fledged member, boys were now required to endure an initiation that involved some public display of deference or humiliation. The first evidence of such initiations was a photo of a boy kneeling in front of a teacher in the 1964 *El Gabilan*, with the caption, "The boys had to polish the shoes of the Block "S" members and teachers." Within the next two years, the club decided that having initiates perform at a school rally dressed as girl cheerleaders would generate more laughs and fun than shoe-shining.

By the late 1960s, the boys' "cheerleader" attire had evolved from gunnysacks to skirts, overstuffed bras that simulated huge breasts, and flowing wigs and lavish facial makeup, all of which displayed highly exaggerated signs of femininity (Figure 3.45). By the early 1970s the boys' imitations of girls' dress, comportment, and bodies had devolved from mocking exaggeration to cartoonish caricature.

At first glance, the 1960s gender play of boys cavorting publicly while dressed like girls seems an example of what the sociologist Harold Garfinkel called a "status degradation ceremony," a ritual that lowers an individual's identity and rank within a status hierarchy.[50] One might assume that, in this case, it was "degrading" for high-status boys to embody, display, and occupy ritual space defined as lower, as feminine. I can attest, as I noted in the opening paragraphs of this chapter, that participating in this Block "S" initiation performance did feel embarrassing. But was it really *degrading* for me or for the other boys? I am reminded of a story my father once told of a tackle on one of his SHS football teams of the 1950s, who on bus trips to away games would pass the time by pulling out his crochet needles and some yarn. "Nobody made fun of him," my father emphasized. "He was an all-conference tackle, and the biggest, strongest kid on the team." The boy's crocheting is an example of what the sociologist Barrie Thorne called

Girls! What Would Mama Say?

Figure 3.45. *El Gabilan*, 1967

"earnest crossing," akin to an effort by a grade school boy to join a playground activity that only girls do, like playing jacks or jumping rope.[51] Attempts at this sort of crossing of gender boundaries puts a boy at risk of symbolic pollution via his contact with a debased feminine activity, his masculinity and likely also his sexuality called into question by his peers. This is not so, though, for boys who have already established their masculine cred as sports stars, especially if it is on the gridiron. Boys like that "biggest, strongest lineman" on my dad's 1950s football team, and boys who are being initiated into the Block "S" Society, are mostly inoculated against the stain of femininity.

Those Block "S" initiations were in some ways the opposite of an individual boy's "earnest crossing" into a girls' activity like crocheting or jumping rope. The Block "S" boys' cheerleader performances were anything but earnest attempts to be taken seriously as cheerleaders. Instead, their performances overtly mocked feminine dress and comportment, the disdainful parody becoming more extreme each year. As the fake torpedo breasts inflated and the red lipstick smeared across their faces, the boys distanced themselves from girls. The boys' masculinity was neither threatened nor degraded in this ceremony; if anyone was symbolically "degraded" it was girls and their bodies, dress, and activities. Rather than somehow softening the cultural boundary between girls and boys, these performances reinforced the hierarchical divide between them, while also cementing the boy athletes' honored masculine status vis a vis other, non-athletic boys.

The Block "S" boys' cross-dressing performance was a ritual rich with gendered meanings, and part of what gave it its symbolic power was undoubtedly the laughs it drew from its audience. The broader cultural context surely mattered here, the high school ritual perhaps influenced by the popular 1959 film *Some Like It Hot*, where the

Butch Hazelaar and John Montes try their hand at cheerleading while the Varsity Pom-Pon Girls and Cheerleaders take on the role of football players.

Figure 3.46. *El Gabilan*, 1963

characters played by Tony Curtis and Jack Lemmon disguised themselves as women, with comedic effect, in order to get close to a character played by Marilyn Monroe. It is also possible that the Block "S" initiation was not only tolerated, but perhaps even introduced by, the men coaches of the time—some of whom, like my father, had experienced similar rituals in high school. I found in my father's scrapbook from his high school years at Oakland (California) Technical in the 1930s a typed message that read, "Dear (about to be a man) Messner: Wednesday you will be initiated into the BLOCK T and as you are about to be a man you will make your debut in a ballet dancers outfit, Plus rouge, lipstick, and powder. And lots of it. And 1 wig, any color but you would make an awfully pretty blond." My father, and likely other coaches of the postwar years, had also experienced similar gender-bending rituals in the military during World War II. For instance, "Polliwogs" (sailors who had not yet crossed over the equator) dressed as women for the U.S. Navy's elaborately theatrical "Neptune Ceremony," the purpose of which was to convert them to "Shellbacks" as they crossed for the first time into the Southern Hemisphere.[52]

The impact of boys' cross-dressing at school rallies likely took on its deepest symbolic meanings when girls simultaneously "crossed" in the opposite direction. The 1960s saw an explosion of theatrical gender reversals for school rallies that included football players dressing as cheerleaders and girl cheerleaders dressing like football players. A playful gender inversion photo in the 1963 book was captioned, "Butch Hazelaar and John Montes try their hand at cheerleading while the Varsity Pom-Pon Girls and Cheerleaders take on the role of football players" (Figure 3.46). And

Figure 3.47. *El Gabilan*, 1966

several photos from the 1966 rally preceding the rivalry game against North Salinas High depicted boys dressed in girls' cheerleader outfits and the girls dressed in football jerseys. A caption poked fun at the efforts of the cross-dressed boys at the rally, all of them stars on the football team: "Class competition was conducted by the 'GORGEOUS'? cheerleaders" (Figure 3.47).

The mid-1960s saw the introduction of other pageants of gender inversion on campus—then popularly referred to as "role reversals" between boys and girls. One such event was the "Twirp Dance," described in the 1964 *El Gabilan* as "the only dance of the year that the girl gets a chance to ask a boy out." The 1972 *El Gabilan* emphasized that letters in the word "Twirp" stood for "The Woman is Required to Pay!" The Twirp Dance was also sometimes called "Sadie Hawkins Night," inspired by Al Capp's then-popular comic strip, *L'il Abner*, which included a running storyline that highlighted the exploits of the homely, buck-toothed, and spindly thirty-five-year-old "spinster" Sadie Hawkins, who could only hope to land a husband by chasing down and capturing an otherwise unwilling bachelor.[53] Yearbook photos of girls grabbing or lassoing their male prey abounded in mid-1960s yearbook depictions of this event (Figures 3.48, 3.49). The misogynist roots of this pseudo-holiday aside, many high school girls found the role reversal of Twirp season to be a moment of empowerment, where they could choose and lead. The event could also be an eye-opening moment for a boy. It was for me: when I lamented in 1969 to my sister Melinda that I had not been "Twirped" by a girl, she snapped back, "Well, now you know how girls feel."

Another annual ritual of gender reversal began in the mid-1960s, this one a complicated mix of earnest crossing (by the girls) and exaggerated parody (by the boys).

Figure 3.48. *El Gabilan*, 1965

In 1966 girls donned football jerseys—but no pads or helmets—for what the *El Gabilan* touted as "THE FIRST Powder Puff football game of the season . . . The bruising Seniors played the crunching Juniors in a memorable grid spectacular. The game ended in a deadlock, 0–0."[54] By the end of the decade, powderpuff flag football games were deeply embedded in the school's ritual sports complex, expanding to a four-team tournament. A caption in the 1971 *El Gabilan* accompanying four pages of action photos of girls muddied from competing on the wet stadium field heralded the sport's growing popularity: "Powder Puff Play-offs are big success. Senior girls tromp over competition with a 2–0 winning streak. Roles are reversed. Boy yell leaders cheer the girls on to victory. Powder Puff Football King, Bruce Lewis was crowned at an all-school rally."[55] The gender-marked language used to describe the boy participants—"Football King," not queen; "yell leaders," not cheerleaders—revealed the limits of the role reversals.

Reflecting the growing popularity of powderpuff football, the early 1970s yearbooks often included several action shots, and two full pages depicting the posed team photos of all four squads. Each girl's name was listed, as were the names of each team's boy coaches. What is evident is that the girls took powderpuff football seriously, approaching the games with preparation and competitive intent (Figure 3.50). What is more, at a time when girls' sports were still receiving scant respect or attention, the annual yearbooks were devoting more and more space to powderpuff football and

Art Hatley appears to be all tied-up as Judy Coulter gets the jump on Twirp Season.

Figure 3.49. *El Gabilan*, 1966

Figure 3.50. *(left) El Gabilan*, 1971

Figure 3.51. *(above) El Gabilan*, 1974

were covering the girls' efforts with increasing respect. The boys who crossed over as "yell leaders" were another story entirely. They clearly took this as an opportunity for comedic theater that parodied girls' cheerleading (Figure 3.51). As we will see in the next chapter, this gender asymmetry only became starker as powderpuff football exploded in popularity in the late 1970s, during a time when many of the 1960s pageants of gender were disappearing.

Closing Out the Long Sixties

People commonly talk retrospectively of the "Turbulent Sixties" as a decade of political upheaval, violence, youth revolt, and deep cultural schisms.[56] Assassinations of revered leaders John F. Kennedy in 1963 and Robert F. Kennedy and Dr. Martin Luther King Jr. in 1968 jolted the nation. The carnage of the American war in Vietnam gestated a huge anti-war movement. Little of this political tumult was hinted at in the Salinas High yearbooks of the sixties, though the 1964 book was dedicated to the memory of President Kennedy. The decade had opened with a civil rights movement for

Figure 3.52. Mexican American Youth Association, *El Gabilan,* 1974

racial justice already shaking the moral and political foundations of the nation, and it manifested in Salinas in the movements for labor justice led by Cesar Chavez and the United Farmworkers Union that stretched into the 1970s.[57] Little of that national or local struggle for racial justice made its way into the *El Gabilan*. The Salinas High School student body remained predominantly white, though the growing Mexican American population—roughly 15 percent of the SHS student body by the late 1960s—and the broader politicization of the "Chicano Power" movement in cities like San Francisco and Los Angeles was reflected at the high school with the birth of a new club in 1969, the Mexican American Youth Association (MAYA). By 1970, according to historian Lori A. Flores, "Chicano Power" student activism was palpable in Salinas, though it was probably more extensive at Hartnell College and Alisal High School than at Salinas High.[58] Still, Salinas High's MAYA club grew by 1974 to forty-four members, who posed for the *El Gabilan* behind an American flag and a Mexican flag, several members raising the fist of Chicano Power (Figure 3.52). In the late 1960s and early 1970s, "the town's Mexican American students began their campaign for an education that included more Spanish-surnamed teachers, a more culturally inclusive curriculum, and less funneling into vocational programs that locked them into low-wage careers."[59] But for the time being the faculty at Salinas High remained almost entirely white. The scant few Hispanic and Black teachers hired would remain token faculty of color at the high school for the next several years.

Nor did the yearbooks directly engage with most of the deep cultural transformations taking place during the decade. There are traces of the loosening mores brought on by the sexual revolution of the early sixties, and the rise of the youth counterculture in the latter part of the decade, seen in the shifting clothing and hair styles of students. Changes in popular music—from rock and roll music of Elvis Presley in the 1950s to the Beatles in the mid-sixties—are hinted at in the yearbooks; for instance, students can be seen in 1966 rocking at school dances to the tunes of the E-Types, a local "British Invasion" knockoff band that enjoyed a brief appearance on the national top-40 list that year. Cultural change was perhaps a bit slow in reaching small-town Salinas during that time. Youth countercultural styles, "anti-establishment" values, psychedelic music, and recreational drug use was flourishing in San Francisco by 1966 or 1967, but not so much yet in Salinas. Images of "hippie" styles like long hair on boys, flowing dresses on girls, and students singing along with acoustic guitars while sitting cross-legged on the school lawn bubbled up first at the end of the sixties, mostly among the students who were active in theater and the arts. But it was not until the start of the 1970s that the entrenched, largely conservative styles, mores, and routines of Salinas High students began noticeably to shift. By 1972 most boys (and even some of the men teachers) were sporting longer hair, often with lengthy sideburns, and that year a relaxed dress code allowed girls to wear pants to school, rather than the mandatory skirt of previous decades.

And here is where we can see the limits of thinking about historical periodization in decades like "the sixties," as though that was a time when distinct political and cultural transformations occurred between 1960 and the end of 1969. Many historians of the United States have argued instead that it is more useful to think of a period they call "the long sixties," often ranging from about 1955 to 1973, bookended on the front end by the expanding civil rights movement and at the other by the Watergate scandal.[60] The feminist historian Alice Echols has emphasized that when we think of "the sixties" as a time of political and cultural challenges to racial injustice, it makes sense to think of that time as starting at least as early as the mid-1950s. "But for women and gays," she emphasized, "the periodization is different. The 60s *remained* repressive until much later in the decade. The Sixties in this case are long because these movements really take off in the 70s."[61]

This was certainly true, as we have seen, for gender relations at Salinas High. Despite the blossoming of a national women's liberation movement in the late 1960s, the yearbooks mostly affirmed continuity in gender relations alongside scant hints of change: for instance, the same 1968 *El Gabilan* that celebrated the crowning of Salinas High student Suzie McComber as Betty Crocker Homemaker of Tomorrow noted that nine girls had formed a club called the Farmerettes. The next year girls were included in the traditionally all-boys' FFA. Few such hints of moves toward equality can be seen in sports, however. The late 1950s through the first three years of the 1970s was arguably the most repressive era for girls' sports, a moment of unparalleled celebration for boys' sports, and the most amazingly theatrical time for ritualized

Girls' Swim Team Undefeated

New to Salinas High this year was the Girls' Swim Team. And what a team they turned out to be! Under the direction of Miss Mary Ann Ray, the girls brought victory to Salinas High by finishing the season with 7 wins and no losses.

Figure 3.53. *El Gabilan,* 1973

pageantry that paid homage to the social divide between what was assumed to be the two "opposite sexes."

Title IX of the Education Amendments, passed in 1972, stipulated that "No person in the United States shall, on the basis of sex, be excluded from participation in, be denied the benefits of, or be subjected to discrimination under any education program or activity receiving federal financial assistance." The passage of Title IX did not result in the immediate evaporation of gender inequities in schools, but the law did create a legal foundation for advocates to press schools to move toward equity for girls' sports.[62] The 1972 *El Gabilan* coverage of girls' sports showed little evidence of the tectonic shift in girls' sports presaged by this new law, though the book did mark one notable change: "a sign of the times: PE classes go co-ed."[63]

For the first time since 1926, the 1973 yearbook depicted girls' interscholastic sports competition, trumpeting, "Girls' Tennis Team Finishes Season 7–1," and adding, "SHS looks forward to seeing this and other interscholastic girls' teams in the future. Being able to compete on the same level as the boys really adds to the spirit and enjoyment of sports."[64] Also "new to Salinas High" that year was the girls' swim team, undefeated with seven wins and zero losses (Figure 3.53). These were remarkable developments, but as we have seen, the appearance of girls' interscholastic sports competition was not exactly "new to Salinas High," but rather, was a *revival* of a practice that had been abandoned nearly a half century earlier. It may seem ironic at first glance that the rebirth of girls' sports at the high school began with tennis and

GIRL S'CHAMPIONSHIP TENNIS

VARSITY

Bertie's form?

TOP: Barbara Lyon, Jan Bryggman, Leslie Bryggman, Roberta Griffin, Linda Kanagy, Coach Emmerson; BOTTOM: Julita Cabanilla, Stephanie Tobossa, Kay Ottone, Julie Shostak, Elaine Tobossa, Lori Netzly.

The Big "E"

Figure 3.54. *El Gabilan*, 1974

swimming, two individual "country club sports" that tended to be populated mostly by white girls, far less so by the girls of color who had disproportionately held up the Girls' Athletic Association (GAA) for decades. As it happened, twenty-three girls appeared in the GAA photo in the 1973 *El Gabilan*, many of them girls of color. The long-standing organization died a quiet death the following year.

The 1974 *El Gabilan* devoted ten pages to powderpuff football, but the five pages allotted to interscholastic girls' sports still paled in comparison with the forty pages of boys' sports, twelve of them alone devoted to football. But the yearbook lauded the forty-six girls portrayed in the girls' swim team photo as "MBL CHAMPIONS AGAIN!!" The tennis teams—eleven girls on the varsity, and twelve on the junior varsity (JV)—also won a championship. The school added two more sports that year for the girls, gymnastics and track. Though there were still no team sports, girls were clearly flocking to the high school's expanding opportunities to play.

Looking forward from the *El Gabilan* books of 1973 and 1974, questions arise concerning the future directions of gender and sports, issues I will explore in the next chapter: When girls' team sports are eventually introduced, will the yearbooks treat them with the levels of respect, support, and excitement routinely afforded boys' sports? Will girls play basketball, baseball, football? When they do play the same sports as boys, will girls' sports have distinct "adapted" rules? As girls' interscholastic sports expands, what will become of the Block "S" society, which since its inception had been a boys-only club for athletes? If girls start streaming into interscholastic sports, especially if they receive equitable financial support, public attention, and respect, what will become of cheerleading? Will high-status girls be content to remain on the sidelines, cheering on others, or will they surge to center stage as athletes?

And who will coach the expanding range of girls' sports teams? In this regard, the future is hinted at in the 1974 *El Gabilan*: The girls' varsity and JV tennis teams were coached by a man, Dan Emmerson (Figure 3.54). The swim team coach, listed as Miss Mary Ann Ray, does not appear in the yearbook as a member of the faculty. No coach appears with the photos of the new gymnastics team, and the fledgling girls' track team apparently was co-coached by a man and a woman, George Anderson and Isabelle MacKay. Despite MacKay's appearance as a track coach, it is curious that other long-time stalwarts of girls' PE and GAA Anna Davis and Jean Madison, not to mention more recent additions to the girls' PE faculty Mrs. Flavia Markert or Miss Paula Baker, were not among the coaches in these fledgling girls' teams. Perhaps these women were not invited to coach, or if they were, perhaps for some reason they decided to opt out? Regardless, this snapshot of the gender composition of girls' sports coaching is an early indicator of what came to be a pattern as girls' sports exploded in popularity at Salinas High School and across the nation.

El Gabilan '75

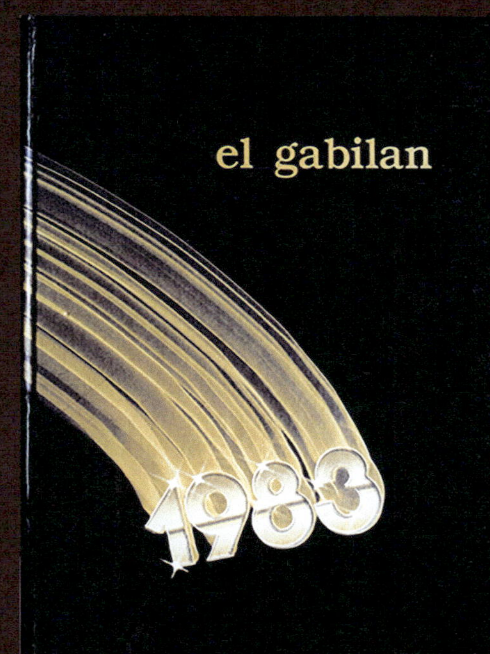
el gabilan
1983

EL GABILAN 84

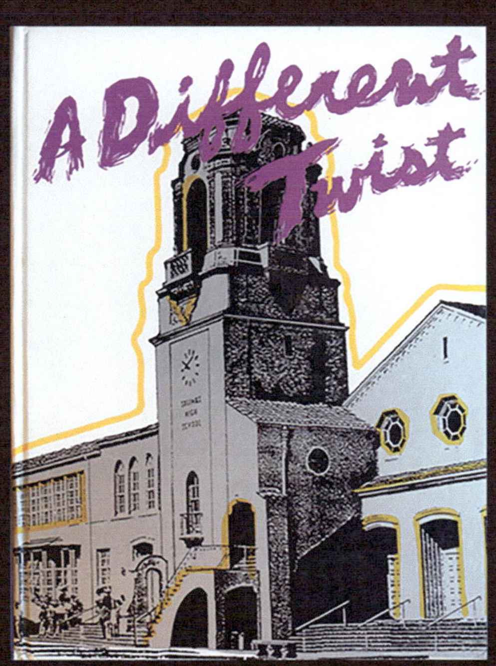
A Different Twist

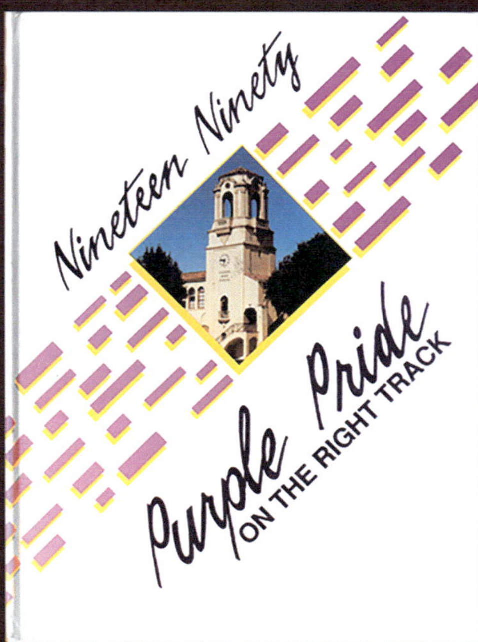
Nineteen Ninety
Purple Pride
ON THE RIGHT TRACK

HOW THE WEST
1
WAS ONE
1993

NOTHING
YOU LIKE
EXPECTED
1995
EL GABILAN

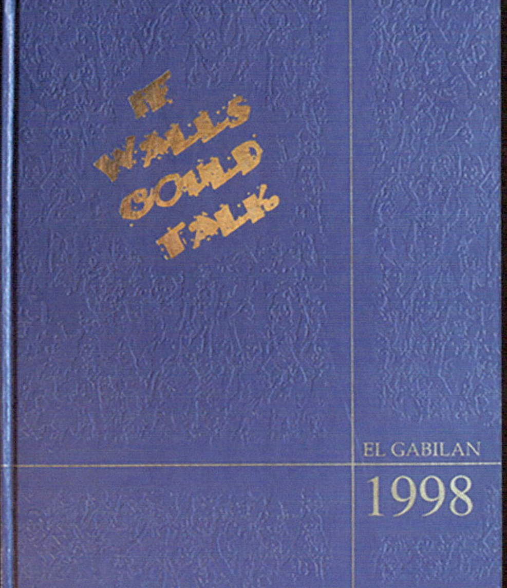
IF WALLS COULD TALK
EL GABILAN
1998

When John Cougar Mellencamp penned his classic song "When The Walls Come Tumbling Down," it's doubtful he had Salinas High School in mind. However, it certainly would apply to the 1990–91 year.

—*EL GABILAN,* 1991

Chapter 4

Boom, Bust, and Purple Pride 1975–1999

THE BLOCK "S" SOCIETY WAS FORMED in 1927 to honor the school's athletes, and every year thereafter, the Salinas High School yearbook routinely included a picture of the members of the exclusive club. But there was nothing routine about the Block "S" photo in the 1975 *El Gabilan*. "There were many new faces in the Block S this year," the caption declared, "for the first time in the history of the club, girls were admitted as members."[1] Girls were not merely *admitted*; they constituted more than half of the sixty-five Block "S" members pictured (Figure 4.2). In this, the third academic year following the passage of Title IX, one of the most visible pillars of athletic boys' honored status on campus now included girls. This change had one immediate impact on the sports pageantry routinely seen in yearbooks of the sixties and early seventies: No longer did it make any sense for new Block "S" members to be initiated into the society by dancing in front of the student body dolled up as caricatures of girls. Not when so many of the new members *were* girls.

The 1975 *El Gabilan* ushered in another landmark shift in the school's athletic gender regime. For the first time since the mid-1920s, Salinas High School introduced two girls' team sports—volleyball and basketball—to join swimming, tennis, gymnastics, and track in the expanding panoply of girls' interscholastic competition (Figure 4.3). Girls were also breaching realms of public leadership in non-sports areas at Salinas High, claiming positions previously held exclusively by boys. In 1977, Alison McAllister was the school's first girl in half a century to be elected president

Figure 4.1. "Rocco Raffo and Fran Perez show the long and the short of Purple Pride," *El Gabilan*, 1991

Figure 4.2. Block "S" Society, *El Gabilan*, 1975

Figure 4.3. Varsity basketball team, *El Gabilan*, 1975

of the Associated Student Body (ASB). In fact, that year eight of the nine elected ASB officers were girls. A decade of shifting consciousness about gender, driven by a vibrant national women's movement and sharpened by new laws like Title IX, was piercing long-standing assumptions and entrenched practices at Salinas High School.

The final quarter of the twentieth century was a boom time for girls' sports at Salinas High and around the nation. But the push toward equal opportunities and greater respect for girls' sports was neither linear nor free from strains or ironies. As more and more girls' sports were introduced, the annual yearbooks gradually allotted more pages to their coverage, but through the 1980s and well into the 1990s, boys' sports still got the lion's share of pages in the book. As girls' athletic teams multiplied, a disproportionate share of the growing number of coaching positions were held by men. And five years after girls celebrated their inclusion in the Block "S" Society, the honorary club for athletes was eliminated following its final appearance in the 1979 *El Gabilan*.

It may also seem ironic that just when girls' sports was gaining traction, getting some respect and movement in the direction of equity, sports was gradually being nudged away from its mid-century position at the center of the school's status system and public pageantry. In the late twentieth-century yearbooks, sports pageantry declined, and sports imagery was more contained, no longer spread all over the books' pages as the undisputed symbolic hallmark of student life. Simultaneously, the meaning of cheerleading (and to a lesser extent the marching band and other groups so central to the mid-century sports spirit complex) was hit with challenging questions about its value, eventually shifting cheer's emphasis away from purely supporting boys' football and basketball and pouring more energy into the cheerleaders' own competitive activities.

Slashed Budgets and Crumbling Walls

Salinas High School was party central in the late 1970s and early 1980s. At least a cursory reading of the yearbooks of that era gives that impression. The books' free-wheeling "anything goes" tone made me wonder more than once just where the adult supervision might have been during those years (a question also raised at the time about youngsters referred to as "latchkey kids," a term for those who had less adult supervision in the home due to living with dual-income parents or a single parent). One of the school's largest clubs depicted in the 1977–79 yearbooks was the "Ten Gallon Club." A drawing accompanying the 1979 club photo depicted a cowboy imbibing an overflowing mug of beer, and the list of the club's officers included positions for "Distributor of Beverages" and "Inventory Chairman."[2] Other party-themed clubs that came and went during these years included the Toga Club, fashioned after the popular 1978 film *Animal House*, and a raucous group of students pictured in a 1981 club photo who called themselves the "Abusers." Elsewhere in that same book were shots of boys drinking with the captions, "chug-a-lug!"[3]

The 1982 *El Gabilan* was themed "ROCK 'N' ROLL ~~SALINAS~~ HIGH SCHOOL," most likely echoing the Ramones' 1978 punk anthem that disparaged school principals, teachers, and studying history, proclaiming instead, "I just wanna have some kicks; I just wanna get some chicks" (Figure 4.4). Indeed, party themes permeated that yearbook, including a shot of a boy with a Jack Daniel's hat, and numerous stoner-inspired captions of kids throughout, such as "Dazed and confused," and "Stoned Blue."[4] If there was an anti-establishment tone during these years, it was a decided

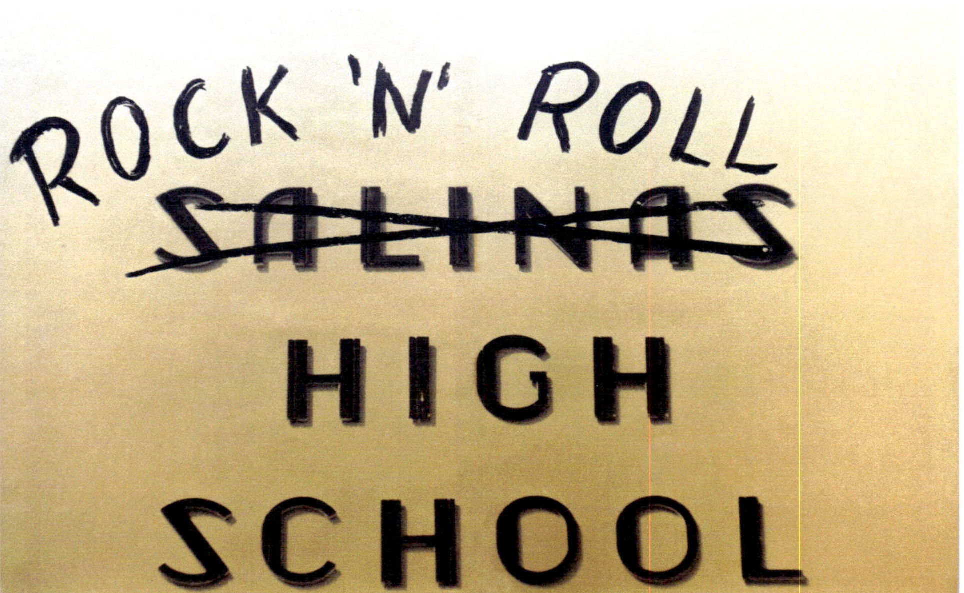

Figure 4.4. Annual yearbook theme, *El Gabilan*, 1982

turn away from the peace-and-love mood of ten years earlier, instead asserting students' rights to be free of adult supervision in order to party. A 1982 two-page photo collage of kids having fun was captioned with lyrics from the popular Pink Floyd song of the day: "We don't need no education . . . Teachers leave us kids alone."[5]

By 1985, party themes were receding from the yearbook, perhaps in part due to a turnover of faculty yearbook supervisors, but more likely due to a shifting social context that made it impossible to ignore mounting problems within the school and in the larger community. The 1987 *El Gabilan* recognized the issue of student alcohol consumption playfully, with a photo of Director of Student Activities Bill Getris at a school dance, "guarding the punch bowl." Heavy-handed law enforcement followed: Under the headline "Our Narc," the 1989 *El Gabilan* devoted a page to the story of police officer Mike Groves who, posing undercover as SHS senior "Mike Johnson," purchased drugs from students, leading to the arrests of twelve students and nine adults.[6]

Striking a less punitive tone in the early 1990s, the school attempted to address alcohol and drug consumption by shifting the values of the school's culture. In place of clubs that celebrated partying, the books increasingly documented the emergence of groups that sought to convince fellow students that drinking and drug use was not "cool." By the start of the 1990s and for the next decade, the student Alcohol Drug Abuse Prevention Team (ADAPT) held public events to advocate for "a drug and alcohol free environment" on campus. In 1995, ADAPT made presentations at local junior high schools, and together with the school's marching band, "marched down to Salinas City Hall spreading the word of having a good time and promoting a drug free lifestyle . . . The ADAPT Club also took part in the Drug Signing Assembly. They were joined by the Salinas, Alisal and Palma football teams and members of the media promoting Drug Free Contracts."[7]

"Partying" undoubtedly continued among a swath of the student population, but it was no longer tolerated by the school, nor would it be openly celebrated in the yearbooks. This shift in tone, along with the booming growth of girls' sports in the late 1970s and 1980s at Salinas High School, unfolded in the context of a crushing fiscal bust. California's 1978 anti-tax Proposition 13 "proved catastrophic for cities like Salinas . . . [that] were trying to serve a new and growing population that was also poorer and in need of education, housing and medical care."[8] Bludgeoned school budgets led to deferred building maintenance, staff cuts, wage freezes, and slashed funding for sports and other extracurricular activities. The fiscal crisis deepened at the start of the 1980s, as the "Reagan Recession," marked by double-digit unemployment and deep cuts in federal spending, further challenged Salinas High and all public schools. By 1984, budget cuts had reached a crisis point. Newly formed athletes' clubs responded with "marathons, dances, and candy sales" to raise funds for team uniforms. Parents and community groups organized the Save Our Sports group, and among their fundraising efforts was a raffle for a new car: "All proceeds went to the

Figure 4.5. (*above*) Celebrating the Rotary Club's donation of new lights for the SHS football stadium, *El Gabilan*, 1985

Figure 4.6. (*right*) SHS Sports Booster Club, *El Gabilan*, 1993

S.O.S. fund," the *El Gabilan* reported.[9] There were also "donations of district Boosters Clubs, community service organizations, and supportive citizens who were concerned that sports remain a cherished tradition in our schools."[10]

The 1984 *El Gabilan* mourned the shuttering of the school newspaper *Flashlight*: "After many years of publication, budget cuts have forced the presses to stop."[11] And the 1985 book observed that "school spirit has gone down a bit since the closing of the cafeteria." On the bright side, the Salinas High football stadium received new lights, "donated by the Salinas Rotary Club at a cost of about 15,000 dollars" (Figure 4.5).[12] As public funds for schools dried up, sports boosters clubs and community-based foundations that sought to supplement hollowed-out school budgets became a permanent part of public schools like Salinas High (Figure 4.6). These generous community efforts, of course, were hit-and-miss, and their beneficiaries tended to reflect community groups' values (e.g., funding football stadium lights versus any number of other school needs). The fundraising efforts of school foundations also tended to further widen the gap between public schools in wealthier communities and their counterparts in poorer ones.[13]

Now a half century removed from its moment as one of the most prosperous towns in the United States, Salinas in the 1980s and 1990s fell on hard times. Reflecting a national trend of deindustrialization, a series of plant closures in the 1970s and early 1980s—Firestone Tire, Smucker's, Peter-Paul candy, Spreckels Sugar—evaporated hundreds of solid blue-collar jobs in Salinas.[14] As key pillars of Salinas's economic foundation crumbled and the tax base eroded, the town's demographics shifted dramatically. From small city of 29,000 people in 1960, 90 percent of whom were white, Salinas expanded to 80,000 people in 1980 (38.8 percent Hispanic) and to more than

100,000 in 1990 (50.6 percent Hispanic); by 2000, Salinas had swelled to 150,000 people (63 percent Hispanic).[15]

A large proportion of Salinas's Mexican American newcomers—especially the most disadvantaged—settled outside the Salinas High School district, in the Alisal and North Salinas areas of town. But Salinas High in the 1980s and 1990s was not entirely insulated from the town's demographic transformation. From 1975 to the early 1980s, students with Spanish surnames made up about 10–12 percent of the students pictured in the graduating senior classes of the high school, and from there the numbers climbed: 16 percent in 1985, 25 percent in 1987, 35 percent in 1990, and 39 percent in 1999. Given the large number of Spanish-surnamed seniors whose names appeared among the "shutter shy" students whose senior portraits did not appear in the yearbooks, the proportion of Spanish-surnamed students in the school was actually substantially higher (e.g., closer to 49 percent in 1999) than a count of pictured seniors would suggest.[16] Added to the modest clusters of Asian American, African American and other non-European-origin students at the school,[17] the swelling numbers of Spanish-surnamed students meant that by the late 1990s, white students constituted fewer than half of the student body.

Salinas High School's rapid transformation from a white-dominated school to a minority-majority school was not without strain and conflict. One student struck a hopeful tone in a 1988 *El Gabilan* feature on interracial dating: "Many of the racial barriers have been knocked down by the youth of today. Still, those walls remain high in the eyes of our parents."[18] But not every "racial barrier" had been knocked down among the students, it turns out. While reading the 1991 *El Gabilan,* I had noticed an odd anomaly on the pages that depicted that year's MEChA club (Movimiento Estudiantil Chicano de Aztlan, a club that had become widespread in Southwest U.S. high schools and colleges)[19] and the Bilingual Gate club: A single page had been neatly sliced out, a quarter of an inch from the binding, and a fresh page had been glued in.[20] I had no idea what to make of it. Then, when talking about my project with my niece Jennifer Rios—a 1991 Salinas High student and MEChA member—she asked me if I knew about "the big yearbook scandal" of that year. I asked her to tell me about it.

> A few members of the yearbook staff thought it would be amusing to put placeholder names for the student members in the Bilingual Club photo while they were waiting for the roster of actual names. What's not amusing is that the placeholder names they used were racist in nature and depicted the mostly Latinx students with derogatory names that do not need to be repeated. This egregious error was discovered after the book had gone to print and the finished copies arrived at the school. The error was caught, thankfully, before the books were passed out to students. The school sent every book back to the printer, and the printing house replaced the page in question, which I'm sure cost a pretty penny.[21]

Racial tensions in the school also contributed to escalating concern with violence, on and off campus. In 1993, school counselor Art Hunsdorfer organized the Conflict Resolution Team (CRT). Often disproportionately made up of Latina students, the CRT worked in subsequent years to "stop the violence, stop the hate" on campus (Figure 4.7). That same year, the *El Gabilan* announced the arrival of the school district's first woman superintendent, Mrs. Aurora Quevedo, who was "born and raised in Mexico City," and who aimed to promote "communication and positive leadership" to better address "the rise of gang violence, school population, and the need for equality between students, teachers, and races."[22] The 1980s and 1990s activities of the MEChA oscillated between organizing celebrations of Mexican culture and political advocacy. The latter included a 1991 effort to "demand equal representation among student leadership. [MEChA] President Jose T. Gonzales said, 'For too long, we have stood back and allowed decisions to be made for us, and now is the time to take control of our own situation. We need more positive Chicano role models. Power to the people—refuse to lose!'"[23] The 1995 yearbook included photos of MEChA students working to defeat California's anti-immigrant Proposition 184 (Figure 4.8).

Public infrastructure for law enforcement, libraries, and schools thinned in the 1980s, and with an electorate that was loath to vote for higher taxes, Salinas reeled from rising poverty rates and escalating violence. Some community members imagined one source of civic revival in Salinas High School's deceased alum John Steinbeck. In 1977, partly "to rectify Salinas' disdain (and disregard) for Steinbeck," citizens established the Steinbeck Foundation.[24] Many years of fundraising and maneuvering resulted in the 1998 opening of the National Steinbeck Center on Salinas's Main Street. The historian McKibben noted that then–Salinas mayor Alan Styles "proclaimed enthusiastically that the new center would 'put Salinas on the map . . . as a tourist center' rescuing the downtown economy with a projected attendance of hundreds of thousands of visitors a year, a wildly unrealistic figure . . . That dream never materialized."[25]

Meanwhile, Salinas High School was hit with a particular trouble of its own. Following the Loma Prieta earthquake in 1989, inspectors found wood rot, termite damage, rusting pipes, and dangerous asbestos. The walls of the old school were literally crumbling. Much of the aging building was condemned, and in subsequent years a generation of students witnessed a series of failed school bond measures as they waited to see if their school would be knocked down, rebuilt, or simply left to rot as they made the best of their high school years in portable classrooms (Figures 4.9 and 4.10).

Not surprisingly, the yearbooks annually bemoaned the doldrums of the 1990s, frequently remarking on the decline of "school spirit." The school gamely attempted to pump up sports-based "Purple Pride" (Figure 4.1), featuring all-school football rallies in The Pit, but in the *El Gabilan* books of the 1990s, the sports pageantry of previous decades was muted in importance as other issues pressed for attention. Where yearbooks of previous decades depicted high school life as a mostly self-contained

Figure 4.7. SHS Conflict Resolution Team, *El Gabilan*, 1999

Figure 4.8. MEChA students oppose anti-immigrant legislation, *El Gabilan*, 1995

world, insulated from troubles in the community, nation, or world, the *El Gabilan* books of the 1990s evidenced a turning outward to social issues that had pushed into and through the once protective (and now crumbling) walls of the school. In this context, the mustering of Purple Pride clearly sparked some spirit and fun. But no amount of school spirit could magically transform portables into sparkling new classrooms or create a new cafeteria, auditorium, or gymnasium. Nor were the shoulders of sports pageantry wide or strong enough to fully bear the weight of growing poverty, racial inequality, violence, drug and alcohol abuse, and the decline of public

Figure 4.9. (*left*) Demolition, *El Gabilan*, 1995

Figure 4.10. (*below*) Life in the portables, *El Gabilan*, 1998

support for schools. Yet, amid all of this, girls' sports continued to grow, and eventually prosper.

Female Studs and Courtside Cuties

In 2022, Susan (Springer) Garcia was inducted into the Salinas Valley Sports Hall of Fame (HOF). Of the nearly one hundred individual HOF inductees through 2024, twenty-four are former Salinas High School athletes or coaches. Of that SHS twenty-four, Springer Garcia is one of two women (the other being Gina Miller Ucelli, a star setter on the 1982 and 1983 SHS volleyball team). Springer's inscription on the HOF website reads, "By the time Susan Springer Garcia graduated from Salinas High in 1979 she was not only the most decorated track and field girl in the history of the Salinas Valley, but likely the most dominant of any Salinas-area track athlete."[26] As a junior and a senior at SHS, Susan Springer amassed seven Central Coast Section (CCS) titles in discus and shot put while setting CCS records in both events. I had read the *El Gabilan* yearbooks of that era, and I was puzzled: I had never heard of Susan Springer. So I returned to the 1979 yearbook, and yes, there she was: a single photo freezing Springer in time, her hair flying as she completes a powerful and graceful hurl (Figure 4.11). But it took some detective work to be certain this was Susan Springer, as the photo had no caption. In the two-page yearbook section for girls' track and field, the athlete who four decades later would be lauded as "the most decorated track and field girl in the history of the Salinas Valley" was named only in the team photo, and none of her records or championships were mentioned.[27]

Figure 4.11. Shot put and discus champion Susan Springer, *El Gabilan*, 1979

Susan Springer's yearbook photo, coupled with the book's silence concerning her sterling athletic accomplishments, are indicative of the *El Gabilan*'s late 1970s and early 1980s mix of growing visibility for girls' sports alongside continuing inequities in quantity and quality of coverage. As girls' sports teams began to receive more space in the annual yearbooks, depictions of girl athletes evidenced growing levels of respect, alongside residues of past sexist or ambivalent treatment. For instance, the 1980 *El Gabilan* devoted two pages to girls' tennis, trumpeting the varsity team as "Champs 9 Years In A Row," but also including a shot of eight of the girls in a happy pose, with the caption "Courtside Cuties" (Figure 4.12). The use of a trivial, perhaps sexualized caption reflected what

Figure 4.12. SHS girls' tennis team, captioned "Courtside Cuties," *El Gabilan*, 1980

1970s and 1980s women's sports researchers labeled "the female apologetic."[28] For female athletes of that era (or for sports media), to emphasize signs of femininity like wearing long hair and makeup, displaying "cuteness," and other signs of heterosexual femininity could be seen as "apologetic" behavior that neutralized the potential stigma of masculinization or lesbianism that athletic girls risked when engaging in masculine fields. A similar mixed message—an ambivalent stew of respect with disparagement—can be seen in a 1982 basketball action shot, labeled "Female Studs," juxtaposed with a cartoon drawing of a player getting bonked on the head by a basketball (Figure 4.13).

The messages may have been mixed, but the trend was clear: girls' sports teams at Salinas High were growing in number, and the yearbooks were gradually treating them with greater respect. For a time though, the yearbooks remained stingy in their allotment of pages devoted to girls' sports. As Table 4.1 shows, there was a gradual movement toward parity in coverage of boys' and girls' sports in the yearbooks of the final twenty-five years of the century. From 1975 to 1982, the books devoted an average of thirty pages to boys' sports and thirteen pages to girls. During each of those years, the inclusion of two pages for girls' powderpuff football, not an interscholastic sport, literally puffed up the total girls' sports page numbers. From 1992 through the end of the decade, the number of *El Gabilan* pages devoted to boys' sports dipped slightly—football was reduced to four pages in 1993—as the girls' pages continued to climb. But the increase in girls' sports coverage in the yearbooks of the 1990s was puffed up by a new source. While cheerleading squads had been included in the "Clubs" section of the books until 1991, starting in 1992 cheerleading was included as a girls' sport

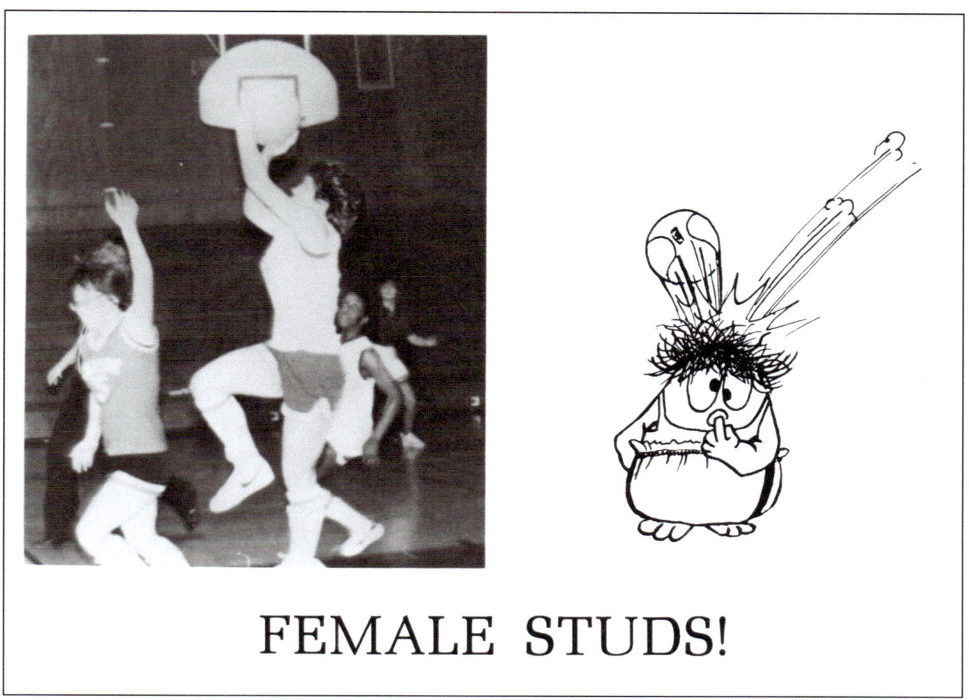

Figure 4.13. SHS girls' basketball team, *El Gabilan*, 1982

TABLE 4.1

Average yearbook pages devoted to boys', girls', and coed sports, 1975–1999

	Boys' teams	Girls' teams	Coed teams[a]
1975–82	30.5	13.3[b]	1.8
1983–91	26.1	13.2	3.4
1992–99	24.6	20.4[c]	5.4

[a] Cross-country and track and field were coed squads, but boys and girls competed separately.
[b] Includes 2 pages per year, 1975 to 1982, devoted to powderpuff football, an intramural sport.
[c] Includes 5.3 pages per year, starting in 1992, devoted to cheerleading.

(a topic I will take up later at greater length), contributing an average of 5.3 pages in the "Sports" section of the yearbooks from 1992 to 1999.

Equity, Difference, and Title IX

The law of the land since 1972, Title IX immediately placed a powerful tool in the hands of advocates for girls' sports in schools.[29] The year Title IX was passed, girls' sports made up only 7.4 percent of the nearly four million athletic opportunities in U.S. high schools.[30] By 1978—the date by which all schools receiving federal funds were required

Figure 4.14. SHS girls' softball team, *El Gabilan*, 1986

to be in full compliance with Title IX—girls' share of high school sports opportunities had grown dramatically to 32.3 percent, though most educational institutions in the United States were still far from compliance with the law.[31] The Reagan administration stripped the legal enforcement teeth out of Title IX during much of the 1980s; as a result, schools' movement toward equity slowed. In 1988, though, Congress passed the Civil Rights Restoration Act—over a presidential veto—and this put enforcement teeth back into Title IX. The next decade saw the continued growth of girls' high school sports opportunities—girls were 40.1 percent of high school athletes in 1999—sometimes stimulated and punctuated by battles fought in the courts over Title IX compliance in high schools and colleges.[32]

These national political battles place into perspective the continuing lopsided allocation of pages devoted to boys' sports in Salinas High School's yearbooks ten, twenty, or twenty-five years following the passage of Title IX. It is hard to measure the impact of the stubborn legacy of decades of celebratory pageantry of boys' sports in the yearbooks. But there are two factors that can be seen in the books that help to explain the persistent second-class status of girls' sports in the *El Gabilan* from the mid-1970s and through the 1990s. First, there were simply more boys' sports than girls' sports in these years. A snapshot of the 1990 yearbook illustrates this fact. That year, girls occupied 30 percent of the school's athlete positions (shy of the national 1990 average of 35.4 percent).[33] Salinas High boys that year had the opportunity to play in eleven sports, girls in only eight, a disparity made more acute by the fact that some sports offered more teams for boys (eighteen) than for girls (twelve). For instance,

Figure 4.15. SUHS girls' baseball team, *El Gabilan*, 1923

the school offered boys' varsity, JV, and freshmen basketball teams, but only varsity and JV for girls.

Second, as girls' sports grew in number and popularity, many of the sports they were offered were different from the sports that boys played. It is doubtful whether there was any talk of creating a girls' baseball team in 1977, the year the school added a girls' softball team. After all, at least some of the girls who suited up for this new team had likely played Little League Softball, a national youth sport founded in 1973 in the wake of girls' successful legal challenges to Little League Baseball for the right to play baseball with the boys.[34] Echoing this development in youth sports, softball took off as a regular girls' team sport in high schools across the nation, including at Salinas High (Figure 4.14). Of course, there was no natural, anatomical reason to channel girls into softball rather than baseball.[35] In fact, there is a rich history of girls' and women's baseball, from the World War II–era All American Girls' Professional Baseball League (made famous by the 1992 film *A League of Their Own*) to the girls' interscholastic baseball teams fielded by Salinas High in the 1920s (Figure 4.15).[36]

Girls at Salinas High did play some of the same sports that boys played in the 1980s and 1990s—cross-country, track and field, swimming, tennis, basketball—but several of the team sports organized for girls were different from the sports that boys played. The 1985 *El Gabilan* noted, for instance, that "because of the popularity of the game in the Summer Olympics, the rest of the nation caught volleyball fever."[37] The next

Figure 4.16. SHS varsity volleyball champs, *El Gabilan*, 1990

Figure 4.17. SHS freshman football team, *El Gabilan*, 1990

year, the yearbook gushed that "the popularity of [girls'] volleyball surprised many a football fan."[38] The girls' volleyball teams were popular and successful, but their size (and one would assume, their annual operating costs) paled in comparison to the boys' football program. Again, to use 1990 as a point of comparison, the girls' varsity and JV volleyball teams had a total of 26 athletes, a scant 9 of them on the league-champion varsity team (Figure 4.16). By contrast, 121 boys played on the 1990 varsity, JV, and freshman SHS football teams, nearly as many as the entire number of girls (156) who played across eight sports that year. The freshmen football team alone fielded 42 players (Figure 4.17).

Not surprisingly, football also gobbled up an outsized share of space in the annual yearbooks—roughly eight pages each year through 1988, when the sport was demoted to six pages. Nationally, the game of football was a political hot potato in 1980s and 1990s debates about Title IX. Pointing to the ways that high school football absorbed a lion's share of athletic department funds, advocates of equity fought for more money, more sports, more teams, and more playing fields for girls. Meanwhile, defenders of the status quo argued that perhaps football should be thought of as being in a category of its own (as though the game was played by a privileged third sex), and as such should be exempt from Title IX equity discussions.[39]

For some at Salinas High, the gradual march toward equity and respect for girls' sports was moving at a frustrating snail's pace. When I asked Nancy Getris,[40] a member of the SHS volleyball and basketball teams between 1982 and 1986, what it was like being an athlete at the school, just over a decade after the passage of Title IX, she recalled the time fondly. But then she paused and said, "I remember the girls, we never got as big of crowds as the boys. And the girls teams, we would always go support the boys, but the boys would never come and support us." More than a decade later, Getris would return to coach the SHS girls' freshman basketball team for a couple of years, and this persistent lack of reciprocity still irked her: "If you were the freshman boys' coach and you saw the girls' team come and support you, you would think that you would say, 'Hey, let's go support the girls.' Yeah. It never happened." The 1995 *El Gabilan*, which included a full-page tribute photo collage celebrating the school's "1994 Central Coast Section Football Champions," also reported a bit of pushback from physical education teacher Melanie Miller. "Women are becoming more and more involved in athletics and not recognized for their outstanding athletic ability. For the first time, Ms. Miller established the Salinas High School National Girls and Women in Sports Recognition Week . . . 'I felt that the boys always got the recognition, and it was time for the girls to receive some as well,' stated Ms. Miller."[41]

"She's a Champion!"

One form of recognition that was increasing, starting in the mid-1980s and accelerating in the 1990s yearbooks, was the occasional feature that celebrated an outstanding girl athlete, often accompanied by an action photo. Headlined, "She's a champion!" the 1984 *El Gabilan* included a sidebar feature on sophomore Jenny Sowerwine, who competed "on the YMCA Gymnastics Class II Team."[42] The 1990 yearbook spotlighted track and field senior sensation Aimee Cohon, who starred in the 400 (which she ran in 58.8 seconds), the long jump, and as the anchor in both the 4×100 and 4×400 relays (Figure 4.18). The next year, the yearbook celebrated swim team MVP Erin Ramsey for winning the Monterey Bay League (MBL) diving championship and finishing fourth in the CCS (Figure 4.19). In 1995, the yearbook reported that record-setting cross-country runner "senior Joanna Peschkoff won the City Meet for the second year in a row."[43]

Figure 4.18. (*left*) Record-setting track star Aimee Cohon, *El Gabilan*, 1990

Figure 4.19. (*above*) Champion diver Erin Ramsey, *El Gabilan*, 1991

These celebratory features stood in stark contrast to the combination of silence, insult, or ambivalence that framed the efforts of the school's girl athletes in previous decades. But these stories also illuminate two other patterns in the final two decades of the twentieth century with respect to girls' sports. First, nearly all the girls showcased in the book as star athletes were white girls. This was likely not a result of a discriminatory decision to ignore star girls of color. Rather, it reflected a structural factor; in the two decades following Title IX, the school's teams were disproportionately populated by white girls. As we saw in the previous chapter, Salinas High's first girls' sports teams in the mid-1970s, tennis and swimming, were individual "country club" sports to which white, upper middle-class girls likely had greater access. But even when the school began to introduce team sports, and despite this being an era when Salinas High was becoming more racially diverse, the girls' teams included a scant number of Asian American, Latina, or Black girls. Again, to take 1990 as an example, in a year when roughly 50 percent of the school's senior class was white, about 77 percent of the girls on sports teams appear to be white.[44] As in previous decades, Japanese American, Chinese American, and African American girls were still overrepresented, given their very small numbers in the school. But Latina athletes were few and far between on most of the school's sports teams, with the exception of soccer—added as a girls' sport in 1994—and in some years softball. In 1999, white students constituted less than half of the SHS student population, but white girls still populated about two-thirds of the positions on sports teams.

The influx of white, middle-class girls into sports represents an historic sea change. In the decades preceding Title IX, girls of color had participated in the Girls' Athletic Association (GAA) program far in excess of their proportions in the school. Now, in a period where resources and respect were starting to flow toward girls' sports, white girls were rushing to play. A second pattern, linked to the disproportionate whiteness of girl athletes in the eighties and nineties, is the way that sports participation was becoming "part of the package" of building an impressive résumé for college admission and future professional life. Take multisport star Starry Sprenkle, for example. The 1998 *El Gabilan* profiled the junior "Shining Star" volleyball, softball, and basketball player, noting she was carrying a 4.0 GPA, and quoting her saying that she was motivated by "the drive to wipe out the prejudice against women in sports."[45] The next year, the yearbook celebrated Sprenkle's contributions as a member of the league co-champion volleyball team, and her standout season in basketball as "the sixth leading scorer in the Monterey Bay League" (Figure 4.20). Elsewhere in the book, we see that Starry Sprenkle was a member of the school's jazz band, president of the Key Club, and the winner of Bank of America's Science Certificate Award. Her classmates voted Sprenkle "most likely to succeed" (Figure 4.21).[46]

Starry Sprenkle was a standout in her class, and she also illustrates a pattern that began in the 1990s and continues today: Girls, especially those from professional and middle-class families, participate in sports in great numbers, often encouraged by their

Figure 4.20. (*above*) Starry Sprenkle (*top left*) and varsity volleyball team, *El Gabilan*, 1999

Figure 4.21. (*right*) *El Gabilan*, 1999

Most Likely To Succeed

Success is their middle name! Starry Sprenkle and Alfred Fung.

parents and peers, and come to see sports not simply as a fun pursuit but also as one of a cluster of activities that are empowering, status-enhancing, and part of a package of curricular and extracurricular achievements they will need to be admitted to selective colleges and universities. This package can also include leadership in community service clubs like the Key Club. And one of the most striking developments evidenced in the yearbooks of the 1980s and 1990s is the rise and numerical dominance of girls as elected ASB officers, a good number of them also athletes. With the caption, "Officers Without Gentlemen?" the 1990 *El Gabilan* pictured the elected leaders of the senior class—Whitney Welsh, Michele Burruss, and Kandi Kelly (two of them also cheerleaders and one an athlete)—and crowed that the three "led the class of '90 without the help of the male species. Hooray for Women's Lib!!"[47]

As boys receded from leadership in student government and in many clubs, the yearbooks did at times feature college-bound boys whose athletic accomplishments were one element in an impressive résumé. But often, for boys athletic stardom seemed more of a stand-alone accomplishment than part of a larger package of résumé-building as it was for many standout girls.[48] This was part of a national pattern for girls, encouraged and promoted by organizations like the Women's Sports Foundation, who started to disseminate a research-based message in the 1990s that "It is no accident that 80% of the female executives at Fortune 500 companies identified themselves as former 'tomboys'—having played sports."[49] Sports participation was good for girls' physical health, national advocates like the Women's Sports Foundation announced; sports also enhanced girls' self-esteem, and built leadership qualities and confidence to make it in a man's world.

Senior Studs and *Futbol* Heroes

As girls' sports expanded at Salinas High, boys' sports certainly did not disappear. In fact, for the latter half of the 1970s, and into the 1980s, the yearbooks presented boys' sports in ways that echoed the previous decades. Boys' sports, as Table 4.1 shows, was receiving a lion's share of space in the "Sports" section of the yearbooks, with football and boys' basketball routinely getting eight and six pages, respectively, of the thirty or so normally allotted to boys' teams. Images of football and boys' basketball games, pregame rallies, and their accompanying pageantry were also peppered liberally through the pages of the books. For instance, the opening pages of the 1982 *El Gabilan* included a full-page photo spread, "A Shining Season," celebrating the football team's accomplishments.[50] Football also retained its role as a public anchor for an honored form of masculinity (Figure 4.22).

As girls' sports expanded and received a bit more space in the yearbooks, boys' domination of the books' pages began gradually to erode. In 1989, the football team's yearbook pages dropped from eight to six. Boys' basketball also was cut down to size, reduced to four pages in 1992. And starting in 1993 the school's three football teams shared only four pages in the yearbook. Even the 1995 MBL and CCS champion varsity football team that coach John Felice called "the greatest football team in the 74 year history of football at Salinas High School" received only two yearbook pages (with the JV and freshmen teams receiving one each) (Figure 4.23). Still, the masculine bombast remained, even if the yearbook space for it was

Figure 4.22. *El Gabilan*, 1981

Figure 4.23. MBL and CCS champion football team, *El Gabilan*, 1995

constrained. "Boys play football," senior Ray Lee boasted in the yearbook, "MEN play 'pit-style' football."[51]

The yearbooks' declining number of pages for football and boys' basketball meant that girls' sports could receive a bit more space, without cutting into the already modest coverage of boys' baseball, swimming, wrestling, water polo, golf, and tennis. More so than in girls' sports, the Salinas High boys' teams of the final quarter of the century reflected the growing racial-ethnic diversity of the school. In 1977 SHS introduced boys' soccer. Then, and in subsequent years, the team's players were predominantly, sometimes almost exclusively, Latinos (Figure 4.24).

On a few occasions, a girl breached the boundary of boys' sports. Titled "She's proven there's equal opportunity for all," the 1985 *El Gabilan* devoted a full-page feature to sophomore Cynthia Stephens, who was credited with being "the first girl ever

Figure 4.24. SHS varsity soccer team, *El Gabilan*, 1979

Figure 4.25. Cindy Stephens with the boys' football team, *El Gabilan*, 1985

in Salinas High on a boys' tackle football team" (Figure 4.25). The accompanying text added, though, that "Cindy never played in any games. Wrong timing too much pressure and too much attention were the reasons Cindy quit before the season started."[52]

The 1996 yearbook noted two girls who did successfully join boys' teams. "One thing that took most people by surprise," read that year's *El Gabilan* coverage of the boys' water polo team, "is that there was a girl on the team and played just as well as the guys. 'It's nothing new. I've been playing with guys for years,' says Senior Dottie West."[53] That same year, Angela Lovorato joined the boys' JV baseball team and said, "I like playing baseball because I like seeing the reactions of the other teams faces

Figure 4.26. SHS track team, *El Gabilan*, 1992

when they see me."[54] But Salinas High's sports teams remained mostly sex-segregated in the 1980s and 1990s. Two teams—cross-country and track and field—were combined coed squads. The girls and boys practiced and traveled to meets together, but their interscholastic competitions remained sex-segregated (Figure 4.26).[55]

Sports in the 80s and 90s at Salinas High was in many ways still a "man's world," including the ways that the school, so troubled by slashed budgets, crumbing walls, and concerns about violence and drug and alcohol abuse, was loading hope onto the shoulders of boys' football and basketball teams to bolster "Purple Pride" and revive a sagging school spirit. But interscholastic sports in the final two decades of the century seemed to be losing its centrality in student life, for three reasons. First, the 1990s saw the rise in popularity of "extreme" or "lifestyle" sports that were not part of the regular menu of interscholastic sports offered by schools. The 1995 *El Gabilan*, for instance, devoted a two-page photo spread titled "Extreme Athletes" with shots of students skateboarding, surfing, bicycling, horseback riding, snowboarding, and waterskiing. "These people don't get letterman's jacket for what they're doing," the accompanying text read. "Some of these people put in the same amount of work and effort but don't always get the same recognition. . . . this is more than a hobby but a way of life. Maybe even one day a career."[56] The yearbooks regularly devoted pages to alternative sports in subsequent years, reflecting a national trend of young people turning away from school-based sports and toward sports that offered them more opportunities for self-expression, less adult supervision, and sometimes less emphasis on competition.[57]

A second contributor to the decentering of school sports in the 80s and 90s yearbooks was the growing focus on students' work and leisure outside of school hours. Increasing numbers of students held paid jobs during the school year, and the yearbooks began to show photos of students working in fast-food jobs, restaurants, or clothing stores. Some students needed money to help support their families. Many needed cash to participate in an expanding teen consumer culture—to buy and maintain a car, participate in recreational and leisure activities, or to build a stylish wardrobe.[58] In the mid-1980s, the *El Gabilan* started featuring fashion photos of students, often presented in a way that highlighted the varying styles of different student subcultures: over the years, the books featured several pages of full-color posed shots of students decked out and labeled variously as skaters, yuppies, grunge, goth, beach, metal, casual, or sporty (Figures 4.27, 4.28, 4.29).

Third, the sports limelight dimmed in the 1980s and 1990s as the yearbooks devoted more attention to academics, service-oriented clubs, and social issues that affected students' daily lives both inside and outside the walls of the school.[59] The books shifted the spotlight onto efforts by students, parents, faculty, and administrators to address the pressing issues of racial inequality, violence, drug and alcohol abuse, HIV/AIDS, and environmental decay, as well as the shrinking budget and crumbling walls of the school. In the process, sports photos and stories were gradually re-contained in the "Sports" section of the yearbooks. To be sure, some shots of sports games and rallies continued to spill into other parts of the book, but far less so than in previous decades.

Shifting Pageantry

Coinciding with the party atmosphere that peppered the late 1970s and early 1980s yearbooks, the *El Gabilan* continued to highlight the sports-based pageants of gender that had so permeated the imagery in the 1960s and early 1970s books. Powderpuff football, introduced in 1966 at Salinas High, was a popular annual gender inversion ritual by the mid-1970s. Girls formed four teams—freshmen, sophomores, juniors, and seniors—donned football uniforms, practiced, and played flag football games against each other in front of a crowd. Some boys from the football team joined the event—a few as coaches for the girls' teams and a handful as cheerleaders, decked out in attire that exaggerated girls' bodies, hair, makeup, and comportment. The annual event was intended as fun for all, but the distance between the gender performances of the girls and the boys, noted in the previous chapter, seemed only to become more extreme by the late 1970s. The yearbooks regularly depicted the girls' team photos and reported which teams had won or lost games (Figure 4.30). The rare action shots of the girls' games depicted athletes competing hard for victory.

The boy "cheerleaders," on the other hand, seemed each year to try to outdo the previous year's efforts to caricature the most extreme expressions of femininity. And the photos of their performances, framed in ironic humor, were splashed all over the yearbooks (Figures 4.31, 4.32). A 1977 shot of boy cheerleaders with huge fake breasts was captioned "My New Living Bra."[60] In 1978, several shots of boys mimicking girl cheerleaders were scattered throughout, with captions including "Senior Men?,"

Figure 4.27. (*above left*) *El Gabilan*, 1988

Figure 4.28. (*above right*) *El Gabilan*, 1992

Figure 4.29. (*left*) *El Gabilan*, 1992

Figure 4.30. Junior class powderpuff football champs, *El Gabilan,* 1975

"Charlie's Angels," You Sexy Things," and "Take It All Off!"[61] In 1981, a photo of girls in football jerseys, juxtaposed with a shot of boys as cheerleaders, drew the caption "THE EQUAL RIGHTS AMENDMENT FINALLY MAKES ITS WAY INTO SALINAS HIGH???"[62] And likely referencing the popular 1981 Rick James song "Super Freak," the 1982 book wrote of the boys dressed in drag, "THEY ARE VERY KINKY GIRLS."[63]

It is fascinating to consider the meanings of powderpuff football as gender pageantry during the years when girls were so rapidly moving into fields previously dominated by boys, like sports and student leadership. In this transformative moment, girls were pushing boundaries, breaking through barriers, and seeking recognition and respect as equals. Some boys and men of the 1970s were supportive of girls' and women's equality, some were vehemently opposed, and many were just confused and unsettled from being decentered from positions of public leadership and respect to which they had been traditionally entitled. Viewed in this context, the boy athletes' extreme performances as girl cheerleaders can be seen as attempts to distance themselves from disparaged forms of femininity, ironically affirming their masculine status.[64]

There were a couple of passing mentions of powderpuff football in mid-1980s yearbooks, but by 1983 the event had otherwise disappeared from the Salinas High yearbooks. By the mid-1980s the school had also discontinued the cringeworthy annual student "Slave Auction." The 1975 book had included a shot of "Gerald, Ben, Willie, and Cliff auctioneering girls off at Salinas High's Slave Day" (Figure 4.33).[65] Freshman girls were auctioned off on Slave Day 1977, and the *El Gabilan* noted, "Many of these girls had to fix a lunch for her master big enough for an army! Others had to carry their masters' books to his or her class."[66] In the next few years, it appears that boys too were sometimes auctioned off, but a 1983 photo suggested that for a boy to

Figure 4.31. *El Gabilan*, 1978

Figure 4.32. *El Gabilan*, 1982

be a proper slave, it is perhaps more convincing if he is dressed like a girl (Figure 4.34). These "auctions" seem to have included mostly white students, and the master-slave spectacle was overtly themed as being about gender, not race. Still, the ritual was recapturing and celebrating one of the harshest eras in American history. Most likely someone at Salinas High in the early 1980s—administrators, teachers, students, parents—saw it this way, and put the kibosh on future slave auctions.

Powderpuff football and slave auctions disappeared from the yearbooks at roughly the same time that faculty and administrators presumably shifted the emphasis of the

Figure 4.33. (*above*) SHS slave auction, *El Gabilan*, 1975

Figure 4.34. (*left*) *El Gabilan*, 1983

school and its yearbook away from overt celebration or covert tolerance of students' alcohol and drug use. Perhaps the party was over, or at least the tone was shifting as the yearbooks became gradually more serious, and perhaps also less willing to endorse rituals that echoed traditions of treating women or people of color as property. But that does not mean that a gender pageantry, rich in meanings, entirely disappeared from the *El Gabilan*. The annual "role reversal" Twirp Dance continued through the 1990s. "TWIRP," the 1998 *El Gabilan* reminded readers, meant "The Woman is Required to Pay," and the event regularly included the crowning of a "Twirp King." As some of the school's ritual pageantry disconnected from sports, Halloween celebrations helped to fill the gap, and each year the *El Gabilan* devoted a few pages to chronicling the October costumed revelry, and also, by the late 1990s to celebrations of Dia De Los Muertos, the Mexican Day of the Dead. One sports-related public ritual that not only persisted but also expanded its scope and carnivalesque pageantry was the school's homecoming celebration.

Homecoming Week culminated with a parade on Main Street, complete with elaborate floats and costumed students, the ritual crowning of the homecoming queen (and eventually also a homecoming king) during the football game, and a postgame dance. Started in 1961, by the 1980s homecoming had taken center stage in the school's sports pageantry, its growing prominence linked with the school's efforts to deploy sports to boost "Purple Pride" during an otherwise difficult time. Homecoming festivities received four pages in the yearbooks of this era—two covering the parade of floats, and two the crowning of the homecoming queen. Notably, in some of these years there was no mention of the football game that the event was supposedly built around. By the 1990s, the choice of queen, which in earlier years seemed more of a ritual crowning of the school's most popular, conventionally pretty, (mostly) white girls, had morphed in three notable ways. First, homecoming queens and their court began to reflect the expanding racial and ethnic diversity of the school. Second, there was a clear effort to emphasize that the homecoming queen was chosen not due only to her popularity or her looks, but for her range of accomplishments. For instance, the *El Gabilan* page devoted to 1993 homecoming queen Lori Villafuerte and her court emphasized, "It's a time to overlook beauty and recognize their achievements over the past four years at Salinas High School." Among the many of Villafuerte's accomplishments listed next to her photo were three years on the principal's honor roll, captaincy of both the volleyball and basketball team, and athlete of the year honors (Figure 4.35).[67]

By the latter half of the 1990s, SHS began also to name a homecoming king alongside the queen. These honorees reflected the school's racial diversity, and the yearbooks included lists of their accomplishments. This move toward equal-opportunity royalty revealed a gender asymmetry alluded to above. High-achieving girls tended to fold athletic successes into a larger package of school honors and community service; while this was also true of some boys, it continued to be possible for athletic stardom

Figure 4.35. (*above*) Homecoming queen Lori Villafuerte, *El Gabilan*, 1993

Figure 4.36. (*top right*) Homecoming king JoJo Hernandez, queen Julissa Mendoza, *El Gabilan*, 1998

Figure 4.37. (*bottom right*) Homecoming king Jason Gustus, queen Jocelyn Tumacder, *El Gabilan*, 1999

to form a singular foundation for a boy's status on campus. For instance, 1998 honor roll student and homecoming queen Julissa Mendoza had been voted "Most Involved" by the class of 1998, and her long list of achievements included serving as president of MEChA, ASB secretary, and tutor for the Migrant Center. Mendoza's counterpart, homecoming king JoJo Hernandez, was MVP on the basketball team and a DJ for the Hip Hop Club (Figure 4.36).[68] Similarly, 1999 homecoming queen Jocelyn Tumacder and king Jason Gustus were standout athletes, and both were voted by their classmates as having the "funniest laugh." But Tumacder's accomplishments stretched far beyond her role as a basketball player and football cheerleader: she was also senior class president, an elected officer of two clubs, an honor roll student, and a member of the National Honor Society. Gustus was an award-winning football and basketball player who also served the I Help Program during Thanksgiving (Figure 4.37).[69]

"Cheerleading Is a Sport!"

In the decades following World War II, the *El Gabilan* heaped lavish attention on cheerleaders, pom pon girls, the marching band, majorettes, drill teams, and rooters' clubs. Coalescing in the 1950s through the early 1970s, these groups in the sports spirit complex orbited boys' football and basketball, the gravitational center of campus life, providing support, spirit and pageantry. As girls' sports began to contest for equity and respect in the late 1970s, as funding for sports and other school activities eroded in the 1980s, and as myriad social issues distressed the school and the community in the 1980s and 1990s, boys' sports was nudged away from the center of student life, in the process losing some of its gravitational pull.

The trajectory of the school's marching band illustrates how some groups in the sports spirit complex became semiautonomous during this era. From the yearbooks' focus on the band's mid-century role primarily as halftime entertainment at football games, starting in the mid-1980s the *El Gabilan* regularly noted the marching band's successes in their own competitions. The 1986 yearbook trumpeted, "Awards! Awards! The Cowboy Band and Colorguard of more than 60 members won numerous awards."[70] The 1988 yearbook informed readers, "It may have seemed as if the band only played during football games, but this was far from true. During the school year, they competed in eight different competitions."[71] At a time when cheerleading was predominantly a white girls' niche, the band's color guard became a space made up disproportionately of girls of color (Figure 4.38). The 1991 *El Gabilan* signaled the tension between the band's dual roles, first praising the group for its' "numerous awards [and] undefeated season," then adding, "Before thought of first-place trophies dance in the heads of band members, a halftime show must be put together for the football season."[72] Adding competition to its halftime entertainment role meant more practice and more funding for travel and uniforms than in previous eras. But if there were tensions built into the new dual role of the marching band, the late-century transformation of cheerleading was even more fraught.

From its mid-century position of honor at the apex of the school's status hierarchy for girls, would cheering in the post–Title IX era be toppled from its perch, lose its allure for girls, perhaps even whither and disappear? Or might it spin off and become something different? In the immediate wake of the reintroduction of girls' sports teams, the final years of the 1970s were a time of stasis for cheerleading at Salinas High. As in the recent past, the cheerleading squads remained predominantly white. Photos of them doing their job—promoting "spirit" at all-school rallies and leading

Figure 4.38. SHS marching band and color guard, *El Gabilan*, 1992

the cheers at boys' basketball and football games—were liberally spread through the yearbooks (Figure 4.39). Meanwhile, some cheering tasks appear to have been farmed out to other groups, including a Track Interest Club and a Swim Boosters Club. Mat Maids provided spirit for the wrestling team, had official cheering uniforms, and in some years appear to have been more than half girls of color. And in 1988, the school introduced a squad of soccer cheerleaders who routinely included mostly Latinas who rooted for the boys' soccer teams (Figure 4.40).

By the early 1980s, cheerleader photos were less ubiquitous in the yearbooks, though the number of cheer squads—still made up mostly of white girls—remained stable. Meanwhile, across the nation the cultural prominence and even the very existence of cheerleaders was being called into question. In popular films like 1984's *Revenge of the Nerds*, it was common to see cheerleaders skewered as privileged, narrow-minded airheads, as mean white girls who aligned with male jocks to bully other kids and dominate campus life.[73] In 1986, cultural studies scholar George Kurman began an article on the puzzling persistence of cheerleading with a stinging question:

> In spite of feminist "consciousness-raising" and contrary to much apparent good sense, cheerleading as an institution continues to flourish. More girls, it often seems, would rather be cheerleaders than be athletes or scholars; cheerleaders rather than in the counterculture or gainfully employed . . . Nation-wide, school girls vie ardently for positions on cheerleading squads . . . Cheerleading summer camps and clinics prosper. National and regional cheerleading organizations proliferate. Squads increase in number and variety at many schools. Why?[74]

The *El Gabilan* books of the late 1980s and early 1990s reflect some of these critical questions—acknowledging the negative stereotypes about cheerleaders, and

Figure 4.39. Varsity cheerleaders, *El Gabilan*, 1975

Figure 4.40. Soccer cheerleaders, *El Gabilan*, 1989

consistently presenting cheerleaders in a way that buttressed their crumbling status. Alongside action photos of cheer squads in the 1991 *El Gabilan* (Figure 4.41) the accompanying text noted that "Few observers realized the sacrifice the cheerleaders made for the often-maligned activity. Arduous practices, summer camps, weekly travel, and snide remarks all came with being a cheerleader, in addition to outrageous costs. The uniforms alone ran $400, to which the girls themselves had to

Figure 4.41. SHS cheerleaders, *El Gabilan*, 1991

pay."[75] A caption added that all three SHS cheer squads had swept the Macy's Competition.

These comments hinted at several ways that cheering was then in the process of reconstituting itself. Foremost, the line between cheering and sport was becoming blurry. By the start of the 1990s a few cheerleaders were also participating on the cross-country, swim, or other of the school's sports teams. But this was not common, perhaps due in part to the time-consuming nature of being on a cheer squad. More impactful was the fact that cheering itself was morphing into a more athletic, competitive activity. Girls regularly attended summer cheer camps where they were introduced to new cheers and where they learned to perform stunts that required much greater strength and athleticism than was needed by previous generations of cheerleaders. The mid-1980s ushered in a growing tension between cheerleaders' traditional tasks of supporting boys' teams and devoting effort and time for their own cheer competitions. The 1984 yearbook observed that for the cheerleaders, it had been "a thrill to cheer for an undefeated [football] team, they all agreed," adding that the cheerleaders were victorious in their own competition, bringing home, "the ultimate award in spirit, 'The Spirit Award.'"[76] The 1989 yearbook noted that "The SHS

Figure 4.42. *El Gabilan*, 1989

JV and Varsity squads were rewarded for their time and effort by competing at Great America against other schools. The JV placed fourth and Varsity claimed eighth out of twenty-seven" (Figure 4.42).[77] Cheering was morphing into a hybrid activity—part traditional spirit-boosting for boys' football and basketball rallies and games, and part a stand-alone athletic competition in its own right.

Nationally, by the early 1990s, many were claiming that cheer *is* a sport, with its own regional and national competitions.[78] Competition-only high school cheer squads began in the early 1990s, and by the mid-1990s it was "the fastest growing sport for girls."[79] This claim was echoed in the Salinas High yearbooks. In fact, in 1992 the *El Gabilan* had moved cheerleading squads from the "Clubs" or "Activities" section of the yearbook to the "Sports" section of the book. This relocation was completed without explanation, but it was consistent with the national trend of viewing cheer as a sport. Still, the 1993 yearbook pointed to continuing tensions in the meanings of cheer's hybrid aims, quoting varsity cheerleader Melissa Reed as saying, "A lot of people stereotype us, but it's a lot more than that." The book then praised the squad's competitive accomplishments: "When our talented Cowgirls are not cheering on our Cowboys they are competing in cheerleading competitions and winning them . . . At the Northern California Cheerleading competitions held at Great America, the girls came in first place."[80] The 1994 *El Gabilan* expanded the pages devoted to cheerleading in the "Sports" section from four to six, and also ramped up its support for the activity: "Cheerleading is not just fun and games, it's a sport that supports others through good and bad seasons." The book's editors seemed intent on rescuing cheerleaders from persistent negative stereotypes: "From members of the Leadership class to being elected as club presidents, these students are truly dedicated to the school."[81]

But tensions still inhered in cheer's hybrid meanings. On the one hand, the constitution of cheer as a sport coincided with 1990s "girl power" narratives that emphasized individual empowerment of girls.[82] Perhaps the cheerleaders' growing athleticism had helped to hasten the demise of boys' negative caricatures of girl cheerleaders in the yearbooks of previous decades: if cheerleaders could no longer be thought of simply as ornamental feminine bodies whose sole job was to support boy's athletic endeavors, then what were they? On the other hand, critics like Alaska high school author Marty Beckerman, author of *Death to All Cheerleaders*, concluded that "cheerleading is nothing more than a perfect example . . . of what is wrong with our generation."[83] The *El Gabilan* continued to echo this tension, consistently coming down on the side of rescuing cheer from criticism. Accompanying a shot of cheerleaders doing athletic leaping toe-touches at a football game, the 1999 yearbook insisted "Cheerleading is a sport and it's harder than it looks . . . First place was on their minds as they practiced for the Nationals held at Disneyland."[84]

Figure 4.43. Stephanie and Lindsay Scattini, *El Gabilan*, 1999

Declaring cheer a sport did not entirely make it so. Cheerleading was something different, occupying "a contested space in American culture."[85] Cheer had become a competitive, athletic activity, but it was not yet considered an interscholastic sport in the Monterey Bay League, nor was it "counted" as a girls' sport in legal Title IX equity determinations. But tethering cheer to sport bolstered a faltering public respect for the activity. And including cheer in the "Sports" section of the yearbooks added beef to the page counts of girls' sports: four pages starting in 1992, six in 1996, and eight pages in 1998 and 1999. Cheer's escalating athleticism also affected the cheerleaders, making them more susceptible to a range of physical injuries. And taking place as it did during the fiscal crisis that had pummeled the school's ability to support extracurricular activities, the development of cheer as a competitive activity in the 1990s meant that the girls and their families had to raise hundreds, perhaps thousands of dollars to purchase uniforms, and to fund travel to Los Angeles, San Jose, and other venues for competition.

It is unlikely that anyone in Salinas absorbed more of these costs than the Scattini family. In 1992, Melissa became the first Scattini to be an SHS cheerleader, and sisters Stephanie, Lindsay, Mary Lynn, Victoria, and Jessica followed in her footsteps over the next two decades (Figure 4.43). The girls' father, Jon Scattini, told me that his daughters cheered at every level—freshman, JV, and varsity.[86] Over a span of twenty-three years, Scattini estimated the cumulative price tag of new uniforms each year, annual summer cheer camps, and travel, food, and lodging for trips to San Jose and Los Angeles for cheer competitions, to be in excess of $150,000. The school, he added while shaking his head, paid "zero" of the costs.

> It's not like football, where they hand you the fricking gear and the uniform. You had to pay for everything. And you had to get new outfits every single year, always tailor-made to each girl's body. So, wow. All these cheerleading uniforms cost a minimum of $500 every single year. And we had to buy tons of them. I was on the Boosters, and all the money made by the Boosters goes to the football program. I bitched about it. I said, parents of cheerleaders spent all this fricking money. We got nothing from all the Boosters' work. So why don't we divvy up this money equally? So cheerleaders get part of the money? And they said no, because cheer is not a sport. It's an activity. That drove me nuts. Cause I said the best athletes are cheerleaders. Obviously.

During the years that his six daughters were cheerleaders at Salinas High, Jon Scattini worked for UPS—first as a driver, then in middle management—and for many of those years the girls' mother, Mary, was not employed. It was, Jon said, "Twenty-three years of just shelling out money, money, money." This sort of expense clearly strained a middle-income family like the Scattinis, and it likely precluded some girls from lower-income families from participating. But for girls from families with sufficient resources, cheer had become (like sports, student leadership, and community service) "part of the package," especially for college-bound high-achieving girls.

At the turn of the twenty-first century, historians Adams and Bettis asked, "If cheerleaders are one of the last bastions of traditional femininity, what does it mean when they too want to leave their poms and megaphones behind to be tough athletes who are competitors themselves?" This question makes sense only if we think of femininity as some singular, stable definition of girlhood, frozen in time. Instead, dominant conceptions of femininity and masculinity are always historically shifting. As the epitome of postwar heterosexual femininity, the high school cheerleader of the 1950s and 1960s sat at the apex of the gender status hierarchy for schoolgirls. With the rise of feminism and the revival of organized sports for girls in the 1970s and 1980s, the postwar definition of cheerleader femininity was destabilized. By the end of the 1990s, cheerleading had incorporated athleticism and competition, and in so doing restabilized itself as a high-status activity for girls, perhaps cracking the door open for boys to reenter the activity.

Whither the Coach?

As Salinas High added girls' sports teams in the latter half of the 1970s, the number of coaching jobs grew quickly. Flavia Markert, a recent addition to the girls' physical education faculty, was named the first coach of the newly formed girls' varsity basketball team in 1975 (Figure 4.3), and PE teacher Carol Knight took over the new girls' volleyball team in 1976. But longtime girls' PE teachers Anna Davis and Isabel MacKay were nowhere to be seen among the growing legion of coaches at Salinas High. Instead, several of the new girls' teams were coached by men. George Anderson headed the fledgling girls' track team (Figure 4.44), and in the twelve years he coached girls' tennis until hanging up his racquet in 1984, Dan Emmerson's teams won the league championship every year (Figure 4.45). For three years in a row at the turn of the decade, the *El Gabilan* included a feature titled "Special Thanks To Coaches": In 1978, fourteen of the sixteen coaches thanked were men; in 1979 it was thirteen men and one woman; in 1980 the yearbook acknowledged thirty men and two women coaches.

The influx of men coaches into girls' sports at Salinas High reflected a broad trend. There is little national data on the gender of coaching in high school sports over time, but national research at the college level shows a dramatic erosion of women's leadership and control of college women's sports in the decades following the passage of

Figure 4.44. (*above*) Girls' track coach George Anderson, *El Gabilan*, 1975

Figure 4.45. (*left*) Girls' tennis coach Dan Emmerson, *El Gabilan*, 1984

Title IX. In 1972, over 90 percent of women's college athletic programs were headed by a female administrator; by 2000, that had dropped to 17.4 percent. And as coaching salaries and status rose in women's sports, men became more attracted to these jobs, and were more likely to be hired (by predominantly male administrators). In 1972, women were the head coaches of over 90 percent of college women's teams. By 2000, that had dropped to 45.6 percent. Meanwhile, male coaches continued to preside over 98 percent of men's college teams.[87] These data illustrate a common dynamic identified by sociologists who study sex segregation in work and occupations: When the status and pay of an occupation rises, men tend to be pulled into the occupation, and women are squeezed out. This shift has the reciprocal effect of further raising the status of the occupation (if men do it, it *must* be important).[88] And women coaches were almost never given the opportunity to break the sex bar that kept coaching in boys' and men's sports an almost entirely male occupation. This was even true at the level of volunteer coaching in youth sports. In my book *It's All for the Kids*, I illustrated the barriers to women's efforts to break into AYSO soccer and Little League Baseball and Softball coaching, a realm dominated by men.[89]

High school coaching is, of course, not the same as college coaching, which is often a full-time salaried job. Nor is it the same thing as being a volunteer coach for your kid's AYSO team. High school coaches, in the past, were nearly always school faculty—often PE instructors—who were paid very little for the many extra hours they worked as coaches. But by the mid-1980s, the yearbooks hinted at two shifts in this tradition. First, as coaching positions expanded in number starting in the mid-1970s, more and more of the jobs were filled by members of the community whose names did not appear on the school's faculty roster. Even as the school's faculty grew in size, the number of full-time physical education teachers plateaued; by the early 1980s, PE was no longer mandatory for juniors and seniors, thus arresting the demand for PE teachers. Those who did coach were paid little or nothing, making many of these jobs tantamount to volunteer labor. Whatever the cause, by the 1980s there was less continuity and more turnover among coaches in most of the sports. Science and PE teacher Gary Affonso, a notable exception to this rule, began his career at Salinas High in the late 1960s coaching lightweight football, eventually transitioning in the late 1970s and early 1980s to a few years coaching the coed cross-country squad, and then settling in as head coach of the girls' varsity softball team from 1979 through 1998 (Figure 4.14). When I interviewed Gary Affonso, well into his retirement, he recalled that varsity coaches were paid a $600 stipend during his years, and JV or freshman coaches probably less.[90] Affonso said he never resented the token pay for his coaching work. "Philosophically, you do it because you enjoy it, you enjoy the kids." But he acknowledged that daily after-school practices and travel for games had its costs. "Coaching also takes time from your family, so there should be some compensation." It's likely that the time commitment, coupled with little or no compensation, contributed to the high turnover among non-faculty coaches (Affonso called them "walk-ons").

Figure 4.46. Coach Joe Chappell and the MBL varsity basketball champs, *El Gabilan*, 1995

Nobody bucked the trend toward high turnover in the coaching ranks like Joe Chappell. Having inherited the job from my father, Russ Messner, in 1972, Chappell served as varsity boys' basketball coach at the high school for forty-one years, coaching 1,107 games and retiring as the winningest basketball coach in Central Coast Section history.[91] Joe Chappell also illustrates a second trend evident in the yearbooks of the last quarter of the twentieth century. In contrast with the ways that early to mid-twentieth-century yearbooks treated coaches as campus celebrities, as "leaders of men," even the most successful coaches of the late twentieth century were given few such plaudits. In 1995, one of the years that his team won the MBL championship, Joe Chappell appeared in the *El Gabilan* as usual, with little fanfare, standing alongside his players in the team photo, with a humble quote, "It was good to see all the students pull together and work as a team" (Figure 4.46).[92] That same year, champion football coach John Felice received nothing close to the near-deification that the *El Gabilan* had bestowed on football coach Harry Shipkey in the 1920s and 1930s.

One apparent exception illustrates the rule: Several yearbooks in the 1970s and 1980s praised Bill Getris, former star college basketball player and beloved campus character. For several years in the 1960s, Getris coached boys' lightweight basketball, winning a fistful of championships along the way (Figure 3.22). But the 1976 *El Gabilan* full-page dedication to "'Wild' Bill Getris" shows that he won students' appreciation not for his work as a coach, but for his many years as director of student activities. "Mr. Getris can be found helping at almost every rally, dance, game and fund-raising activity," the yearbook dedication observed. "He is more than a teacher to students—he is a friend" (Figure 4.47). Getris would continue to serve students and the school until his retirement in 1992. But he was not quite done: in 1997 and 1998 Bill

Figure 4.47. Yearbook dedication to Bill Getris, *El Gabilan*, 1976

Figure 4.48. Coaches Nancy Getris and Bill Getris, *El Gabilan*, 1998

Getris returned to the high school to co-coach the girls' ninth-grade basketball team with his daughter Nancy Getris (Figure 4.48).

By the mid-1980s, many of the coaching jobs were a revolving door at Salinas High, and this may have opened some possibilities for women to coach. The 1985 *El Gabilan* trumpeted the hiring of Marilyn Croswhite, who was named head coach of the combined boys' and girls' track team (Figure 4.49). That same year, math, science, and PE teacher Melanie Miller was hired, briefly coaching the girls' swim team and then rotating in and out of volleyball and girls' basketball over the next decade. In 1986, the yearbook noted the success of the champion girls' volleyball teams, coached by two women, Leslie Brandlin and Cindy Lenners.

The late 1980s even saw a couple of women tapped to coach boys' teams. The 1987 *El Gabilan* asked of the boys' water polo team, "A lady's sport? Well Sonia Raines seemed to think so. She was the first woman in SHS Water Polo history to coach the team. 'I didn't think I could take orders from her,' added Greg Rose. 'It worked out pretty well although she yelled at us a lot.'"[93] The following year Raines coached varsity and JV boys' water polo and joined with Sally Channing to coach the boys' swim team (Figure 4.50). "Regardless of their gender," the *El Gabilan* noted of the two coaches, Raines and Channing "gained respect from the boys. 'I'd never had a woman coach before,' Brian Breschini recalled. 'It took a while for us to listen and find out she knew what she was talking about.' Chris Tieg added, 'She was tough . . . She worked us twice as hard so we didn't think she was a pushover.'"[94]

The *El Gabilan* did not once ponder any potential stresses, strains, or contradictions when men—"regardless of their gender"—coached girls' teams. "Coach," after all, is a position, a status and a cultural symbol historically gendered as masculine. To describe someone as a "woman coach" (or woman lawyer, woman doctor, or woman judge) is to "gender mark" the position as inherently male, thus subjecting the woman crosser's job performance to sharp critical scrutiny, of the sort that I regularly saw in the early 2000s when I observed women coaching youth sports.[95] But by the end of the 1980s the number of Salinas High coaches who were women was ticking up. In the first years of the 1990s the coaching staff at the high school was about half women and half men, and most of the girls' teams were coached by women. However, once again illustrating that history rarely moves in a linear manner, by the late 1990s the coaching staff was once again mostly men, including for most of the girls' teams. When I asked about her time coaching the freshman girls' basketball team in 1997 and 1998, Nancy Getris said of the school's coaching staff, "Now I think about it, it was all—it was all men. I was the only female." By my count in the 1999 *El Gabilan*, every one of the school's fifteen boys' teams were coached by men.[96] The three coed squads (swimming, cross-country, track and field) were headed by three men, with a man and a woman co-coaching the JV swim team. All but two of the girls' fourteen teams—JV volleyball and freshmen softball being the exceptions—were coached by men. Taking into account head coaches and assistant coaches, I counted forty-seven men and

Figure 4.49. Track coach Marilyn Croswhite, *El Gabilan*, 1985

Figure 4.50. Water polo coach Sonia Raines, *El Gabilan*, 1993

only three women coaches at Salinas High in 1999; not a single woman was listed as coach for a varsity sport.

"Farewell to the Twentieth Century"

The 1999 *El Gabilan*, themed "A Step In The Right Direction," projected an optimistic, forward-looking mood as students finally began to move out of the portable classrooms. In the wake of the August 1998 ribbon-cutting celebration, the editors wrote on the first page of the yearbook, "In the midst of Presidential impeachment, bombing Iraq, and with the Y2K problem looming on the horizon of the year 2000, our main building was completed and the first class of Seniors in five years shared the halls once again with its alumni. The first Seniors since the class of 1994 will have had the chance to graduate with part of the new school fully operational. That's **A Step In The Right Direction.**"[97] Students now had access to fifteen new classrooms, and the yearbook that bade "Farewell to the Twentieth Century"[98] also looked forward to the school's "final phase of construction [which] includes reconstruction of 44 classrooms, shops and a new large gymnasium."[99] Indeed, Salinas High's original, too-short crackerbox boys' gym, which in recent years had been lovingly dubbed "The Corral," would soon be demolished and replaced by a larger, better gymnasium.

Would the new gym, in a new century, be an equal-opportunity space for girls' and boys' sports? Would girls' sports reach full funding and numerical equity with boys' sports? Would cheerleading in the new century continue to occupy a liminal space between its traditional role of providing spirit for boys' sports, and its emergent role as a competitive athletic activity? Or would it continue to morph toward becoming a full-fledged sport? And if so, would boys once again join cheer, as they had in the early twentieth century? What role will sports play in the next century in the school's

Figure 4.51. Alcohol and Drug Awareness Prevention Team rally, *El Gabilan*, 1999

pageantry? Would girls continue to surge into positions of school leadership, with sports participation, cheerleading, and community service becoming part of a varied package of achievement, especially for college-bound girls?

And how will Salinas High School deal with the continuing dramatic shifts in the racial and ethnic composition of the community (Figure 4.51)? The 1999 *El Gabilan* noted that as the population of Salinas had grown to 122,000, the high school now had about 2,000 students and 150 staff. In the past quarter century, Salinas High had transformed from a predominantly white school—the 1975 senior class was about 75 percent white—to a majority-minority school, with roughly half of the school's students in 1999 Hispanic. By the end of the century, many school activities, elected offices, and sports had begun to reflect the school's racial diversity, but the faculty and coaching staff remained disproportionately white. In some ways, Salinas High had made "a step in the right direction" during the final years of the decade, but with respect to gender equity in coaching, it looked like one step forward, and two steps back, as coaching reverted to an almost entirely male activity. Would that change in the 2000s? And as the new century began, would the student population's growing diversity become a resource that, added to the renewed pride brought on by the revived architecture of the school, would be mustered to bear the weight of mounting tensions, persistent inequalities, and concerns about drug and alcohol abuse and violence?

A SIGN
OF THE
TIMES
2001
SALINAS
HIGH
EL GABILAN

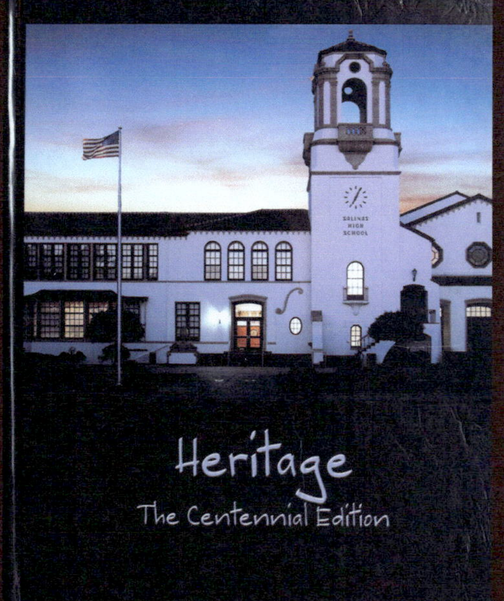
Heritage
The Centennial Edition

Salinas High School
MY BOOK
221 sheets 442 pages
12 1/4 x 9 1/4 in
student ruled 2573
© 2008 Salinas High School, Salinas, CA. 93901

SALINAS HIGH 2011

OUR
ROOTS

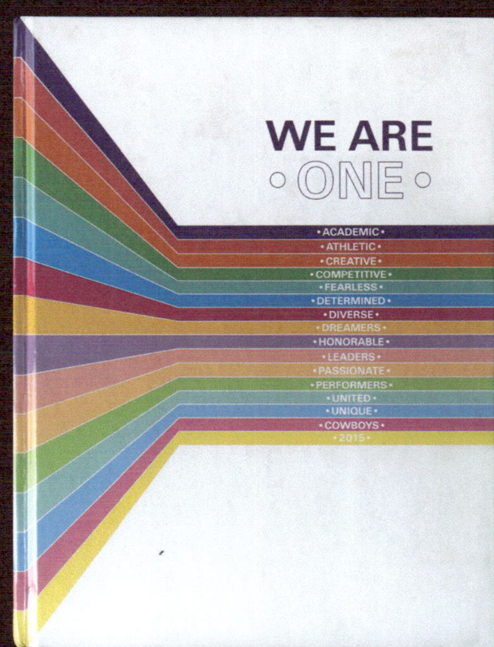
WE ARE
• ONE •
• ACADEMIC •
• ATHLETIC •
• CREATIVE •
• COMPETITIVE •
• FEARLESS •
• DETERMINED •
• DIVERSE •
• DREAMERS •
• HONORABLE •
• LEADERS •
• PASSIONATE •
• PERFORMERS •
• UNITED •
• UNIQUE •
• COWBOYS •
• 2015 •

OUR
GOLDEN
YEAR
19
EL GABILAN

a NEW era
EL GABILAN 2020

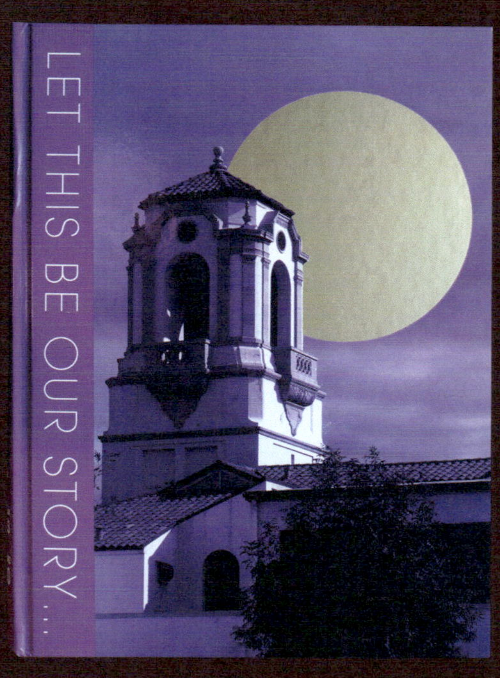
LET THIS BE OUR STORY...

> Despite extraordinary gains in participation, acceptance, and appreciation of girls' and women's sports, female athletic excellence can still pose a contradiction in terms, while the identification of sports with masculine prowess remains firmly in place. This is the paradox of "progress" in women's sports.
>
> —SUSAN K. CAHN, *COMING ON STRONG*, 2015

Chapter 5

"Who Runs This World?" 2000–2024

CASUALLY AND WITHOUT COMMENT the *El Gabilan* yearbooks of the new century introduced images that a few decades earlier would have seemed jarringly out of place: routine shots of girls wearing their Block "S" jackets. In the middle decades of the twentieth century, images of boys in their Bock "S" sweaters or jackets were ubiquitous in the yearbooks. The few mid-century girls who had earned membership in Girls' Sweater Society never appeared in the yearbooks wearing their "S" sweaters, other than in the single Girls' Athletic Association (GAA) group photo. In stark contrast, twenty-first century girls are seen in the yearbooks proudly sporting their Block "S" jackets in daily student life, as members of academic clubs (Figure 5.2), and sometimes even in their senior portraits (Figures 5.3, 5.4). That it is now so routine for girls to wear the Block "S" as a symbol of public pride is a testament to the extent which the twentieth-century stigma that was attached to female athleticism is fading.

If the final quarter of the twentieth century was a time of explosive growth for girls' sports in the United States, the first quarter of the twenty-first century may seem to be a time when high school girls and boys are finally competing on a level playing field. Kindled by swelling sports enthusiasm from girls and their parents, sparked by public activism from high-profile women athletes, and fueled by Title IX, U.S. high schools in the new century continued to add interscholastic sports teams for girls (Table 5.1).[1] The expansion of opportunities for girls did not happen unimpeded. Periodic

Nina Oropeza

Nina Oropeza is a name most people fondly know on campus. They may know her as the Captain of the Varsity Girls Basketball team, the President of A.S.B. or the girl who's in all their AP classes. In fact, one of Nina's many talents is to multi-task, and do it well. What not everyone may know is that Nina has been playing basketball since the second grade, or that she spends most all of her time dedicated to making our school days more enjoyable. Nina's great, innovative ideas and amicable nature have led her to a long history of leadership. Nina was bothered by people's apathy about school and had ideas on how to make it more fun. Beginning in her sophomore year, Nina was a student senator. As a junior, Nina was elected Junior Class President and this year ASB President. She and her staff have created many fun activity days at school for everyone to participate in. In addition to leading the school, she also leads the Girls Basketball team with class and patience to many victories. Basketball has been a passion of Nina's since the 2nd grade when she started on a team at the YMCA. She has played continuously since then and all four years at SHS, two on Varsity. After high school, she plans to continue playing basketball and will likely be United States President.

Number 25, Varsity Team Captain

Nina conducts a lunchtime activity during Spirit Week.

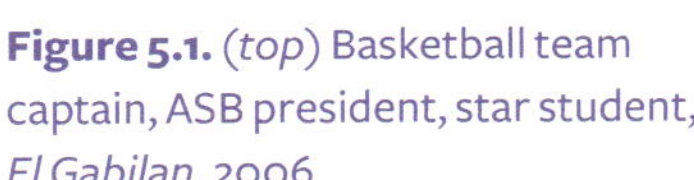

Figure 5.1. (*top*) Basketball team captain, ASB president, star student, *El Gabilan*, 2006

Figure 5.2. Veronica Tonus (*left*) with fellow National Honor Society officers, *El Gabilan*, 2006

Figures 5.3 and 5.4. Senior portraits, *El Gabilan*, 2014, 2015

TABLE 5.1

U.S. high school sports participation rates

	Boys participants	Girls participants	Girls as % of total
1971–72	3,666,917	294,015	7.4%
1981–82	3,503,124	1,853,789	35.5%
1991–92	3,429,853	1,940,801	36.1%
2001–02	3,960,517	2,806,998	41.5%
2011–12	4,484,987	3,207,533	41.7%
2022–23	4,529,795	3,318,184	42.3%

Note: The NFHS has compiled national data on boys' and girls' high school sports participation since 1971, publishing this data annually. National Federation of State High School Associations. 2023.

flare-ups of backlash—spiking in 2002 when President George W. Bush ordered hearings by the U.S. secretary of education to investigate claims that some boys' and men's sports were being undercut by Title IX—were eventually doused by well-organized feminist legal defense teams and by surging popular opinion in favor of girls' and women's sports.[2] As opportunities expanded, girls flocked to play. Belying skeptics who believed most girls were not interested in sports, high school girls illustrated the oft-repeated slogan from the popular 1989 baseball film *Field of Dreams*: "If you build it, they will come."[3]

Reflecting this national development, in the first two decades of the new century Salinas High School added a handful of new girls' sports and expanded its support for girls' teams. In contrast with the *El Gabilan*'s scant treatment of girls' sports in past decades, the annual yearbooks played a part in building respect and equity for girls' sports. Continuing a trend that picked up steam in the 1990s, the yearbooks devoted roughly the same number of pages to boys' and girls' teams in the "Athletics" section of the books. In fact, partly driven by the yearbook staff's decision to include about 8 pages on cheerleading in the sports section each year from 2000 through 2009, the average number of pages devoted to girls' sports during those years outstripped those devoted to boys' sports, 32.1 to 25.8.[4]

Just as significant as the number of pages is the transformation in the ways the yearbooks presented girls' sports. Whereas girls' sports had frequently been depicted with insult or condescension in the 1950s and 1960s, and with ambivalence in the 1970s and 1980s, the yearbooks of the 2000s, 2010s and early 2020s routinely treated girls' sports in much the same way the books presented boys' sports: by foregrounding the athletes' skills, their passion for the game, and their triumphant moments of success (Figures 5.5, 5.6, 5.7). And sometimes, a photo of a dramatic girls' sports moment was used as the two-page opener for the yearbook's "Athletics" section, an honor that in the past was nearly always reserved for a football photo (Figure 5.8). It is also notable what we can see in the left background of this 2023 photo: boys leaping to their feet to cheer on the girls' team.

Girls were also forging ahead as standouts in the classroom and leaders in student government. For several years in the 2000s, Bank of America awarded prizes to high-achieving SHS students in various academic fields. Boys were among the awardees, but more often it was girls who received these top awards (Figure 5.9). Girls also disproportionately populated many of the school's clubs, including as leaders. And while a few boys participated in the yearbook class, girls repeatedly dominated the yearbook staff, including in most years the top editorship positions.

This chapter's title—taken from a heading in the 2017 *El Gabilan* lauding the "Fantastic Four" all-girls Associated Student Body (ASB) leadership—posed a question (likely drawn from a popular Beyonce song),[5] "Who runs this world?" and affirmatively answered, "GIRLS." Indeed, year after year the *El Gabilan* of the past quarter century documented the extent to which girls had come to dominate elected positions in the ASB. The yearbook staff did not shy away from hailing this fact: "Mrs. Big Stuff," read the heading of the half page that featured the four girls who had been elected 2004 ASB officers, led by President Laura Ochoa.[6] This theme echoed year after year: Four "fearless leaders," all girls, led the way in 2009. No longer were boys running the show, and increasingly over the next decade, girls of color moved to the forefront of the school's leadership (Figure 5.10).

Figure 5.5. (*above left*) Volleyball passion, *El Gabilan*, 2010

Figure 5.6. (*above right*) Golf champs, *El Gabilan*, 2010

Figure 5.7. (*left*) Yu drives for a clutch hoop, *El Gabilan*, 2023

Figure 5.8. Lead shot for Athletics section of the *El Gabilan*, 2023

Achievement

Seniors recieve awards for their excellence from the Bank of America

Michelle McCoy
Liberal Arts

Shila Soni
Science & Math

Stefanie Williams
Fine Arts

Erin Hogeboom
Applied Arts

Bank of America Awards 55

Figure 5.9. Academic awardees, *El Gabilan*, 2003

JENNIFER ROGEL

"Being ASB president was challenging but worth it. I had the opportunity to work close with the ASB class, Mr. Dover and Mrs. Vicky to put together memorable events such as back to school week, homecoming and #standwithParkland. Looking back at my term as ASB president, I am very proud of all the work the ASB class did, they really cared about SHS and they really understood that our only goal was to make it an amazing year. Safe to say that we achieved that, this year has been filled with breathtaking events and I'm so thankful to have been the president. This year we witnessed an amazing amount of school spirit starting with the football jamboree and it's not difficult to have so much school spirit when you love your school and want them to be the best. I'd like to thank everyone that voted for me and I hope I did you proud."
-Jennifer Rogel-Sanchez

039

Figure 5.10. ASB president Jennifer Rogel-Sanchez, *El Gabilan*, 2018

The yearbooks' recurrent imagery of girls' achievement and leadership is a stunning 180-degree flip from the early and middle decades of the twentieth century, when boys seemed to own student leadership, especially the position of ASB president. As we can see in the 2006 *El Gabilan*'s feature about basketball team captain, ASB president, and star student Nina Oropeza that leads off this chapter (Figure 5.1), girls' athletic accomplishments during this era were routinely acclaimed as one piece of their academic achievements, campus leadership, and future promise.[7] When we look at this public imagery, it seems that girls, including girl athletes, have finally arrived as equal citizens at Salinas High School. But have they, fully?

To what extent are girls truly running "this world" of Salinas High School? In her recent ethnography of a U.S. high school, sociologist C. J. Pascoe observed that high school girls today still face structural inequalities in schools, agonizingly routine experiences of sexual harassment, and persistent fears of sexual violence. As a result, Pascoe says, girls survive by asserting "boss-girl feminism," a set of skills that position them to be "individually empowered to navigate sexist interactions that seem unchanging."[8] This and other studies that point to the continued barriers that girls face in schools should give us pause before we run a collective feminist victory lap.[9] Surely, compared with what we see in yearbooks of the past, high school girls' twenty-first-century emergence as campus leaders is a dramatic historical development. But mostly outside the frame of what yearbooks show, sexist attitudes and practices still create challenges for girls. Research on girls of color in schools presses us to consider how race and class privilege might position some girls more than others to benefit from gender progress in schools.[10] And are the many skills that girls are developing as school leaders readying them to "run the world" as adults, or perhaps instead to provide a huge range of service and caretaking—in public life and in the home—that keeps other peoples' lives afloat and running smoothly?[11] Sports, as is so often the case, provides a window into contemporary paradoxes of girls' progress: the dramatic social ascent of high school girls' sports is interwoven with stubbornly persistent challenges to achieving full equality. And as always, shifts in gender relations in high schools and their sports are interwoven with changes in communities.

"The Jewel of Main Street" in a New Millennium

"It's all behind us now." The theme of the 2000 *El Gabilan* seemed to breathe a collective sigh of relief and evidence a renewed sense of pride, as "The school year brought a new 19,000 square-foot fine arts and technology building . . . a new 27,000 square foot main gym, boy's and girl's locker rooms and a 73,000 square foot two-story classroom wing," including "thirty-eight classrooms, library, cafeteria, and state of the art computer labs . . . all finally taking Salinas High School into the twenty-first century." The decision to retain the original face of the school's Main Street–facing structure provided a sense of continuity and pride: "The tower that was still standing after eighty or so odd years was a symbol itself of how things had stayed the same, even in the ever-changing world we lived in."[12] The triumphant mood continued in 2001, with the yearbook staff declaring, "'Portable High' has how returned to its original title of luxury, 'The Jewel of Main Street.'"[13]

As the high school was celebrating its renewal, the city of Salinas at the turn of the century was trying to dig itself out from its reputation as a national leader in gang-related violence and homicide.[14] Crushing poverty was especially acute among the swelling Hispanic population that had nearly doubled in size between 1990 and 2000, and now comprised 64 percent of Salinas's 151,000 citizens. The city's fiscal crisis led to a temporary closure of its public libraries in 2002, and public schools were "struggling over funding, and issues such as representation and power."[15] By the 2010s, Salinas seemed to be setting itself on a more prosperous path. City leaders joined with the local agricultural elites and Silicon Valley interests to inaugurate "a new era of Ag-Tech that transformed the city . . . by 2017, Steve Forbes was calling Salinas the Ag-Tech epicenter of the nation."[16]

This was more than a symbolic rebranding of Salinas. By 2016, rates of violent crime were dropping. The city had moved away from self-defeating over-policing, instead instituting programs that created "many more opportunities and support" for young people.[17] Public schools were a big part of this effort. Increased funding and hiring of diverse support staff and teachers boosted bilingual education. New programs replaced longstanding practices of academic tracking that for too long had served kids from privileged backgrounds as launching pads to universities, while channeling students of color from poor families to vocational tracks and too often to discouragement, alienation, and high dropout rates. Partnered with agricultural technology (ag-tech) firms, Salinas schools created STEM (science, technology, engineering, math) training programs "that prepared students primarily for work in agriculture [and] channeled Salinas's high school students" to local community colleges and California State Universities.[18] Despite their successes, these ag-tech training programs were criticized for constraining students' occupational choices. Schools like Salinas High invested more broadly in programs like AVID (Advancement Via Individual Determination), "created to support and prepare promising students who came from poor and underserved minority-majority communities."[19] As a result of these changes, Salinas's public schools today sit near the center of some notable recent successes. However, a 2018 study by researchers from Hartnell College and Stanford University cautioned that as Salinas's ag-tech economy had ballooned to a $2 billion industry, "the city's poverty rate is 22.4%, compared to Monterey County's rate of 17.09%."[20]

As Salinas became more diverse, so did its flagship high school—and its annual yearbooks increasingly reflected and celebrated that diversity. By my count, 48 percent of the 430 graduating seniors in 2000 were students with Spanish surnames—the vast majority surely students of Mexican descent.[21] The year 2009 was the first that Spanish-surnamed students comprised more than half of the graduating seniors, and the proportions grew steadily in subsequent years, topping 60 percent in 2017. About two-thirds of the 2022, 2023, and 2024 senior classes were Spanish-surnamed students. During the twenty-five-year period covered in this chapter, students of East Asian descent (the largest groups being Chinese Americans and Japanese Americans) consistently comprised between 3 and 5 percent, as African American students ranged between 2 and 4 percent of the graduating senior class. The most recent publicly available school-wide data show that in the 2020–21 academic year 72.5 percent of Salinas High's 2,660 students identified as Hispanic, 20.0 percent white, 2.1 percent Asian, 1.7 percent Filipino, and 1.5 percent African American, with the remaining 2.2 percent reporting two or more races or other. Two-thirds of the student body were categorized as socioeconomically disadvantaged, 9.8 percent as English learners, and 10.7 percent as students with disabilities.[22] How did the school, and its sports programs, serve this increasingly diverse student population?

"Committed for the Future"

High school students join sports teams for a range of reasons—for fun and friendship, to develop physical fitness, to enhance their status with peers. And some students dream that success in sports will translate into a college scholarship and upward mobility. The *El Gabilan* yearbooks of the 2010s and early 2020s frequently featured students who had gained entrance to a university at least in part based on their athletic accomplishments. The 2019 book showcased five "committed athletes"—three boys (two in baseball, one in football), and two girls (soccer and volleyball)—noting that "With time, practice and dedication, a handful of students get into their dream schools not only on their character and grades, but also because of their achievements in extracurricular activities."[23] Under the heading "COMMITTED FOR THE FUTURE" the 2022 book devoted a page to seven student-athletes who were off to college to play their sports (Figure 5.11). As I was working on this chapter in 2023, the SHS athletic booster club's Facebook page and the local *Monterey Herald* newspaper trumpeted the SHS Female Athlete of the Year Tina Panziera's having committed to play softball at UC Davis, Brooke Hibino's signing to play volleyball at UC Davis, and Sabrina Moore's commitment to play beach volleyball at the University of Washington.[24]

When a student wins an athletic scholarship, the community celebrates, partly because it is such a rare accomplishment. But when a high school athlete "commits" to attending a college to play a sport there, it does not necessarily mean that the school is giving the student-athlete a "full ride" scholarship; some colleges give partial athletic scholarships (sometimes as low as $500 a year), while some give no scholarships.[25] When I interviewed athletic director Art Hunsdorfer, he said that that several SHS athletes each year go on to play on local community college athletic teams, but only a small number win scholarships at Division I colleges.[26] I counted 1,070 athletes

Figure 5.11. Student-athlete college commits, *El Gabilan*, 2022

in team photos in the 2023 SHS yearbook.[27] If a half-dozen or so of them earn athletic scholarships each year, this is a small "handful" indeed. And certain students, it turns out, are better positioned to get these rare athletic scholarships. Research by Kirsten Hextrum might surprise those who think of high school sports as an escalator to success primarily for young people from poor or working-class families, especially African American youth.[28] Hextrum's meticulous analysis of college sports admissions data reveals that the beneficiaries of the system are disproportionately white students from relatively privileged suburban schools. Since 1981, "white women have retained between 70% and 87% of the total spots on college women's sports teams."[29]

There are several reasons this, and it starts before high school. Elementary and middle school youth who grow up in families with robust financial resources have greater access to a range of sports and thus have substantially higher sports

Practicing a few times a week, **Sophomore Laura Porter** works hard year-round in order to prepare for the club volleyball competition season from December to July. "We compete every weekend all across Northern California and Utah," said **Porter**. She hopes that one day she will get a college scholarship for volleyball as a setter.

Figure 5.12. *El Gabilan*, 2003

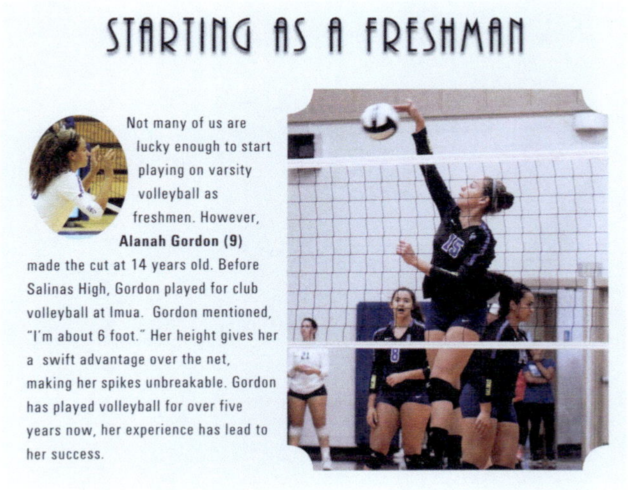

STARTING AS A FRESHMAN

Not many of us are lucky enough to start playing on varsity volleyball as freshmen. However, **Alanah Gordon (9)** made the cut at 14 years old. Before Salinas High, Gordon played for club volleyball at Imua. Gordon mentioned, "I'm about 6 foot." Her height gives her a swift advantage over the net, making her spikes unbreakable. Gordon has played volleyball for over five years now, her experience has lead to her success.

Figure 5.13. *El Gabilan*, 2019

participation rates.[30] Girls of color face multiple barriers to sport participation.[31] And kids whose parents can afford to hire private coaches, and can pay the considerable cost of years of club sports and travel teams, have a leg up on those who develop their skills primarily in school sports.[32] This shows up when the yearbooks spotlight star athletes. In the 2003 *El Gabilan*, sophomore Laura Porter said that through her experience in club volleyball, "she hopes that one day she will get a college scholarship for volleyball" (Figure 5.12).[33] Similarly, 2018 softball star Mia Victoriano noted that she'd been playing softball for seven years, including for a club team, the Salinas Storm.[34] The next year, the yearbook trumpeted that six-foot-tall ninth-grader Alanah Gordon was "STARTING AS A FRESHMAN," on the varsity team, adding that Gordan had played club volleyball before starting high school (Figure 5.13).[35]

In addition to the advantages in competitive experience and skills training that some high school athletes enjoy due to family resources, there are structural factors that benefit student-athletes from more privileged backgrounds, including especially a misalignment of opportunities in particular sports between high school and college. Put simply, in the "major sports" of football, basketball, and track and field—sports to which poor and African American youth have greatest access—the high school "base" of the participation pyramid is massive, while the college "tip" is very narrow. More than a million U.S. boys play high school football annually, and there are about 19,000 scholarship football players at Division I colleges.[36] At Salinas High, I counted 184 boys appearing in the 2023 yearbook's three football team photos; one or two of

Figure 5.14. Lacrosse team, *El Gabilan*, 2015

Figure 5.15. Field hockey, *El Gabilan*, 2019

these boys each year might win a football scholarship. In contrast, when high schools "sponsor sports that are relatively noncompetitive in college recruitment"—such as rowing, fencing, and gymnastics for boys, and rowing, beach volleyball, and fencing for girls—the athletes who compete in these sports have a much higher chance to win college scholarships than their counterparts in football, basketball, or track and field.[37] This is especially true for schools that sponsor what the NCAA calls "emerging sports," included in which are sports that SHS has added in recent years: water polo, lacrosse, and girls' field hockey.

Under the heading, "The Beginning of Something New," the 2015 *El Gabilan* announced the introduction of lacrosse, "The New Sport on the Block" for Salinas High boys and girls (Figure 5.14). As early as 2003, the yearbook had shown some students forming an informal lacrosse club, but in 2015 the school joined others in the district in adding it as an interscholastic sport. Adapted from Native American games, lacrosse has long history in the U.S. northeast, especially in elite prep schools and Ivy League colleges. The sport's emergence in a West Coast public school like Salinas High, according to the yearbook, "has opened many opportunities for our students."[38] The following year, Salinas High added a girls' sport, field hockey (Figure 5.15). Athletic director Art Hunsdorfer told me that "At the time, our principal Judith Peterson was really into adding more female sports on campus, which was great. I wouldn't say we were really lacking. It was just trying to meet the needs of everybody. And field hockey was one of those sports that she grabbed onto and said, 'we need that at this school.'"[39] In the 2017 *El Gabilan*, field hockey coach Laura Prevatt alluded to some challenges in getting the new sport started: "A lot of the girls were nervous because some were playing field hockey for the first time."[40] But the sport grew, and the school eventually fielded both varsity and junior varsity teams.

Participating in sports rarely leads to athletic scholarships, but college-bound students often view sports as one element in building a deep résumé for college applications—a trend first evident in the 1990s yearbooks. And here again, national research shows two things very clearly. First, universities' admissions officers have in recent years placed less weight on GPA and entrance exam test scores and more emphasis on a range of extracurricular activities, including sports participation. Following suit, high schools have increasingly emphasized the importance of extracurriculars as part of the package that college-bound students consciously create.[41] And second, "Since the 1970s, upper-middle-class students have become increasingly active in school clubs and sport teams, while participation among working-class students has veered in the opposite direction."[42] As a result, universities' strategies of "seeking exceptional talent (as currently defined) in extracurriculars favors wealthy students."[43]

For a student, adding sports participation to an already busy list of academic and extracurricular activities isn't easy, or without strain. A story in the 2001 *El Gabilan* pointed to the "enormous time commitment" for members of the girls' volleyball team—2 to 2.5 hours a day for practice, plus travel and matches. A handful of students that year quit the team, leaving only eight girls to play. One of them, Sarah Hernandez, said she was just too busy: "I love volleyball, but I just didn't have time to play this year. Between college applications and coordinating activities for ASB there was no time left for volleyball."[44] National data shows that due to the expanding options to play a range of sports, together with girls' tendency to participate in a wide range of non-sports extracurricular activities such as student leadership, some are deciding to limit their participation in sports.[45]

In a school with a roughly 70 percent Hispanic student body, and only 20 percent white-only students, it is striking how the athletes on Salinas High's water polo, swim and dive, golf, tennis, lacrosse, and cheer teams continue to be disproportionately white (by my count, about 60 percent on those 2023 squads were white), with a notable sprinkling of Asian Americans (Figure 5.16).[46] Football, baseball, softball, field hockey, boys' and girls' basketball, cross-country, and track and field teams more closely approximate the range of the school's racial and ethnic mix. Two sports—wrestling, which I will discuss more later, and soccer—are mostly populated by Hispanic students. From the inception of boys' soccer at SHS in 1977, the boys on the teams have been predominantly, sometimes exclusively, Latinos (Figure 5.17). By contrast, the girls on the school's soccer teams have tended to be about half Latinas, with several white girls, a few Asian Americans, and an occasional African American girl (Figure 5.18).

In other words, boys' soccer teams tend to be ethnically homogeneous, while the girls' teams reflect the school's racial and ethnic composition. How do we explain this divergent pattern? We know that in most of the rest of the world, including Mexico and Latin America, *futbol* (what we call soccer) is the most popular sport, and American football is rarely a part of these national sport contexts. Boys who migrate to the

Figure 5.16. Girls' tennis team, *El Gabilan*, 2007

United States from Mexico, and also U.S.-born Latino boys, tend already to be experienced and skilled at *futbol*, and are ready and able to step into the game, claim it as their own, and dominate on the field. Non-Latino boys in the U.S. also often play youth soccer, but their playing options include a wide range of sports, and they are inspired by a deep well of cultural heroes in other sports, including football, a sport most girls do not have access to. By contrast with their brothers, white and other non-Latina girls have a shallower history of team sports opportunities and fewer national sports heroines. Women soccer stars took on huge and inspiring cultural significance for American girls with the successes of the U.S. Women's World Cup team—especially following their dramatic 1999 victory in Pasadena, California—creating a continuing groundswell of excitement about the sport among girls and their families. Sociologist Rachel Allison has argued that in the United States, soccer "is a sport on the rise." While the game retains "earlier linkages of elite soccer to men, ethnic minority communities, immigrants, and the working class," in recent decades "the sport became embedded in emergent processes of racial and class distinction among white, middle- and upper-class suburban families," especially for girls.[47] Research points to the ways that stubborn historical barriers and informal prejudices have slowed Latinas' inclusion in youth and school sports.[48] But at Salinas High, a growing number of

Figure 5.17. Boys' soccer, *El Gabilan*, 2018

Figure 5.18. Girls' soccer, *El Gabilan*, 2022

Latinas do play on the school's soccer teams, and increasingly in other sports too, where they are sometimes pathbreakers into sport fields where other girls have rarely tread.

Coed Squads, Crossers, and Grapplers

I have long found sports fascinating in part because of the ways that they reveal the tensions between our cultural ideals of equality and deeply engrained assumptions about natural differences between boys and girls, men and women. In recent decades, previously male-dominated social institutions like universities, medicine, law, and politics have started to integrate women, but sport is an institution that remains mostly sex-segregated. From youth sports through professional competition, nearly all sports are neatly divided in binary categories: girls and women on one side, boys and men on the other. High schools are no exception. Advocates of sex-segregated sports have long claimed that differences in body size, musculature, and even emotions logically translate into organizing separate sports for boys and girls. Critics of this point of view have claimed that separate can never be fully equal, that sex-segregated sports teaches kids outmoded ideas of male superiority and female frailty, and denies children the opportunity to build cross-sex friendships and mutual respect.[49] More recently, critics have claimed that sex-segregated sports discriminate against transgender or gender nonbinary young people who do not neatly fit into binary sex categories.[50] The *El Gabilan* yearbooks offer windows into several points of tension in an interscholastic sports system that is committed to gender equity while simultaneously maintaining separate and often different sports for boys and girls. In what follows, I will explore two such points of tension. First, school sports systematically separate boys and girls, but what happens when the boundary between sexes is blurred, as when boys and girls practice together, or when a girl "crosses" the boundary and competes against boys? Second, if separate sports for boys and girls are supposed to be equal, what does it tell us about gender beliefs when girls play different sports than boys play?

The 2002 *El Gabilan* posed a question to a few of the school's tennis players: "'Should tennis be co-ed?' of four responses, two girls said no, and one yes. The one boy said no."[51] Professional tennis, of course, is a sport that includes mixed doubles, where man-woman teams compete against each other. At Salinas High the boys and girls have separate tennis seasons—the girls in the fall, the boys in the spring—so there is not even the possibility for mixed doubles. However, a few sports teams do routinely blur this gender boundary. Salinas High's cross-country, track and field, and (in some years) swim and dive athletes have long been joined into coed units that, though they compete in separate boys' and girls' contests, do routinely practice together and travel to meets together (Figures 5.19, 5.20, 5.21).

Most likely these sports combine their routinely large girls' and boys' teams for logistical and financial reasons: sharing fields, tracks, and pools for practices and for meets makes sense, as does combining travel and sometimes also coaches. But research suggests that there are ancillary benefits when boys and girls join on sports teams. In her study of a youth coed swim team, sociologist Michela Musto observed that when young people practice together as teammates and are treated equally by their coaches, they tend to develop mutual respect as athletes, and sometimes as leaders. This is especially evident when a girl competes well, sometimes winning, in a head-to-head swim with a male teammate.[52]

In previous chapters I introduced the idea of "earnest crossing," which takes place when an individual crosses into an activity deemed inappropriate for their sex. For

Figure 5.19. (*above left*) Track team, *El Gabilan*, 2004

Figure 5.20. (*above right*) Cross-country team, *El Gabilan*, 2007

Figure 5.21. (*left*) Track team, *El Gabilan*, 2009

instance, we saw an occasional girl in the 1980s and 1990s joining the SHS boys' football or baseball teams. In recent years, a few similar crossings were shown in the yearbooks, rarely with much fanfare or comment. The 2003 *El Gabilan* showed a girl, sophomore Kalistyn Lemke, in the JV football team picture, but made no comment about it. In a 2010 senior profile, "Sarah Epperson the football player" said the highlight of her season was "Los Gatos because I got in for five plays" (Figure 5.22).[53]

Crossing the gender divide in sports is rare and tends only to work in one direction (a girl joining a boys' team). So it got my attention when I read a caption stating that a boy pictured in the 2008 yearbook was "the only boy on the Girls Varsity team yea!" This same boy also appeared in the girls' varsity soccer team photo, but not wearing a uniform like the girls on the team. I asked Art Hunsdorfer about this, and the longtime athletic director's reply was clear: "We have never had a boy play on a girls team at Salinas High School."[54] There are reasons for this. Title IX regulations

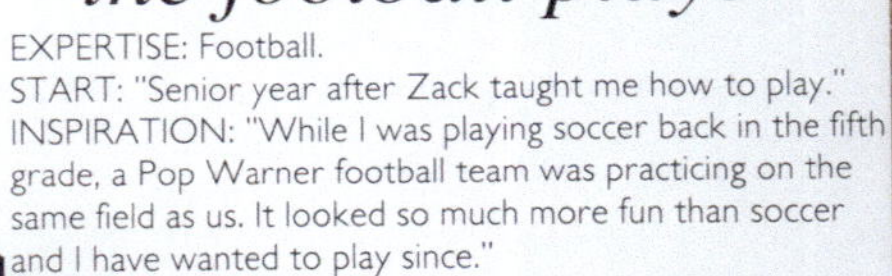
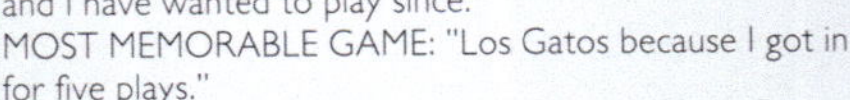

Figure 5.22. *El Gabilan*, 2010

stipulate that if there is no "equivalent" sport for a student to play with their own gender group, then they have a right to cross—for instance, there is no equivalent of boys' tackle football for girls, so a girl who wants to play football has the right to go out for the team. But there are other more murky reasons that the gender-crossing door tends to swing only one way, and the recent emergence of the occasional transgender woman who wants to compete in girls' or women's sports has raised this issue to the level of hot public debate.[55] Hunsdorfer told me in 2023 that "We have not seen any transgender or nonbinary students attempt to play sports at Salinas High School. There is a policy within the district but I really don't have specifics about it mainly because I have not dealt with it. I am sure I will have the policy down once it hits my office."

No doubt transgender students will one day test the boundaries of Salinas High's sports policies, as they have in many high schools around the nation. But thus far one of the most dramatic challenges to embedded assumptions about gender differences has come from girl wrestlers. The first girls who wrestled at Salinas High were true pioneers into male territory. Two girls appeared in the wrestling team photo in 2000, and the following year only one girl, sophomore Sarah Rios, competed. She stated that "One thing I like about wrestling is that everybody comes together at the last moment, even though we argue in practice. It's PUNK ROCK!"[56] Since there were so few girls in wrestling, early crossers like Rios often had to compete against boys. The fact that wrestling is a sport organized by weight class means that competitors always wrestle against individuals who are roughly the same size, and this tends to mitigate the fact that boys tend on average to be taller and heavier than girls (a difference that will make it difficult for most girls to play competitively, for instance, on a boys' football or basketball team).

By the middle of the decade, the number of girl wrestlers had begun to grow (Figure 5.23). As the 2007 *El Gabilan* crowed that girls were "the sport's best-kept

Figure 5.23. Girls' wrestling team, *El Gabilan*, 2007

secret," it also addressed cultural questions about femininity that tend to crop up when girls participate in a sport that requires physical aggression and muscular strength. "One very common error in judgement would be that girl wrestlers are big, muscular, rough, tough, Manley chicks who are closer to men than women in appearance. In actuality, that is not the case. 'You can spot a few girls applying makeup before a match!' says sophomore Andrea Orozco."[57] In 2009, the yearbook reported that "As many as 5,000 high school females had participated in wrestling in 2006–7, a number that has tripled in the last 10 years. California continues to ignite a fire for wrestling, an epidemic of women pioneers who continue to tear apart the label of a *girl's sport* . . . Our Salinas High team took 8th at State, and 3rd at CIF."[58]

By the middle of the 2010s the yearbooks were delivering little or no apology for the empowering experience of being a girl wrestler at Salinas High (Figure 5.24). The sport had grown, and girls were mostly wrestling other girls in matches, though the 2015 yearbook quoted senior Alexandra Babayeva on the value of wrestling against boys: "When I wrestle the guys at practice, and I pin them, it inspires me to continue."[59] The 2018 yearbook quoted senior Aricelli Castillo on the same topic. "It's harder to wrestle the boys because of the different body types, but we try our best." The yearbook editors followed by noting that "many of the girls see this as an opportunity to improve their skills and take down the gender oppressive roles of the sport."[60] By the start of the 2020s it was clear that the girls who were pinning these "gender oppressive roles" to the mat were mostly Latinas, like 2022 champions Mariela Rodriguez and Ailyine Acosta (Figure 5.25).[61]

STATE BOUND

Figure 5.24. (*above*) *El Gabilan*, 2016

Figure 5.25. (*right*) *El Gabilan*, 2022

Separate . . . and Different

Some sports at the high school are played only by boys and some only by girls: boys have baseball teams, and girls play softball (despite having played baseball at Salinas High one hundred years ago); boys play tackle football and girls play flag football or field hockey. These differences reflect and reinforce entrenched views about boys' and girls' supposedly natural bodily differences. Even when they both play the same sport, the boys' and girls' games are sometimes governed by different rules. We saw in chapter 3 how mid-twentieth-century girls' basketball was regulated by "adapted rules" that severely circumscribed competitors' physical movements and limited their bodily contact with opponents. Today, girls' basketball is far closer to the boys' game than in the past, though the ball girls play with is slightly smaller in diameter than the boys' ball.

Adapted rules sports are not simply a residue of the past, when girls and women were viewed as vulnerable and needing protection. Even the recently introduced sport of lacrosse has different rules for boys and girls. I did not grow up with lacrosse, so at first I did not know how to interpret what I was seeing in the yearbooks: boys wearing helmets with full faceguards and protective equipment on their shoulders,

Figure 5.26. Boys' lacrosse, *El Gabilan*, 2019

Figure 5.27. Girls' lacrosse, *El Gabilan*, 2019

forearms, and hands, and girls wearing only eye guards and perhaps protective mouthpieces (Figures 5.26, 5.27). When I asked Art Hunsdorfer about this, he confirmed that there are different rules for girls' and boys' lacrosse: "The boys are all suited up in helmets and shoulder pads and the whole bit and they're beating each other with sticks. And then the girls' game, they do not wear helmets, they have eye guards from the ball, and it's not as aggressive. There's different rules. Yeah, very different rules."

Similar to the ways that "body checking" rules in women's ice hockey prevent the sorts of collisions that are a normal and celebrated part of the men's game, the gendered rules (and different protective equipment) in lacrosse delimit levels of physical aggression among girls.[62] In the fall of 2023, Salinas High School introduced another new sport for girls, flag football (Figure 5.28). Perhaps the ultimate adapted sport, flag football includes many of the same strategies and skills as boys' tackle football, minus the body armor and violent collisions.

In an age of increasing gender equality, why do schools continue to channel girls into less aggressive, adapted sports? Why do boys pitch a hardball overhand, while girls hurl a softball underhand? Why do boy lacrosse players don helmets and pads, while their girl counterparts need simply to protect their eyes? And why do defenders in girls' football stop an opponent by yanking loose her flag, while boy footballers slam a ballcarrier's body into the turf? Some have replied that adapted sports for girls continues a long history of protective legislation that treats women as "the weaker sex," in effect barring them from participating in higher-status, higher-reward

Figure 5.28. Girls' flag football, *El Gabilan*, 2024

positions in public life.[63] I think there is an equally important question here: Why do we tolerate, even celebrate, violent collisions in boys' and men's sports, when we know that routine action in these sports occasionally ends with a tragic injury, and frequently results in long-term debility? The fact that this question is rarely asked, I think, says a lot about our unspoken assumptions about boys, men, and masculinity. And the game of football shines a spotlight on this question.

Tackling Football

By just about any measure, football remains the king of sports at Salinas High School. Consider participation rates. Based on my count in team photos in the 2023 *El Gabilan*, far more athletes play football—184 on the school's three teams—than any other single sport. For the boys, track and field is a distant second, with 54 participants, followed by baseball and basketball with 42 each, and soccer with 37. For the Salinas High girls, swimming and diving is tops with 54 on the team, followed by cheer with 52, track and field with 49, volleyball with 45, lacrosse with 43, and basketball and field hockey with 41 each. These local numbers resemble national distributions. In 2022–23, 1,208,761 U.S. boys played high school football. Track and field (604,983), basketball (537,438), baseball (478,451), and soccer (450,455) lag well behind football's

Figure 5.29. Homecoming, *El Gabilan*, 2022

numbers. For U.S. girls, track and field is tops with 486,355 participants, closely followed by volleyball (470,488), soccer (377,838), basketball (373,366), and softball (344,952).[64]

The cultural centrality of football at Salinas High School stands out even more than the large numbers of boys who play the sport. The "Athletics" sections of the *El Gabilan* in the twenty-first century pared down the space allotted to football so that the sport got roughly the same four pages as most other sports. But football and its supporting pageantry continued to play an outsized role in other sections of the yearbook, clearly occupying the center of the athletic universe of "Purple Pride." Homecoming Week—joined at the hip with football—continued to be a "front and center" autumn ritual (Figure 5.29). And though activities like cheer and band now have their own independent competitions, their roles in the sports spirit complex on campus are still centrally concerned with promoting the pageantry of football, and to a lesser extent basketball.

The opening pages or "Student Life" sections of the yearbooks of the new century consistently devoted prime coverage to football pageantry, frequently spotlighting Cowboy championships or victories against rivals Palma High or North Salinas High. "It was great to finally beat them!" senior Chris Choate said of the football team's 24–13 win over Palma in 2003, the first victory since 1970. A caption noted that "Nearly 7000 people . . . were witness to the game that will never be forgotten."[65] The opening page of the 2011 *El Gabilan* was a faux newspaper, with the headline "SALINAS HIGH BEATS PALMA 53–0" (Figure 5.30), and the 2014 yearbook featured the football team's having spoiled North High's inaugural game at their new Robobank Stadium by beating them, 35–10 (Figure 5.31). Under the headline "WE ARE NO 1" the 2018 yearbook celebrated the varsity football team's win over Palma, and the following year, "THE STREAK LIVES ON! Our Cowboys victoriously take the win against the Chieftains!" (Figure 5.32).[66] The opening "Student Life" section of the 2020 *El Gabilan* devoted two pages to celebrating "the 100th season of Friday night lights," of SHS football, noting that the varsity team beat North High 71–7. Salinas High's rivalry with Palma, the sports powerhouse Catholic high school just a few blocks away, took on a decided edge in recent decades. On more than one occasion, yearbook crowd shots at games against Palma depicted SHS students holding up signs reading "PUBLIC SCHOOL"—expressing a particular angle on Purple Pride. On September 27, 2019, the crowd chanted "three-peat, three-peat, three-peat," as the varsity beat Palma for the third year in a row.[67] The 2023 book again trumpeted in its opening pages that the football team had won "bragging rights" by beating the rival Palma Chieftains 47–14.[68]

What explains the continuing centrality of football at Salinas High and at other high schools? In 1994, journalist and former Stanford basketball player Mariah Burton Nelson tackled this question, and the title of her influential book placed a fine point on her answer: *The Stronger Women Get, the More Men Love Football*.[69] Nelson's argument about the ideological meanings of football in a time of feminist progress for women was consistent with the emergent scholarly research at the time, including some of mine. In a 1988 article, I observed that the movement of women into previously male-dominated professions, including their impressive rise in organized sports, challenged traditional assumptions about "natural" male superiority. I argued that "Football, based as it is on the most extreme possibilities of the male body (muscular bulk, explosive power and aggression), is a world apart from women, who are relegated to the role of cheerleaders/sex objects on the sidelines rooting their men on. In contrast to the bare and vulnerable bodies of the cheerleaders, the armored male bodies of the football players are elevated to mythical status, and as such give testimony to the undeniable 'fact' that here is at least one place where men are superior to women."[70]

Thirty-five years after writing that article, I do not think that my argument was wrong, but I now think that there is more to football's popularity besides offering boys and men an opportunity to identify with a mythical ideal of superior manhood. After all, while it is true that lots of men love football, many women do too. Football's draw is not, in other words, simple masculine backlash against feminism. Football is an inherently exciting, action-packed game played on a large field, situated in stadiums that seat hundreds, even thousands of spectators. At Salinas High School, football remains at the center of the school's ritual complex through which faculty, students, alumni, and members of the community create and celebrate a collective identity.

EL GABILAN

26 S. Main Street, Salinas, CA 93901

50 cents

Thursday, May 26th, 2011

SALINAS HIGH BEATS PALMA 53 - 0

By Tara Storm

THE INCREDIBLES

Ms. Beach, Mr. Grahl, Ms M Cullough, Mr. Mandon, Zalin, Mr. Patheal, and Hinton - the new staff memb on campus - are ready to their colleagues in the f against illiteracy and for the "Cow phobia, Way."

Figure 5.30. (*left*) Opening page, *El Gabilan*, 2011

Figure 5.31. (*below*) Cowboy victory, *El Gabilan*, 2014

Figure 5.32. Victories over rivals, *El Gabilan*, 2019

Figure 5.33. New turf ceremony, *El Gabilan*, 2003

For football to continue to anchor "Purple Pride" takes ongoing investment—of time, emotion, and money. The 2003 *El Gabilan* included a two-page spread that celebrated the "new turf ceremony" at The Pit (Figure 5.33). The $700,00 cost of the new artificial turf had "caused a lot of controversy among community members and students concerning the price tag." The previous year, the muddy grass turf had gotten so bad that athletic director Art Hunsdorfer was told that the field was unsafe to play on. The school district said it could not afford the price tag of installing artificial turf. "I told them there's *no way* we're not gonna have football in The Pit next season," Hunsdorfer told me. "I said we will raise the money." A large agribusiness firm donated $250,000, and two others also made sizable donations; their corporate logos are now stenciled on the walls of the tunnel leading into the field. The *El Gabilan* reported that the student body contributed $20,000, and "The Boosters Club also gave a substantial donation, contributed partly from local businesses."[71] The school did not miss a Cowboy home game in The Pit. This sort of effort speaks to the depth of community commitment not simply to the game of football, but to maintaining the ritual meanings and collective identity that the game continues to anchor.[72]

Given this civic investment in boys' tackle football, it is not surprising that difficult questions about the health costs of playing the game are so often brushed aside. When I did life history interviews in the 1980s with former athletes for my first book, *Power at Play*, I was stunned by the stories I heard from former college and pro football players, most still in their thirties and forties, about the cumulative damage to their bodies, including chronic pain from compacted spines, arthritic fingers, and damaged knees, hips, and shoulders that required multiple surgeries.[73] After that, I was never able to watch football with much enthusiasm. To be sure, it is a lovely game to watch from a distance: Passing, catching, running, and tackling all require high levels of skill and precision that commentators sometimes say reminds them of ballet. But football action only resembles ballet when viewed in slow motion on TV. Close up and in real time, the game of football is a spectacle of powerful, armor-clad bodies violently crashing into each other, often at high speed.

In the past twenty years or so, growing awareness of head injuries has led to the development of better helmets and concussion protocols in football and other sports. A few years ago I contributed to a panel discussion on head injuries in sports at the University of Michigan. A neurologist who works with athletes dashed cold water on any comfort people might feel in knowing about improved helmets or concussion protocols. A body of evidence, he said, points to the conclusion that the CTE (chronic traumatic encephalopathy) commonly found in autopsies of former football players and boxers is not caused by the occasional dramatic concussion, but by the cumulative impact of small and medium bumps and blows to the head that routinely happen, play after play, in football. These dangers are seeping into the public consciousness. A 2014 Bloomberg poll found that 50 percent of parents said that they would not want their sons to play football.[74] And a 2023 *Washington Post* article examined how growing public awareness of "the toll of a sport linked to brain damage" has contributed to a decline in the number of boys who play tackle football. The national survey data showed that "Among kids and teens, white and Black males are playing tackle football at declining rates, while Hispanic boys increasingly take up the sport."[75]

Salinas High School has no shortage of boys who are enthused to play football each year. High school girls do not play tackle football, but for the occasional "crosser."

But the tradition of powderpuff football continues at Salinas High. During the first decade of the century, there were very few references to powderpuff in the yearbooks, and it appeared that the event was withering away. Powderpuff football stormed back in the next decade. Alongside action shots of girls passing and running the ball, the 2010 yearbook declared, "Men created football, but women perfected it,"[76] and the 2011 book echoed that sentiment: "Who said girls can't play football?"[77] By 2014, powderpuff had morphed from an entirely intramural activity to one that culminated with the school's winning team competing in a jamboree with four other local high schools. A two-page spread in the 2015 *El Gabilan* declared, "Girls Gone Wild! Powderpuff Championship!" and senior Brianna Rodriguez declared, "Who says girls can't play football? Powderpuff is life!"[78]

The yearbooks' coverage of powderpuff football over the past fifteen years primarily featured photos of the girls competing (Figure 5.34). Boy powderpuff cheerleaders were rarely depicted, and when they were, they no longer displayed the exaggerated girls' clothing, makeup, or gigantic fake breasts that were so much a part of the powderpuff pageantry from 1960s into the 1990s. Instead, powderpuff was framed as a story of empowered girls seizing male territory, if only temporarily: "FEAR THE FEMALE," declared the 2019 yearbook, "Powderpuff football takes over the Pit" (Figure 5.35).[79] Powderpuff had clearly evolved into a chance for girls to show what they can do on the gridiron. With the school adding interscholastic flag football in 2023–24, the future of powderpuff was unclear. Powderpuff football did happen that year, but there was no sign of it in the 2024 yearbook. The event's obvious popularity may give it legs for a while, but now that girls have a team and a full season to play flag football, powderpuff may have outlived its purpose.

Pride, Pageantry, and Spirit

The middle decades of the twentieth century saw the development of the sports spirit complex, an amalgam of groups and activities that orbited around boys' sports, often with the sole purpose of anchoring the pageantry and sparking the spirit that celebrated the centrality of football, and to a lesser extent boys' basketball (Figure 3.31). In recent decades football did not lose its gravitational power. But two social changes that began in the 1980s and 1990s and accelerated in the new century upset the singular focus of the sports spirit complex. The first, of course, is the dramatic rise of girls' interscholastic sports. The second is the way that central players in the spirit complex—notably the marching band and especially the cheerleaders—have undergone transformations in their own organizations, meanings, and purposes.

The twenty-first-century Salinas High marching band continued to perform at football games and marched down Main Street for the school's homecoming parade (Figure 5.36). But the yearbooks frequently highlighted the band's life independent of football. The 2002 *El Gabilan* praised the marching band's many hours of practice "in

Figure 5.34. (*right*) *El Gabilan*, 2017

Figure 5.35. (*below*) *El Gabilan*, 2019

Figure 5.36. Homecoming parade, *El Gabilan*, 2001

preparation for their band reviews held in various counties of California."[80] And the 2008 book noted, "Like our sports teams, the marching band represents SHS in competitions and shows how great our school is despite the bad reputation we have acquired over the years."[81] This latter phrase likely referenced the school having been placed on athletic probation in 2006, including a two-year ban on postseason play for the football team.

Cheer remains one of the most fascinating sites of gender turbulence in the new century. In some ways, it always has been. We saw that in the early twentieth century the "yell leaders" were always boys. Mixed-sex squads emerged during the years surrounding World War II, and by the mid-1960s "cheerleaders" were always all girls whose high-status position placed them at the center of the school's spirit complex. Following the passage of Title IX in 1972, girls' sports accelerated, and questions arose as to whether cheer, as a high-status girls' activity, would survive. It did, but only by shifting toward athleticism and competition. The new century saw the continuation of cheer as a hybrid activity—providing support and spirit for the school's sports (with an emphasis on football) while also developing into a competitive sport in and of itself (Figures 5.37, 5.38). These dual aims created challenges for cheerleaders that centered on the increasing professionalization of cheer as a competitive sport and the concomitant shifting gender meanings of the activity.

As cheer leaned into becoming a serious sport in the new century, including practices run by dance choreographers, cheerleaders faced challenges in how to prioritize

Figure 5.37. (*above*) Qualifying for nationals, *El Gabilan*, 2009

Figure 5.38. (*right*) "Competition Bound," *El Gabilan*, 2018

the time they allotted to supporting the school's sports versus emphasizing their own competitions—not to mention the time devoted to being a student, participating in clubs, serving in ASB leadership roles, or participating on other sports teams. Junior Jenny Broom stated in the 2000 *El Gabilan*, "Having two different practices for [cheer] competition and one for basketball practice is really hard and putting stress on me."[82] Most striking, yearbook depictions of cheer revealed, year after year, the continuing strains built into the ways that cheerleaders are seen, or want to be seen, by their peers. At the center of this tension we see cheerleaders navigating the shifting meanings of gender in sports, schools, and the broader culture.

As I read these yearbooks, one repetitive theme that was impossible to miss was what I came to think of as "cheerleaders' protest apologetic." Here a few examples, drawn from the many: In 2001, a year the cheerleaders won first place in the Great

America Cheerleading Competition, senior Breanna Panelli declared, "With injuries, practice, and dedication, who would say it's not a sport? People base our talents not only on our outward appearance, but by mistakes we may make. Cheerleaders understand that others disregard us as a sport and just for that, we excel in every aspect."[83] The following year, school principal Dr. Pawlick "officially declared cheerleading a sport," with junior Natalie Dill noting, "We have competitions just like sports. We also practice just as hard, sometimes harder than some sports."[84] In 2006 senior Jenny Navarez protested, "I think us cheerleaders work just as hard or even harder as any other sport and for us not to get any credit for that is whack."[85] That sentiment was echoed in the 2007 yearbook by Allison Kuska's declaration, "We work just as hard as other sports and we aren't stereotypically dumb."[86] With editorial zeal, the 2010 *El Gabilan* staff seemed intent on rescuing the school's cheerleaders from negative stereotypes: "Whoever said 'cheerleading is not a sport' is in need of a serious reality check . . . These girls are as committed as any pro sports player . . . cheer takes fierce attitude, drive, determination, and strength! Stunts can be dangerous if not taken seriously and executed perfectly . . . So it is safe to say that cheer IS a sport. In any other sport, if you miss a catch, all you drop is a ball."[87]

The "cheer is a sport" declarations continued into the yearbooks of the 2010s, though they were harder on the protest, more muted on the apology: "Athlete by nature, Cheerleader by choice," the 2012 *El Gabilan* stated,[88] and the 2013 yearbook declared, "You Lift Weights, We Lift People!"[89] In 2018, the school seemed to rectify the longstanding tensions inherent in the hybrid tasks of cheer by delineating two squads: "sideline cheer" that focuses on leading cheers at games, and "competition cheer," which focuses on sport competitions. Subsequent yearbooks, however, did not depict separate sideline cheer and competition cheer squads until 2024, when the book showed three squads of sideline cheerleaders, and two squads called "Song Pom Cheer" and "Showcase Cheer." Athletic director Art Hunsdorfer told me that sideline cheer is not a CIF-recognized sport, but competition cheer is. At Salinas High, he said, it is mostly the same students doing both. However, he added, in recent years a few boys, some of them football and water polo players, have joined competition cheer during the spring season.

The girl cheerleaders with high-flying gymnastics skills do require larger and stronger teammates to lift and to safely catch them. But if the redefinition of cheer as a competitive sport has opened the door for boys, very few have chosen to enter. As important in cracking the door open for boys might be a recent broadening of the cultural definitions of masculinity. Perhaps boys like Gabriel Lopez, who in 2019 "decided to try out for the cheer team because of his passion for dance and flexibility" (Figure 5.39),[90] or boys who are put off by traditional competitive sports, or perhaps also boys with queer or nonbinary gender or sexual identities (as viewers of the popular 2020 TV docuseries *Cheer* have seen) might find cheer to be a more inviting place for them than in the past.[91] That said, high school cheerleading remains primarily a girls'

Figure 5.39. Gabe Lopez and the cheer team, *El Gabilan*, 2020

terrain. Cheer was 100 percent girls at SHS from 1966 until senior Joe Thompson joined the squad in 2004. The number of boys shown in the yearbooks' cheerleader squads in subsequent years can be counted on one hand. The inclusion in 2023 of one boy, Sean Montemumo, meant that 98 percent of the school's three (varsity, JV and freshman) cheer teams were girls (Figure 5.40). Of the 93 cheerleaders pictured in the school's five cheer squads in the 2024 yearbook, every single one appears to be a girl. Nationally, the numbers are similar. In 2003, 97 percent of those who participated at all levels of cheerleading in the United States were female.[92] In 2023, 97 percent of the 153,820 U.S. high schoolers in "competitive spirit" were girls.[93]

Cheer remains a coveted position on campus and apparently an influential one in the community. The 2014 *El Gabilan* credited varsity cheerleader Quinn Houchini for having "convinced the Salinas City Council to allow the homecoming parade after the Council had decided that police officers had better things to do than blocking off Main Street for it."[94] As in the past, the girls who occupy this position stand out as exemplars of femininity, but not in the same ways that they did in the 1950s or 1960s. Cheer remains a high-status activity for girls precisely because the transformation of the activity has been a key part of how femininity itself has been more broadly redefined—by fusing successful performances of conventional feminine attractiveness (including the ubiquitous smile) with athleticism, competitive zeal, and leadership. As such, high school girls who cheer embody the currently elevated definition of femininity. And the 2022, 2023, and 2024 cheer team photos show that compared with the past,

Figure 5.40. Varsity cheer team, *El Gabilan*, 2023

there are now more girls of color sharing this high-status space on campus—though at a school with only 20 percent white students, white girls are still overrepresented in cheer.[95]

Change and Continuity Inside and Outside Sports

High school sport is both a site of dynamic social change and one that reiterates traditions that link the school and its community to its past. In some ways, the boundary around what is considered sport has shifted. In 2010, Salinas High School created a sports-related academic track. The FAST (Fitness And Sports Training) Academy "focuses on sports medicine and health, attracting many students who are interested in physical therapy as a future career."[96] The athletics department also added new sports and pulled some activities into the fold. Cheer, as we have seen, was incorporated into the athletics department as a competitive sport. We saw also that the yearbooks of the 1980s and 1990s started to devote space to students who participated in "alternative," "extreme," or "external" sports—like biking, skateboarding, surfing, snowboarding, rollerblading, martial arts, horseback riding, or gymnastics—that comprised athletic activities not organized by the school (Figure 5.41). One of those sports, bike racing, became so popular that it moved from a club activity to an official Salinas High School interscholastic sport in 2008. Over the next decade the sport grew, with the team regularly fielding about forty-five competitors, roughly a third of them girls (Figure 5.42).

Figure 5.41. (*above*) Gymnast Patrick McFall, *El Gabilan*, 2000

Figure 5.42. (*left*) Bike racing team, *El Gabilan*, 2017

Figure 5.43. "Coach Alex" and the varsity water polo team, *El Gabilan*, 2006

Coaching at the high school has also seen some changes in recent years. Unlike in the early and middle decades of the twentieth century, today's yearbooks rarely elevate coaches, even the highly successful ones, as celebrities or heroes. The local media in 2023 praised head football coach Steve Zenk for having won five straight league titles (including wins each year over rival Palma High),[97] but the *El Gabilan* came nowhere near to lionizing Zenk in the way that the yearbooks praised Harry Shipkey nearly a century ago. Since Shipkey's time, the number of coaches at the school has expanded dramatically. By my count from team photos, in 2023 there were 125 people coaching Salinas High sports teams.[98] Some of that growth came from the swelling numbers of men coaching the three football teams: 14 football coaches in 2003, 23 in 2013, 26 in 2023, and 25 in 2024.

One thing that changed very little since the 1990s was the gender composition of the coaching staff. From 2000 to 2024, the proportion of women coaches appearing in yearbook photos held steady, hovering around 15 percent (though in 2024, the women coaches nudged up to 21 percent at the school).[99] During that time, women held about 35 percent of the coaching positions for girls' sports teams, while boys' teams were coached 98 percent by men. The rare cases where women coached boys occurred in water polo, volleyball, or in coed squads of swimmers or cross-country runners (Figures 5.43, 5.44). For the most part, boys were coached by men, and two-thirds of the time girls were too. Salinas High is not unusual in this respect. Good

Figure 5.44. Coach Liz Prewett and the varsity boys' volleyball team, *El Gabilan*, 2006

longitudinal data on gender in college coaching exists,[100] but there is very limited national data on high school coaching. California is one of the few states that gathers such data, and the 2023 CIF Census of Coaching Data revealed that women comprised 26.5 percent of all high school coaches in the state that year.[101]

Why are women still so underrepresented in high school coaching? One factor is the stubbornly persistent belief that boys need to be coached by men, an assumption that translates into more than half of the coaching jobs being unavailable to women from the get-go. But how to explain the fact that today men are two-thirds of those coaching girls' sports, despite the fact that so many women now have a deep well of sports experience and knowledge? In 2023 I interviewed Martha Getris-Utschig to explore this question. A 1979 graduate of Salinas High—where she lettered in basketball, volleyball, and track and field—Getris-Utschig later was enshrined in the Hartnell College Athletics Hall of Fame. She retired from her faculty position at Salinas High in 2023 following many years of teaching that included a few years of coaching in three sports (Figure 5.45). Getris-Utschig shed light on three factors that had discouraged her and other women coaches.

Getris-Utschig loved coaching the girls at Salinas High, but she pretty much hung up her whistle after coaching for just a few years. She had felt frustrated, for one thing, with the lack of fairness in the basic allocation of resources. "I always felt like I was struggling, especially when I was coaching basketball, trying to get court time . . . This is hard because I don't want to bash anybody, but when you've got some strong personalities on the men's side who don't want to share the court, it's really tough. [My] sister Nancy [coached] the freshman girls; she couldn't get a key to the gym. She had the first practice on a Saturday; there was nobody there to open the door for her. The

Figure 5.45. Martha Getris-Utschig, *El Gabilan*, 2023

kids are standing in the rain, you know, but she can't get a key to the gym. Are you kidding me? That's just crap."

Getris-Utschig also pointed to a double standard in the ways that women coaches are judged, a story familiar to me from my research with youth sports coaches.[102] "Parents were really hard on female coaches—we're held to a different standard. Men, the football coaches are out there cussing their boys out. And the minute a woman says anything they deem inappropriate then you're getting called on the carpet. I mean, the double standards were just horrific. They chew us up. They chew up female coaches. I'm not sure how Patty Lamar lasted as long as she did. She coached

Figure 5.46. Coach Patty Lamar and girls' JV water polo team, *El Gabilan*, 2004

swimming and water polo a really long time, and she developed coaches, and she was awesome" (Figure 5.46).

Getris-Utschig named a third constraint on women coaches, one that also echoes stories I heard from women youth sports coaches, about the challenges of juggling a paid occupation, community service, and family labor, especially as a mother.[103] "In terms of being a woman and coaching, one of the hardest things is that you finish your day at work as a teacher, then you go off and you deal with these girls, and then you have to go home to your family and take care of them. And you still have papers to grade. Yeah. And it's pushing 11 o'clock and you still haven't made lunches for your own children. It's extremely hard without support. And I had a lot of support, but it was still really tough. It was exhausting. I just remember being tired all the time."

Sport is rarely in the forefront of progressive social change. To be sure, the U.S. Women's National [Soccer] Team's public activism in recent years has helped to

WHAT SPORTS DID YOU PLAY AND WHY?

"Basketball, badminton and swimming are my favorite."
- **Aidan Martin (12)**

"Soccer! Also I like to play basketball, when we shoot to the hoop and score."
- **Joseph Prudencio (11)**

"Basketball, happy when we score and when people cheer for me because it makes me happy."
- **David Sanchez (12)**

"Basketball, soccer, and badminton."
- **Ramiro Reyes (11)**

Figure 5.47. SHS Special Olympics, *El Gabilan*, 2019

inspire a broader movement for equal pay for women,[104] just as National Football League quarterback Colin Kaepernick's taking a knee in 2016 to protest violence against African Americans galvanized movements for racial justice both inside and outside of sport.[105] But usually sport tends to lag a step behind, rather than being a major driver of social change. If athletes at Salinas High were organizing around causes in the past, it was usually to raise funds to support their teams. Some SHS athletes involved in "PE Leadership" helped to staff local Special Olympics events in 2019 and 2020 (Figure 5.47). And in most years over the past three decades, the yearbooks have included a photo of the Fellowship of Christian Athletes club, whose members "play hard, and sometimes they pray hard" (Figure 5.48).[106]

"Achievement, Service, and Character"

Over the past twenty years, the first-year students that appeared in my university courses were already well practiced in community service work from their high school

Figure 5.48. Fellowship of Christian Athletes, *El Gabilan*, 2001

years. Many continued to do service work in college because they cared about connecting their classroom work with the "real world." I have often been inspired by the important work my students have done on campus and in the Los Angeles community—working to end violence, serving unhoused people, creating community food banks, tutoring children. Some high school students also engage in community service because they want to make the world a better place. But there are also other reasons. High schools sometimes require a certain number of community service hours to qualify for graduation; at Salinas High, it is a minimum of forty hours. Ambitious students learn too that accumulating community service experience adds an impressive ingredient to one's résumé on top of strong academic and extracurricular achievements. No doubt for many students, service work is driven by two or more of these motivations.

Student organizations also have multiple motivations that tend to shift over time. During moments of national urgency when social movements are on the rise, high school clubs become more overtly political. But during times when social activism and urgency is on the wane, student clubs bend more into community service, an activity rewarded by the school to the point where, for a few years, it became a public competition that was reported in the *El Gabilan*. "Who's ahead in hours?" the 2010

And the FIRST place goes to...

Anacaren Sanchez
Hours: 824

Emily Erling
Hours: 730

Nicholas A. Clark
Hours: 412

Teyan Birgani
Hours: 147

Figure 5.49. Students with most service hours, *El Gabilan*, 2014

yearbook asked next to a photo of the top ten students, headed by Alicia Zhu, who had accumulated 859 hours of service.[107] The 2014 yearbook honored the four students who were tops in service hours in their respective classes (Figure 5.49).

Student organizations that engage with social issues range from ones that provide help for others (e.g., collecting food for hungry families) to those that aim to bring about changes that address the root causes of social issues. Some organizations oscillate over time between these two poles—providing service and help for others during one era, and shifting to political activism in other times. Salinas High students' engagements with gender and sexuality issues in recent years offer some good examples of this.

Gender-based violence, including sexual assault, harassment, and stalking, continue to plague high schools. There is little mention of gender-based violence in the *El Gabilan*, but from 2013 through 2017 the yearbook showed a small group of boys who had joined the "My Strength" club (Figure 5.50). In the mid-2010s I was conducting research with men who work to prevent sexual assault and domestic violence. The resulting 2015 coauthored book, *Some Men*, included a profile of Gilbert Salazar, a young man who at that time was working with the Monterey County Rape Crisis Center to form My Strength clubs in Salinas middle schools and high schools, groups that aimed inspire boys to become campus leaders in preventing gender-based harassment and violence.[108] It is not clear from the yearbooks whether any of the boys who joined Salinas High's My Strength clubs were also athletes. But nationally, some of the most prominent men in the gender-based violence prevention movement are former

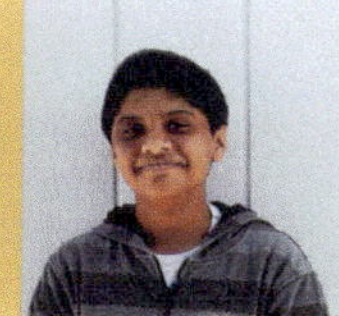

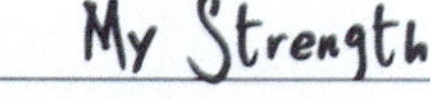

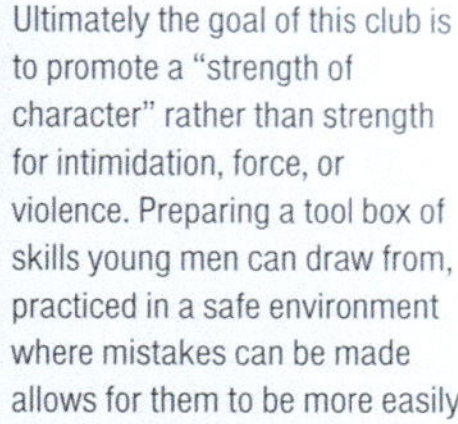

Figure 5.50. My Strength Club, *El Gabilan*, 2014

athletes, and they commonly seek to recruit athletes to serve as campus leaders in their efforts to build support for anti-violence efforts.[109] The fact that many of those at Salinas High who did join My Strength were Latinos would not have surprised Gilbert Salazar, who understood from his own experience that many of these boys were motivated by having experienced horrific violence in the streets and sometimes abuse in their families.[110]

Since it first appeared as a campus club in 2005, the Gay-Straight Alliance (GSA) waged a sustained effort to address gender and sexuality issues at Salinas High. GSA clubs exist in many U.S. and Canadian high schools, and were renamed "Gender-Sexuality Alliance" clubs around 2015.[111] It is not clear how many Salinas High GSA members over the years were also athletes, but athletes have been centrally involved in GSAs in other high schools.[112] Researchers have shown that high schools with GSA clubs tend to have greater levels of acceptance for LGBTQ+ students and declining levels of bullying, absenteeism, depression, and suicidality.[113] The GSA's page in the 2007 *El Gabilan* included a statement that the club "is strongly against discrimination and harassment among students. This group is about building tolerance on campus." And the center photo on that page was captioned, "Not Afraid To Show It: Seniors Brittany Livingston and Brittany Lopez prove that just because you are gay doesn't

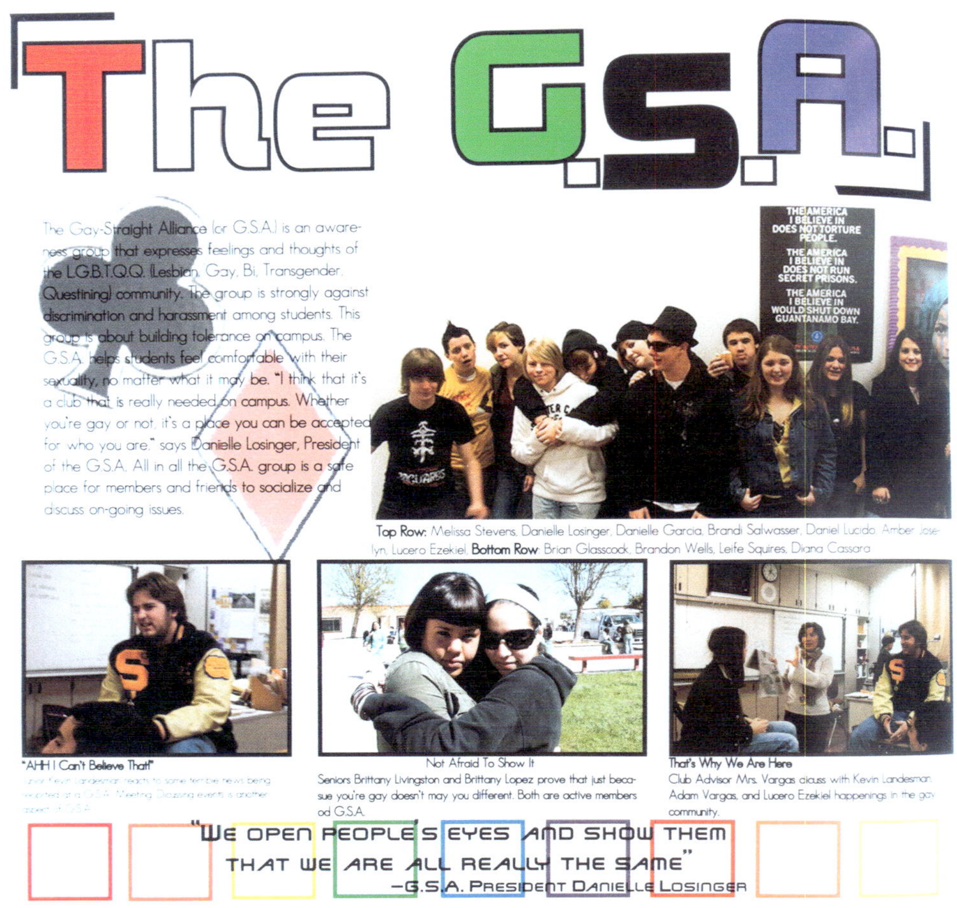

The G.S.A.

The Gay-Straight Alliance (or G.S.A.) is an awareness group that expresses feelings and thoughts of the L.G.B.T.Q.Q. (Lesbian, Gay, Bi, Transgender, Questining) community. The group is strongly against discrimination and harassment among students. This group is about building tolerance on campus. The G.S.A. helps students feel comfortable with their sexuality, no matter what it may be. "I think that it's a club that is really needed on campus. Whether you're gay or not, it's a place you can be accepted for who you are," says Danielle Losinger, President of the G.S.A. All in all the G.S.A. group is a safe place for members and friends to socialize and discuss on-going issues.

Top Row: Melissa Stevens, Danielle Losinger, Danielle Garcia, Brandi Salwasser, Daniel Lucido, Amber Joselyn, Lucero Ezekiel. **Bottom Row:** Brian Glasscock, Brandon Wells, Leife Squires, Diana Cassara

"AHH I Can't Believe That!"
Junior Kevin Landesman reacts to some terrible news being reported at a G.S.A. Meeting. Discussing events is another aspect of G.S.A.

Not Afraid To Show It
Seniors Brittany Livingston and Brittany Lopez prove that just becasue you're gay doesn't may you different. Both are active members od G.S.A.

That's Why We Are Here
Club Advisor Mrs. Vargas dicuss with Kevin Landesman, Adam Vargas, and Lucero Ezekiel happenings in the gay community.

"We open people's eyes and show them that we are all really the same"
—G.S.A. President Danielle Losinger

Figure 5.51. *El Gabilan*, 2007

mean you are different" (Figure 5.51).[114] GSA carved out a visible presence on campus. "The club organized a gender-bender day on November 2nd which promoted transgender equality," the 2010 *El Gabilan* reported. "At club meetings, philosophies about gender and methods of combating offensive slurs were debated."[115] Club members also frequently marched behind a GSA banner in the school's annual homecoming parade (Figure 5.52).

The GSA continues to be a presence on the SHS campus but, echoing a change made at other high schools, in 2022 it was renamed the "Be Yourself Club." I have not seen an explanation of this name change, but it is consistent with a common dynamic at high schools, whereby student groups that may be viewed as "political" are turned away from directly confronting persistent inequalities and injustices and pushed toward promoting goals seen as less inflammatory or divisive, such as celebrating diversity and promoting kindness (a "Kindness Club" did also appear in the 2022 and 2023 *El Gabilan*).[116] But if the default position for student organizations is a depoliticized form of service, there are also moments when national or statewide social

Figure 5.52. *El Gabilan*, 2010

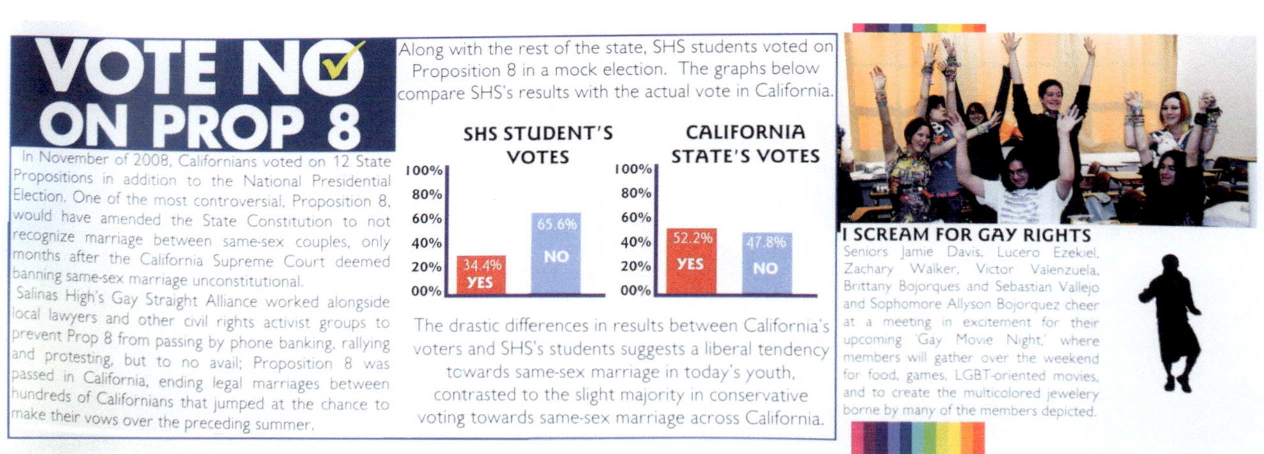

Figure 5.53. *El Gabilan*, 2009

movements galvanize students' political activism. The stakes were high in 2008, for instance, when California's Proposition 8 gave voters the opportunity to eliminate same-sex marriage, which had been legalized recently in the state. GSA members at Salinas High "campaigned against Prop 8, and attended a Youth Empowerment Summit in SF. Polled SHS students said No to Prop 8, though Calif voters passed it 52.2 percent" (Figure 5.53).[117]

A similar back-and-forth oscillation between moments of political activism with longer stretches of community service was evident in other student clubs during a time when Salinas High's student population was becoming increasingly liberal (a mock vote during the 2008 presidential election resulted in 74 percent of SHS students voting for Barack Obama and only 20 percent for John McCain).[118] The Students for a Better Earth Club in some years emphasized promoting recycling, but in 2020, sparked by an international youth-led movement to address climate change, SHS students marched to city hall wearing shirts with Sunrise Movement and Green New Deal logos. Similarly, the 2018 *El Gabilan* showed students in the March for Our Lives, demonstrating for gun control in response to February 14, 2018, mass shooting at Stoneman Douglas High in Parkland, Florida. That spring the SHS debate team also held a public debate on gun control.[119] MEChA students continued a long tradition, stretching back to the 1970s, of presenting Mexican American cultural awareness events that were occasionally punctuated by moments of public political activism. In 2017, sparked by incoming president Donald Trump's anti-immigrant rhetoric and "build the wall" plans, SHS "Dreamers" (immigrant youth covered by the federal Deferred Action for Childhood Arrivals [DACA]) traveled to Washington, DC, and joined in the massive anti-Trump Women's March on Washington (Figure 5.54). Even during the depths of the 2020 COVID-19 pandemic lockdown, face-masked Salinas High students, led by the Black Student Union, joined racial justice demonstrations that blossomed throughout the nation during the Black Lives Matter uprisings (Figure 5.55).

The first quarter of the new century was bookended by two major international jolts—war and pandemic. On the front end, the terror attacks of September 11, 2001, shocked the nation. The 2002 *El Gabilan* noted that "September 11 proved to be a test of our country's nationalism . . . we saw many of the effects of this fateful day around the city and the campus." In response, the ASB sponsored a dance to raise funds for "the September 11 tragedy."[120] The United States' subsequent invasions of Afghanistan and Iraq, followed by many years of war, caused few ripples in the annual yearbooks over the next several years. It is likely that the lack of focus at the high school on the United States' protracted wars in the Middle East was related to the fact that unlike during previous wars (World War I, World War II, Korea, and Vietnam), young men no longer faced the prospect of being drafted.

Twenty years later, the COVID-19 pandemic upset the SHS apple cart much more. Toward the end of what had been so far a normal academic year, students and faculty were abruptly told in March 2020 to shelter at home. Faculty and administrators scrambled to adjust to online learning, and students—already well schooled in social media—shifted their social activities to online modes (Figure 5.56). The 2020–21 school year was an almost entirely locked-down year, including the suspension of nearly all interscholastic sports. "In the midst of a pandemic," the *El Gabilan* staff wrote, "It was up to yearbook students to create a book that will last forever."[121] With adviser Ms. Kelsey Beall, they did just that, creating a yearbook themed "The Bright

A NEW BEGINNING

The Salinas High School Dream academy attended the inauguration and woman's march in Washington D.C. It was an emotional experience for all.

"The amount of protestors out there for and against Trump."

Brandon Dydasco (11)

"Very interesting, very emotional, when Obama's helicopter disappeared it felt like the whole world just dropped on me."

Miguel Rodriguez (10)

"Probably seeing how many people were against Trump and thinking how many people where on his side."

Samantha Torres (10)

Figure 5.54. SHS "Dreamers," *El Gabilan*, 2017

Figure 5.55. Rallying for Black Lives, *El Gabilan*, 2021

VIRTUAL

SPIRIT

WEEK

Cowboys
take on
Quarantine!

COVID-19 may prevent us from attending school but it cannot take away our spirit! Salinas High had its very first virtual spirit week this year. Students were able to participate by sending in or posting pictures and videos of themselves partipating. Across various social media apps, such as Instagram and Tiktok, students are able to connect with each other and share what they are doing to pass time during quarantine. #stayhome

Figure 5.56. *El Gabilan*, 2020

Side" that could not have been better, given the circumstances (Figure 5.57). Similar to during the Great Depression, Salinas's agricultural economy largely mitigated the steep financial losses that hammered neighboring communities more reliant on tourist money. However, farmworkers were considered "essential workers" who could not shelter at home, thus "the deadly virus had a devastating impact on the fieldworkers and service workers who made up most of the population of east Salinas."[122]

Tucked in between and around the tragedies of war and pandemic, the staff of the *El Gabilan* continued to put out an annual book that, over the years, cohered around a thematic trilogy of what the 2004 *El Gabilan* called "achievement, service, and character." While sports, clubs, and other student activities continued to be important in the yearbooks, they frequently were presented in a frame that foregrounded students' academic achievement or community service. For instance, the yearbook praised the 2015 boys' water polo team as much for their cumulative 3.7527 GPA as for their league championship.[123] Homecoming Week continued to include days devoted to goofy celebrity dress-up or pajama days, the week always culminating with a football game

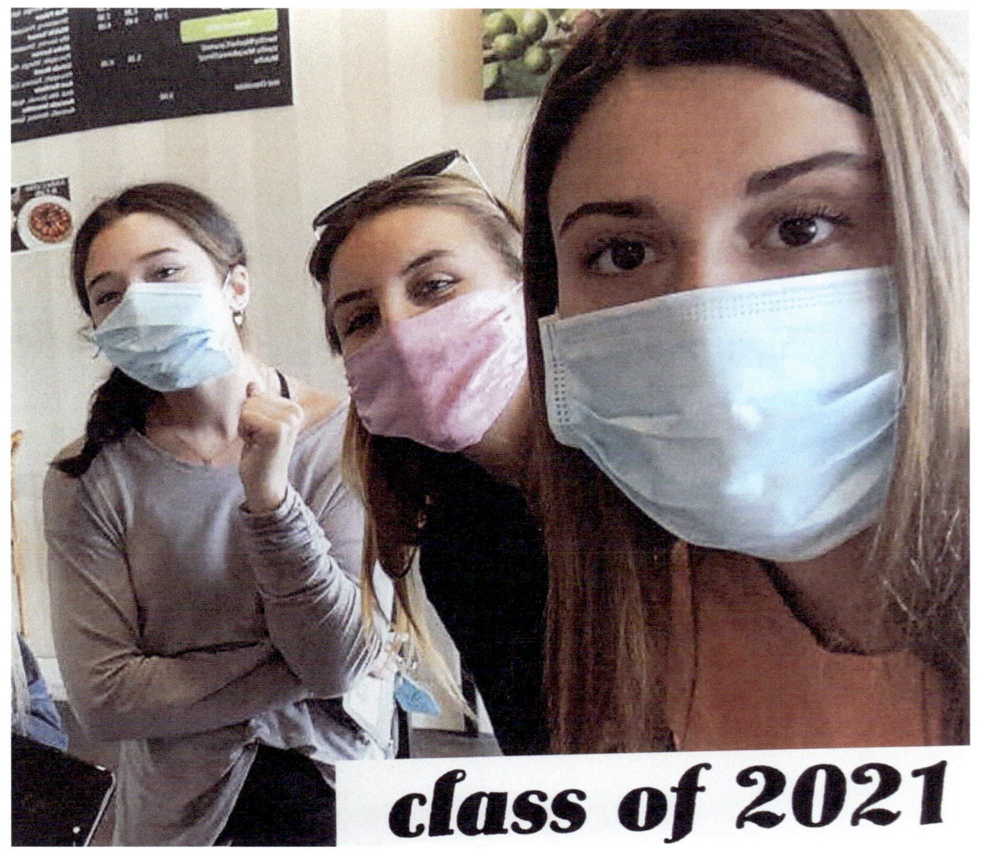

Figure 5.57. *El Gabilan*, 2021

Royalty
And the winner is....

Figure 5.58. *El Gabilan*, 2003

and a "Purple Pride" crowning of "Homecoming Royalty" whose résumés were stunning to read. This was especially true of the girls who were so honored. For instance, standing aside 2003 homecoming king and football player Nick Nance, homecoming queen Abbie Coffee, we learn from the yearbook, was also the ASB president, a football cheerleader, a track and field athlete, and a member of the National Honor Society (Figure 5.58).[124]

That yearbooks in the new century so often featured girls as embodying the school's most honored package of "achievement, service, and character," a theme I introduced at the start of this chapter, says volumes about what has changed, and perhaps too what has not. Most obviously, that girls are so often given center stage in the yearbooks as campus leaders, as academic achievers, and as athletes indicates a tidal wave of progress toward gender equality from a century, or even a half century earlier. Perhaps less obvious is the extent to which our views and expectations of boys have remained relatively unchanged. Feminism and movements for LGBTQ+ rights have somewhat loosened the constraints of narrow conceptions of masculinity, broadening possibilities for self-expression for some boys. But boys who are football stars remain near the center of the school's status system at Salinas High, as in other schools.[125] And we might also wonder about the many girls and boys who are not the leaders, not the academic achievers, not the sports or cheer stars. The yearbook's frame has broadened and has become more inclusive over the years, but the spotlight still shines most brightly on high-achieving student-athletes.

Conclusion

Paradoxes of Progress

THE IDEA TO WRITE THIS BOOK began to gestate in the fall of 2001 when my then-teenaged niece Samantha Rios walked me through a tour of my old high school. I was struck by the familiar feel of the Salinas High School that Sam inhabited at the turn of the new millennium and the school I had attended between 1966 and 1970. I marveled at the school's spanking-new gymnasium, and spoke with Joe Chappell, the boys' basketball coach. My dad had been the varsity basketball coach here at Salinas High from 1947 to 1971; Chappell had played ball for my dad, and then took over the team in 1972. That is over half a century with only two varsity boys' basketball coaches. Nor, it turned out, was Chappell finished: he would continue to coach the team for another decade. This amazing continuity stirred in me deep satisfaction and pride.

On that day in 2001, when I looked around at the new gym, the beautifully remodeled campus, and the increasingly diverse student population, it struck me that as much had changed over the past thirty years as had stayed the same. The old boys' gym that my dad had labored in for most of his adult life (and that I had played in for several years) had been reduced to rubble to make way for the much larger new gym. I asked the coach what had become of the old girls' gym. He said that yes, the old girls' gym was still standing, and was still in use. However, he told me, "It's not called the 'girls' gym' anymore. It's called the 'old gym,' and the new one is called the 'new gym.' The boys don't own the good facilities around here anymore." To emphasize his point, he took me outside the "new gym," and pointed to the top edge of the

Figure C.1. 1920s decorative tiles from the old boys' gym. Author photos, 2023.

building. "Remember the tiles that were on the face of the old boys' gym?" he asked. Yes, this was seared in my memory: the old Spanish colonial revival–style building had sported individual tiles, each of which depicted a different icon of classic athletic performance: a hurdler, a football player, a basketball player, and a baseball player (Figure C.1).

Back in the 1920s, the 1950s, and even in 1970 when I was in school, I doubt that many people noticed that every single one of the athletes depicted on these lovely tiles were men. But around 1999, when they were building the "new gym," somebody did notice. So they carefully removed the tiles from the doomed old boys' gym and fashioned some new ones of a similar style to include side by side with the old tiles on the façade of the new gym. These new tiles depicted women athletes playing basketball, softball, and cheering. And there was another, perhaps less noticeable change: the old tiles represented men all with white skin, but the new tiles showed women and men of various hues, from pale pink to darker brown skin. Fixed to the outer façade of the new gym, the old and new tiles together tell a story of the school's

Figure C.2. Decorative tiles on the new gym. Author photos, 2023.

demographic shift to a majority Hispanic student body, as well as its evolution in who is considered an athlete (Figure C.2).

The gender symmetry depicted on the tiles of the new gym represents a dramatic shift toward acceptance—even symbolic celebration—of girls' and women's presence in sports. And these changes are not merely symbolic. Salinas High, like other high schools in the United States, now offers a range of interscholastic sports for girls. Money is now budgeted for uniforms, travel, coaches' salaries, and awards for girls' sports. Thought is now given to the importance of the girls having access to good practice facilities. Like the decorative tiles on the new gym, Salinas High School yearbooks now depict girls' sports in much more equitable, respectful, even celebratory ways.

In the fall of 2023, I once again toured Salinas High's athletics facilities, this time courtesy of longtime athletic director Art Hunsdorfer. The main gym (now no longer so "new") had changed in another way since my visit twenty-two years ago: It is now called Joe Chappell Gymnasium, so named in 2015 in honor of the retired coach's long

A forty-one year chapter in cowboy history

The history in the "Joe Chappell Gymnasium"

Many of you cowboys may not know that the Salinas High Basketball team hasn't always played at our home court now known as the "Joe Chappell Gymnasium." In 2000 the Salinas High Basketball team left Hartnell and came to a freshly built gym the cowboys still play in today. For years the basketball team felt like they didn't have a home, But finally something happened that really made the cowboys feel like they have found a place that belongs to them. In 2010, with 687 wins and 419 losses, they helped coach Chappell break **CCS record for most wins!** With such an amazing accomplishment the Cowboys and Coach Chappell himself couldn't have been any happier. Years of hard work and dedication from Coach Chsppell and his players over the years paid off. Reaching CCS could not have been possible with all players over the years putting their all into the game.

Figure C.3. Joe Chappell Gymnasium, *El Gabilan*, 2015

and successful tenure. I thought it was fully deserving to honor Chappell in this way,[1] though it also struck me as mildly ironic that the façade of the gym—a testament to a new era of gender equity in sports—should also bear a man's name (Figure C.3).

A more jarring asymmetry greets visitors as they step inside the gym's foyer. There, twenty-nine commemorative plaques are fixed to the walls, honoring the Salinas Cowboys Athletic Hall of Fame coaches and athletes from the past (Figure C.4). All but one of those so honored are men. The sole woman Hall of Famer is Susan Springer, the late-1970s track star we met in chapter 4.[2] One logical reason for the dearth of women honorees, of course, is the fact that more than half a century passed during which there were no girls' interscholastic sports, leaving little to celebrate in terms of athletic or coaching accomplishments. But readers of this book know that there is a deeper story to this: Girls played interscholastic sports at Salinas High in the opening decades of the twentieth century, and women coached them. As I looked at the wall of fame, populated mostly by men coaches of the past, I wondered: Where is Ruth Wing, the 1925–46 stalwart girls' sports coach? Why don't some of the post–Title IX

Figure C.4. Salinas Cowboys Athletic Hall of Fame. Author photo, 2023.

women like Patty Lamar or Martha Getris-Utschig—SHS athletes and later coaches at the school—have plaques on that wall? Hunsdorfer told me that the school will soon be moving to honor more women. But to me, women's absence from the Athletic Hall of Fame in 2023 spoke volumes about past and continuing challenges girl athletes and women coaches have faced.

When I spent a week at Salinas High in September 2023—mostly poring through old copies of the *El Gabilan* that are not in my personal collection—I also hung around campus a bit. In addition to touring the sports facilities, I spent a class period talking with the students who were just embarking on their yearlong task of putting together the 2024 *El Gabilan*. The students in the class—mostly girls, many of them Latinas—listened respectfully, asked good questions, and made earnest statements about wanting their yearbook to be representative of the wide range of students at the school, more so than past yearbooks had. Being with that group of students brought home to me how each *El Gabilan* is so much a collective project where a group of students, guided by their adviser, labors over something about which they care deeply. They know that what goes into the yearbook, and what is left out, is important and meaningful. Every single yearbook I have looked at, from the start of the twentieth century to the present, was created by students like these ones; each book is a product of their creativity, hopes, dreams, joy, sweat, and tears (Figures C.5, C.6, C.7).

During that visit in the fall of 2023, I enjoyed strolling around campus during the lunch hour when the inner court was kinetic with students talking, yelling, and

Figure C.5. *El Gabilan* staff, *El Gabilan*, 1938

Figure C.6. *El Gabilan* staff, *El Gabilan*, 1970

Figure C.7. *El Gabilan* staff, *El Gabilan*, 2024

goofing around during their free time. It was here that the numbers I had seen—that the school was now 70 percent Hispanic—really hit home for me. On my first day there I noticed that the new principal, Hugo Mariscal, was standing, arms crossed, in the center of a concrete area that gave him a 360-degree view of the goings-on. I joined him, and at one point he interrupted our conversation, saying, “Mike, let me introduce you to my troublemakers,” as he signaled to three Latino boys. As the boys approached, the principal switched to Spanish, greeting the boys with fist-bumps, and introducing them to me in Spanish. I also fist-bumped each of the three boys, but was flustered and a bit embarrassed with my monolingual limitations. I asked if I could take a picture. Mr. Mariscal towered over the three boys, embracing them with his long wingspan, and I snapped a couple of shots as the four of them smiled (Figure C.8).[3]

The following day I rejoined Principal Mariscal during the noon hour where he had once again positioned himself, surveilling the yard and talking with students. I told him that the previous night I had phoned my wife, Pierrette, a scholar of Mexican immigration, to tell her how impressed I was not only with the dramatic demographic transformation of my alma mater, but with the scene I had witnessed with the principal and the three boys. In my day, I told Mr. Mariscal, kids who spoke Spanish in school would likely be shunned, perhaps even punished. He nodded and told me that he had moved to the United States from Mexico as a child, and one of his earliest memories as a student in a Salinas public elementary school was having his mouth duct-taped for speaking Spanish. This story underlined for me how meaningful it is that today, not only are Spanish-speaking kids at Salinas High not

Figure C.8. SHS students Christian Rojas, David Quintanilla Galvan, and Julian Espinoza with principal Hugo Mariscal. Author photo, 2023.

punished for speaking their native language, but they also actually have a principal who sees and knows them, speaks their language with them, and embraces them as students.

All this is not to put a too-happy face on the continuing challenges facing so many Hispanic and other youth who attend Salinas High School. Despite improved policies and programs in the city schools, Spanish-speaking kids face uphill challenges. As I discussed in the introduction to this book, we often place burdens on schools that are based on impossible expectations. Schools cannot alone change the existing structural inequalities in society. The high poverty rates in towns like Salinas, the growing gap between the rich and the poor, and the hollowing-out of the middle class are not caused by schools, nor can schools reverse these processes. At worst, schools obfuscate the social causes and possible solutions to economic inequality by uncritically promoting individualist ideas of meritocracy. School-based meritocratic policies typically provide an escalator for youth from well-to-do families and a supporting ideology that justifies the reproduction of long-standing group-based inequalities. But schools can also be a motor for creating democratic citizenship and critical engagement with the social world. Xenophobic, homophobic, racist, and sexist ideas and practices can be challenged as students learn about their history and study the world that they live in. There is plenty of evidence that at Salinas High, this kind of classroom learning, coupled with participation in student organizations, has been a consciousness-raising experience for students that can extend beyond the campus to their current and future families, their future jobs and professions, and future civic engagement in their communities.

High school sport, along with its supportive spirit complex, has traditionally supported conservative beliefs in meritocracy and male superiority. But we have also seen that sport has been—and continues to be—a site of contested meanings about gender and race. As I write the final lines for this book, I can't help but replay in my mind's eye the images of those Salinas High girls and their women coaches who around 1920 were demanding decent fields and courts on which to play sports; the Japanese American girls and boys in the pre–World War II years who starred in athletics; those girls in the mid-1960s practicing to race in the Turkey Trot, as they pressed up against the stubborn constraints holding girls back from competing; the many women coaches, from the early twentieth century to the present, who challenged sexist double standards through their commitment to leading girls' (and occasionally boys') teams; and those tough Latina wrestlers who in recent years are exploding previously entrenched stereotypes of Latina passivity.[4]

One major theme cuts across my analysis of 120-plus years of the *El Gabilan* yearbooks: the relationship between change and continuity. The popular cliché, "the more things change, the more they stay the same" fails to capture this complicated reality. Instead, as a sociologist with an interest in history, I prefer to think that the story I tell in this book illustrates *the unevenness of social change*.[5] Social change can surge, slow, stagnate, or shift directions. Movements toward equality and fairness may have a dramatic impact in one geographical place, while elsewhere not at all. We saw in chapter 5 many examples of what historian Susan Cahn calls the "paradox of 'progress'" in twenty-first-century girls' and women's sports.[6] Akin to the symbolic gender symmetries and asymmetries on the walls of Salinas High's Joe Chappell Gymnasium, the dramatic twenty-first-century shift toward equity and celebration of girls' and women's sports emerges in a dynamic tension with stubbornly persistent inequalities: girls' participation in sports is booming, yet many girls play sports that are very different from those that boys play (softball versus baseball, flag versus tackle football, adapted-rules lacrosse, etc.); more high school girls today are using sports as a means of accessing elite higher education, but that avenue to university is wider for girls from well-to-do families, and it remains a narrow uphill pull for youth of color from poor or working-class families;[7] annual yearbooks now devote roughly equal space and equivalent respect to girls' and boys' sports, yet boys' tackle football still occupies the cultural center of the school's sports universe, despite the routine health dangers built into playing the sport; cheer is now an official sport characterized by exciting competitive athleticism, but cheer also retains its past meanings as a performative activity through which high-status girls support boys' sports, especially football; girls' sports teams have proliferated to a point roughly equal in number with boys' teams, yet boys are still coached almost entirely by men, while two-thirds of those coaching girls' teams are men.

These current paradoxes in high school sports are points of tension that students, teachers, parents, and even yearbook staff members continue to navigate—sometimes with celebration, other times criticizing and chaffing from constraints, and perhaps other times advocating for future changes. A major takeaway I hope readers will get from *The High School* is this: as people grapple with the current paradoxes and strains built into high school sports, they are making history, but there is nothing inevitable about the future directions their actions will take us. As we saw in chapters 1 and 2, the early twentieth-century boom in girls' and women's sports was followed by a backlash that all but eliminated girls' interscholastic competition for fifty years. This alone should disabuse us of any belief in the inevitability of some linear historical move toward fairness and equality. Dr. Martin Luther King asserted that "The arc of the moral universe is long, but it bends toward justice." If this hopeful view of history is to be proven true, it will become so only when people join to push toward that future.

Appendix

High School Yearbooks as Personal and Cultural Memory

THE 1926 *EL GABILAN* FEATURED AN EDITORIAL noting that at that year's convention of California state high school principals held in Pasadena, "The majority of principals thought that annuals were valuable if handled in the right way, but as a rule they are handled incorrectly." *El Gabilan* editor Ralph Berry, assuming a somewhat defensive posture, asserted that "the annual is a lasting history of school activities. It contains the record of the greatest accomplishments of the organizations and individuals of the school; it records facts you might want to remember; and it pictures all students of the school in some phase of every-day school life . . . I believe the annual is indispensable."[1]

Indispensable or not, an annual high school yearbook is never a complete chronicle of everything that happened during an academic year. Rather, guided by tradition, yearbooks highlight what the student editors and their faculty advisers deem to be the most significant events or memorable moments. Nor are yearbooks inherently democratic documents, despite the claim that they picture "all students of the school in some phase of every-day school life." Schools have always had status systems that yearbooks tend to reflect and even celebrate. Over time, the bases of prestige may shift, but yearbooks always track these changes, shining light and devoting ink to the highest-status kids and their activities while consigning others to the margins and shadows. For many of these latter, a single thumbnail headshot may be their sole appearance in a yearbook.

I witnessed this in microcosm in my own family. My sister Terry was the head cheerleader at Salinas High in 1965 and appeared several times in her senior-year annual—dancing with her boyfriend at the Harvest Ball, victoriously hoisting the Rooters' Trophy at a football jamboree, posing with the other cheerleaders on the pages devoted to the squad, and, of course, her senior portrait headshot was there as well. I also made several appearances in my senior yearbook in 1970—as captain of the varsity basketball team and as an officer in the all-boys' Key Club and Block "S" Society. There was a shot of me dancing with Sheila Prader at a school dance and another of the two of us in the advertising section of the book, pitching a couch for a local furniture store. By contrast, my sister Melinda cut a low profile in the 1968 *El Gabilan*. She was neither a cheerleader nor a joiner of clubs. She was not a top student, nor was she conventionally attractive like her older sister Terry, to whom she had been unfavorably compared, year after year, by teachers and kids. Linda was rarely near the high-profile activities on which the yearbook's spotlight routinely shined; she identified with an inchoate youth counterculture that, though it was flourishing in San Francisco, still had very little foothold in Salinas, California. Linda's only appearance in the 1968 yearbook was her senior portrait, situated alphabetically in a sea of 349 other members of her graduating class.

Crafting "a Memory Book"

In the 1968 *El Gabilan* student editor Linda Stevens wrote,

> A yearbook is a collection of portraits and class pictures, snapshots and action photos, headlines and copy. A yearbook is a history, a chronicle of events, a picture story. A yearbook is a challenge, an opportunity, a tradition. The 1968 EL GABILAN is all of these—and a great deal more. For most readers it is a memory book which will be treasured more each passing day, more each passing year. To those of us who have watched it grow, it is also a record of achievement—the reward of endless hours of preparing layouts, cropping pictures, writing copy, proofreading, meeting deadlines, and living within our budget.[2]

Stevens's statement captures the feeling of the yearbook as product of collective labor, commitment, and creativity. Her statement also reveals what yearbooks were like and what it took to produce one during a particular historical moment—because what constituted an *El Gabilan* was different in 1968 from what it was sixty years earlier, and different as well from what it is now. From 1903 through the spring of 1913, the *El Gabilan* was a short, paper-bound quarterly publication composed mostly of student literary productions, a few works of art, and an occasional photograph. Some coverage of sports was routine, and the fourth (spring) issue each year always focused on the graduating senior class. In 1913–14, the book was issued twice, in the fall and in the spring. The following year it became a single annual volume, published at the end of each school year. Most subsequent yearbooks were produced as oversized hardcover books, many with beautifully designed covers (several of which I have reproduced as frontispieces for chapters 2 through 5).

The form and content of the *El Gabilan* changed substantially during the first thirty-plus years of its publication. In the late 1920s and early 1930s the book gradually became more visual, featuring more photos and less text. The black-and-white photos of that era tended to be crystal clear and were usually printed on high-quality glossy stock. In 1938 the *El Gabilan* morphed into a format that seemed more familiar to my generational conception of what a yearbook should look like. The copyright page of that year's book included a seal that marked Salinas Union High School as a "Member, National Scholastic Press Association 1937–38."[3] The NSPA, established in 1921 and still in existence today, maintains a national presence in shaping high school journalism, including student newspapers and yearbooks.[4] I suspect that the NSPA established a national template for high school yearbooks, perhaps in the 1930s, and this may help to explain the ways in which the *El Gabilan* and other the yearbooks from other high schools I have looked at seem generally since that time to have conformed to a set of standards as to what goes into a yearbook and what does not. I inquired with a helpful officer of the NSPA, and he told me that he does not know when the organization created such a national template, but he did point out that the NSPA started giving out its national "Pacemaker" high school yearbook awards in 1993. The judging for the awards is based on an NSPA template that includes specific instructions and standards, including what proportion of a yearbook should be devoted to sports (18 percent), and stipulating that cheer or spirit is to be included in the sports section of a yearbook.[5]

Over the years the *El Gabilan* gradually grew in length, and every few years the book's organizational schema would shift. Sometimes these shifts accompanied the turnover of faculty advisers (in the earliest years, they were called "censors"). Mr. Don Hamburger appears to have been the longest-serving *El Gabilan* adviser, having supervised the production of the book between 1954 and 1983. Following his departure, a series of faculty advisers served shorter stints, and the book tended to change markedly during those years, including adding more focus on social issues (for instance, alcohol and drug abuse, violence, environmental issues). Another change I noted was that during the first several decades that the *El Gabilan* was published—from 1903 through the post–World War II years—the grammar, spelling, and punctuation in the yearbooks tended to be proper, and the text was impeccably copyedited. Starting around the late 1980s and continuing to the present, some of the books included more frequent misspellings, typos, improper grammar (their, there, and they're!), malapropisms, improper punctuation (those apostrophes!), and generally less careful copyediting. The quality of paper used to print the book and the clarity of photos also varied over time; this influenced which photos I chose to reproduce in *The High School.*

Making Sense of Yearbooks as Cultural Memory

High school yearbooks are a rich source of cultural memory, largely untapped by scholars. Andrew Poulson, a scholar who studied college yearbooks as a window into race relations in the U.S. South, described yearbooks as "dense historical documents, issued annually, that are explicitly designed to characterize life at these institutions."[6] But it does not take a professional historian to understand that yearbooks, rich as they may be, are a limited source of cultural memory. Eric Margolis, a scholar who has studied a century of school photos to better understand past race and gender relations in schools, warns that "these large photo collections have significant gaps and historical amnesias."[7] One sort of gap or "amnesia" evidenced in yearbooks relates to social context. Yearbook editors tended to treat their school as an insular cultural space, cordoned off from the broader social issues that shaped life in the school (though this limitation has become less stark in recent years). I attempted to provide historical context to my analysis by couching my reading and interpretation of the yearbooks in relevant scholarly works, for instance Susan Cahn's exhaustive history of U.S. women's sports, the foundational history of cheerleading by Natalie Guice Adams and Pamela Bettis, Carol Lynne McKibben's masterful history of Salinas, and others.

Some gaps in yearbooks are akin to what Tillie Olsen called "unnatural silences"—the ways that the voices, activities and images of some people were muted, rendered to the margins, or perhaps even totally ignored.[8] For decades, yearbooks routinely rendered invisible the less popular and less involved kids within the school, while shining the spotlight most brightly on the most popular and the most accomplished students—who happened disproportionately to be from privileged backgrounds. I sought as much as possible to search out and point to these unnatural silences. My main strategy in using the yearbooks to tell a story about change and continuity was to identify the dominant patterns. Some of this involved simply counting across years and decades, for instance, the number of pages devoted to girls' versus boys' sports; the number of men and women coaches; the racial and ethnic composition of senior classes or student organizations; the number of girls versus boys who were yell leaders and cheerleaders. But while doing this, I also sought to identify and make meaning of exceptions to the rule—the Black or Asian American student during an era when the student body was nearly all white; the rare woman who coached a boys' team; the girl "crosser" who played on a boys' sports team; the few twenty-first-century boys who joined cheer teams that had comprised all girls for decades. I also sought to analyze not just the quantity, but also the quality of how both patterns and anomalies were depicted in the yearbooks. For instance, when the yearbooks did devote some space to girls playing sports during that fifty-year gap in girls' interscholastic sports competition, was it done respectfully? Sarcastically? Insultingly?

Despite deploying these conscious strategies, the things I did *not* focus on, what I chose to downplay or even ignore, constantly bothered me. As I worked on this project, I was continually troubled by the ways that my focus on sports and cheering risked reproducing the very status system I sought to critically analyze. Other eyes, with different sorts of concerns, might have more deeply probed other dimensions of the yearbooks, revealing different stories. For instance, orchestra and theater are activities that tended to include youth who were less visible in the school's status system, some of whom likely formed peer groups that were not simply outside, but defined in opposition to, the school's dominant status hierarchy. School theatrical productions at some points undoubtedly included more countercultural kids, likely too more youth who identified as something other than heterosexual, but the yearbooks rarely accorded music or theater as much space, much less as much honor, as they devoted to sports and cheering.

A different scholar might also have done a fascinating analysis of the rise and fall of student organizations and their meanings for youth culture, gender, race, and students' imagined future lives and occupations. I do touch on this in *The High School*, but not systematically. And it is certainly fascinating to witness the comings and goings of youth hairstyles, clothing fashions, body piercings, and tattoos—again, I touch on this lightly in this book. So too, an analysis of the final section of each yearbook, the advertisements, could be a useful avenue of insight into the growth and development, in addition to decline and disappearance, of local businesses and services and the ways that new technologies (such as automobiles, radios, phonographs, televisions, cell phones, and social media) melded youth culture with consumerism. By the late 1980s this final advertising section of the yearbooks was taken over by "senior ads," paid for by families to celebrate the lives and accomplishments of their graduating sons and daughters. The content of these ads could be useful grist for a cultural analysis of how youth and their families choose to present themselves publicly. A researcher might also wonder about who is included in these ads and who is not. The 2024 *El Gabilan* charged $350 for a full page, $250 for a half page, $155 for a quarter page, and $75 for an eighth page.[9] Which families could easily afford this expense to honor their son or daughter? Which families did not participate because they could not afford to pay the price? And which families could not afford it, but stretched to do it anyhow?

My work on this project was systematic. I examined every page of every yearbook, from 1903 to 2024, taking notes on each book, and discovering storylines and photos that would help me tell what I hoped would be a coherent story of change and continuity. *The High School* contains about 266 photos, nearly all of them reproduced from the *El Gabilan*. That may sound like a lot of pictures, but even one recent yearbook alone, for instance the 2023 *El Gabilan*, contained well over 1,000 images (not counting the 2,651 individual portraits of each student, faculty, and staff member). Part of my task was to choose which photos would best illustrate patterns and general themes. This meant constantly deciding when it made sense to include "extraordinary images" versus "mundane, routine images" from the yearbooks.[10] Most of the images I chose were mundane, routine images that illustrate patterns. But choosing which photos to reproduce also involved the simultaneous challenge of interpreting the meanings of these pictures and the ways in which captions can shape a reader's interpretation of the meaning of an image. For instance, I was attuned to how the images of girls playing sports in the 1950s and 1960s yearbooks, taken together with insulting captions, enforced a "male gaze," a tendency to frame girls' athletic endeavors as ludicrous, the only sensible conclusion from which was that girls were best suited to cheer from the sidelines in support of boys' sporting efforts.[11] But I also sought to read against the grain, to understand photos of girl athletes and women coaches—even during the worst years for girls' sports—as meaningful forms of resistance against institutionalized sexism, as ways that girls and women were challenging the limits placed on them, and projecting the possibility of a very different future. Put in more philosophical terms, the routine yearbook photos of the 1950s and 1960s tended to freeze in time the image of girls as disempowered objects, but a probing reading of these photos (against the backdrop of an understanding of what had happened in previous decades, and what unfolded in subsequent decades) can also reveal girls as active subjects pressing up against constraints, making history.[12]

Interpreting photos from the past can be a slippery process. In *Ways of Seeing*, John Berger cautions against simplistic interpretations of an image that has been "detached from the place and time in which it first made its appearance."[13] In her classic book *On Photography*, Susan Sontag asserted that "Photographs are perhaps the most mysterious of all the objects that make up, and thicken, the environment we recognize as modern. Photographs really are experience captured . . . To take a photograph is to participate in another person's (or thing's) mortality, vulnerability, mutability. Precisely by slicing out this moment and freezing it, all photographs testify to time's relentless melt . . . To photograph is to confer importance."[14] Yearbook pictures are of a particular genre of photo, but they certainly do "testify to time's relentless melt," and their very presence tends to "confer importance" on their subject.

Photographs, however, do not reveal a fully realized "truth" from the past. As I tackled the challenge of interpreting photos, I leaned on ideas I gleaned from scholars like John Ibson, whose analyses of everyday photos from the late nineteenth through the mid-twentieth century yielded amazing insights about men and intimacy.[15] And following ideas from researchers who have studied school rituals, I treat yearbook photos as "visual traces" from the past, partial views of "rituals of the habitual, coming of age ceremonies, patriotic rituals and ceremonies, and degradation rituals and ceremonies."[16] As I looked at these images—some quite old, some more recent—I wondered, "What is the relationship between the image and its audience in the past? What meaning did it hold? How did the photograph speak to its historical viewer?" I also wondered, "What does it say to us now?"[17]

I tried consistently to ask these interpretative questions, sensitized by my years of work in the scholarly fields of gender studies and sport studies. But I make no definitive claim that my interpretations are always the most accurate or correct ones. Even an interpretation of a photo caption must be conducted with some humility. On this topic, Susan Sontag warns that "A caption is only one interpretation, necessarily a limiting one, of the photograph to which it is attached. And the caption-glove slips on and off so easily. It cannot prevent any argument or moral plea which a photograph . . . is intended to support from being undermined by the plurality of meanings that every photograph carries." Sontag concludes, "A photograph is not only an image (as a painting is an image), an interpretation of the real; it is also a trace, something stenciled off the real, like a footprint or a death mask."[18] I wonder about Berger's or Sontag's twentieth-century reflections on the meanings of photographs, in light of the ways that twenty-first-century technologies—cell phones, social media, and selfies—have shifted the meanings of pictures for younger generations. Do photos in yearbooks carry the same meanings? Are they as important to young people as perhaps they were in the past? What will they mean in the future to today's young people?

Yearbooks as Personal Memory

Yearbooks can also be a rich source of personal memory. Many of the books I analyzed had belonged to someone. The 1967–70 ones from my own high school years were full of signatures and messages from my classmates. Most of my copies from 1947 to 1966 had belonged to my father; nothing was written in any of them, except in some cases his name jotted on the inside cover. A few belonged to friends who passed on their books to me: The 1937 and 1938 books belonged to dear friends of my parents, Margaret and Jack Sterling. My friend Debbie Halfpenny gave me her 1972 book. The books I bought online had belonged to people I did not know. I assume some of these books were put up for sale after the deaths of their owners. Some of them were sparsely autographed with mundane inscriptions; some included humorously scribbled remembrances, well-wishes, and inside jokes. "Yearbook inscriptions," the historian Susan Cahn noted, "offer a rare window into informal student culture and ongoing student relationships."[19] There was no way for me to do any systematic comparisons over time, but the individual books I acquired anecdotally suggest that student inscriptions in the yearbooks were more formal in the early decades and became less formal and humorous in the 1950s and 1960s. By the late 1970s and beyond, there were more inscriptions about partying, drinking, drugs, and sex. I was amazed (and a bit envious?) to read in an early-1980s book owned by a boy who was a standout football player, messages written by several girls, each expressing her sexual desire for this boy, including alongside her phone number a description of what she would love to do with him during the summer ahead.

A few yearbooks I acquired were used by the owner as a kind of living document. Jack Sterling had glued the cards for his and his wife Margaret's 1963 twenty-five-year class reunion on page 2 of his 1938 yearbook. The 1936 *El Gabilan* I purchased online belonged to Nettie Wiechring, who had used the book for a lifetime of keeping track and taking stock of her classmates. Wiechring was an editor of *El Gabilan* that year and succeeded in getting nearly every classmate to sign their senior photo. Then, over the years in her neat, tiny script, Wiechring noted whom someone had married, what job they did, and "dec" for deceased. Next to the photo of classmate Richard Clark, custodian of trophies, she jotted, "Killed in WWII." Wiechring also enclosed in the yearbook her diploma, neatly pressed into its original envelope.

That these yearbooks are also salient parts of my personal memory was a powerful motivating factor for me, and this connection was an omnipresent reality all along the way. I am far from a "detached reader" of these books. As I noted in the introduction, Salinas High School is and always has been in my blood. It has been many decades since I resided in Salinas, but the high school remains a profoundly salient place for me: the hallways and classrooms, the grassy inner court, the sports fields, and especially the lovely old building on Main Street with its clock tower and chimes. Seeing photos and reading about these places in the yearbooks triggers memories in me, and a deep sense of nostalgia that colors the whole project. Nostalgia, especially of the sort that is sold to us by corporate salespeople or politicians who hope to convince us that a purchase or a vote will return us to a better, simpler time, can dangerously fog up the lens through which we seek to understand our past and our present. In writing *The High School* I sought not to sidestep nostalgia (probably impossible to do anyway), but to consciously deploy a critical nostalgia to sharpen, rather than obscure, my understanding of the past.[20]

I used my own memories sparingly in writing this book, and my decisions to do so were influenced by what I came to think of as my own varied engagements with Salinas High School over time. I had no direct engagement with the high school for the period of 1905 through 1946, a time well before my birth and before the arrival of my family in Salinas. A salient touchpoint in reading the books of this era, for me, concerned John Steinbeck, because I grew up reading his short stories and novels, and to this day I admire his writings. I have a mostly indirect personal engagement with the yearbooks between 1947 and 1959, as these are the early years of my father's arrival as a teacher and coach at the high school. I was born in 1952, so most of what is familiar to me in these books is based on secondhand memories, stories, or names of people I heard repeated during my childhood.

The period of 1960 to 1966, when I was in elementary school and junior high, is an especially important period of my engagements with Salinas High and the ways that these experiences shaped me. During those years I served as the towel boy for my dad's varsity basketball team, and this included sitting on the bench with the team during games and traveling on buses with them to away games. I felt like the luckiest boy in town. I so admired the boys on my dad's teams and idolized the stars like Rusty

Critchfield. It was during this time that a broadly circulating cultural ideal was cemented into me: Boys who play sports—especially the stars—are the most admired and important kids on campus; they sit atop the status heap. I could see this with my own eyes: hundreds of students and fans applauded these boys at games. The cheerleaders (who, like my sister Terry in 1965, stood atop their own separately gendered status hierarchy) rooted the boys on from the sidelines, and the *Salinas Californian* newspaper celebrated their triumphs. It is hard to overstate the power of this lesson in shaping my preadolescent views about sports and gender at the time. Much of my research and writing as a sociologist, including this book, has aimed to better understand the sources and implications of these beliefs, including the ways that they have changed or have persisted over time.

The period of 1966–70 is salient for me in other ways. The yearbooks from these years trigger direct, personal memories of my own time in high school. Many of the kids depicted in my senior class had been my classmates since grade school, a few even since kindergarten. Reading these books, including the inscriptions from friends and classmates, was an emotionally ambivalent experience. Examining the 1970 *El Gabilan* made me think more about my social position then—as a student, as an athlete, as the son of my coach, as a boy, as a white boy—and how my situated experiences still shape my views and concerns as I read the yearbooks. It is striking to me as I gaze today at my high school classmates' names and faces, and as I read their inscriptions in my yearbook, how much I was tied up in my own imaginings of my status as a basketball player, even though I was not a stellar one. I rarely befriended boys who were not athletes. And even among the jocks, I mostly identified and hung out with white boys. The Black boys on our basketball team mostly hung with each other before and after practices and sat together on bus trips. With the other white boys on the team, I appreciated our Black teammates—especially Sam Singley, who was our most valuable player—but we nevertheless observed an unspoken informal racial divide among our teammates. This saddens me now.

It had also been fully ingrained in me from childhood that cheerleaders were the most desirable and important girls on campus. As a result, I was drawn to girls who were cheerleaders (though this never went beyond a first date, as it turned out, and my longest high school stint with a girlfriend was not with a cheerleader). And here again, there was a racial line. I recalled as I read the 1970 *El Gabilan* that on more than one occasion I had admired a cute Latina who had been in several of my classes over our four years of high school. When she had said hi to me once or twice in the hallways, I quickly flipped the off switch on my attraction to her, and never consciously considered talking to her, much less asking her out. This, too, saddens me.

I share some of these personal details in hopes it might help the reader critically reflect on my own generational standpoint with respect to sports, gender, and race, and how my retrospective views, insights, or blind spots might have shaped how I wrote this book. What I chose to focus on in *The High School*, as well as my interpretations of their meanings, was shaped both by my scholarly foundations in sociology and gender studies, and by my personal background, experiences, and values. I hope readers will find my interpretations compelling. But I know too that each reader will also sift the stories and images in *The High School* through their own memories, interpreting meanings and drawing conclusions in light of their own beliefs and values.

Acknowledgments

I HAVE WORKED ON THIS BOOK for such a long time that it is hard to be confident that I will remember to credit every person who helped and encouraged me along the way. So, first I want to issue a blanket thank-you to the many friends, colleagues, students, and family members who have listened to me talk—seemingly, perhaps endlessly—about "the yearbooks project" for so many years. Thank you all for your patience, encouragement, interest, and even sometimes enthusiasm.

I have completed a good handful of books with Rutgers University Press over the years, and that's due in large part to the pleasure of working with a great editor, Peter Mickulas. I am proud to have *The High School* included in the Rutgers series Critical Issues in Sport and Society, which I coedit with Douglas Hartmann and Jeffrey Montez de Oca. Thank you, Peter, Doug, and Jeff for your support with this project, and especially for your continuing friendship. I am also grateful to Christina Frenzel, who created the companion website for this book: https://www.thehighschoolbook.com/.

Though I retired in the spring of 2023, much of the work for this book was conducted while I was a professor at the University of Southern California. Many thanks to my colleagues and students in the department of sociology and in the gender and sexuality studies department for your years of inspiration and support for my teaching and research. Thanks also to USC Dornsife for financial assistance for the production of this book. Perhaps a quarter of my one hundred personal copies of Salinas High School's *El Gabilan* yearbooks came from my late father Russell Messner's stash, four were my own books, and many others were purchased online. But a few individuals over the years helped me to acquire an *El Gabilan* here and there along the way: many thanks to Karen Campbell, Denise Connolly, Mark Dover, Debbie Halfpenny, Melinda Messner-Rios, Joe Mitchell, Samantha Rios, Willy Rios, and Jack Sterling.

This book is in some ways a love letter to my alma mater, Salinas High School, and I could not have done it without the assistance and support from the current staff, faculty, and administration at the school. Thanks to Elizabeth Duethman, who was the school's principal during the earlier stages of writing, and to Hugo Mariscal, the current SHS principal, for their encouragement and support. Thanks also to Salinas High's Victoria Gonzales, Art Hunsdorfer, Jose Julio Garcia, and the students in Garcia's 2023–24 SHS yearbooks class with whom I spent a thought-provoking class period. Mark Dover, always up to his eyeballs with his work as SHS director of student activities, was never too busy to respond to my queries and to provide help. Mark was central in organizing what turned out to be an invaluable research visit to Salinas High in 2023. Thanks also to Lisa Josephs, archivist at the National Steinbeck Center, for her help during that same research visit.

There are many visuals in *The High School*, the quality of which is due to expert help from three people. The "sports spirit complex" graphic (Figure 3.31) was creatively designed by USC student Avery Redfern. This book includes 266 photographs, nearly all of them reproduced from *El Gabilan* yearbooks. It was a challenge to get up to speed on how to photograph and prepare the photos for my book. Michael Tyler provided expert technical advice and assistance on the front end, teaching me how to grab high-resolution photos from yearbook pages. And Blue Trimarchi at Art Works Fine Arts Publishing in Los Angeles did the final preparation of each of the photos in this book, including magically erasing bends and creases in photos that resulted from my inexpert photography. It's a blessing to have friends like Michael and Blue, who are both generous and technically talented.

This book is mostly an analysis of the text and photos in over a century of yearbooks, but I conducted a handful of interviews that helped me to deepen some of the stories I sought to tell. Many thanks to Gary Affonso, Jo Ann Curtis, Martha Getris, Nancy Getris, Art Hunsdorfer, Jennifer Rios, and Jon Scattini for their time and their trust in sharing their stories with me. My historical and sociological analysis of the yearbooks was also enriched by works by many scholars. Some helpful readings were recommended to me by Rachel Allison, Mario Garcia, Alice Echols, Kirsten Hextrum, Lon Kurashige, Nicole LaVoi, Michela Musto, Ann Owens, Bill Tierney, and Patricia Vertinsky. Several colleagues generously read drafts of one or more chapters along the way, including Cheryl Cooky, Alice Echols, Kirsten Hextrum, Pierrette Hondagneu-Sotelo, Lenn Kimura, Jeffrey Montez de Oca, Carol McKibben, CJ Pascoe, David Rubenstein, Christine Williams, and the anonymous reviewers for Rutgers University

Press. Their comments and suggestions improved the book in countless ways. But of course, any errors or shortcomings in the book are my responsibility.

The High School is dedicated to the memory of the four deceased members of my family of origin—my parents Anita Messner-Voth and Russell Messner, and my sisters Terry Messner and Melinda Messner-Rios, each of whom had their own rich connections with Salinas High School. My guess is that one or more of them might have found it odd that I spent years poring over old yearbooks, but I have no doubt they would be happy and proud to see the result. I know many people in Salinas and elsewhere have fond memories of Anita, Russ, Terry, and Melinda, and I hope that this book will extend and enhance those memories.

I miss my mom, dad, and sisters every day. But fortunately for me, I have a wonderful family that keeps me alive, loved, and connected. I am grateful for the living links with my late sisters, provided by Willy Rios (even though he did go to Palma High School), Jennifer Rios, Samantha Rios, Adam Affonso, and Eric Affonso. My sons, Miles Hondagneu-Messner and Sasha Hondagneu-Messner, never lived in Salinas, but they understand and are a valued part of our family's loving intergenerational ties. Nor did Pierrette Hondagneu-Sotelo ever live in Salinas—and anybody who knows her understands that she mostly has had to tolerate my love of sports, not to mention the uncountable number of hours she has witnessed "an old man with his head buried in musty high school yearbooks." But for over forty years Pierrette has been my brilliant colleague, my unwavering companion, and the relational glue of our family. I sometimes glance in my own rearview mirror to ponder my experience over half a century ago as a mediocre high school point guard who fell well short of his dreams of athletic greatness. And I nevertheless realize that due in large part to Pierrette, life feels like a nothing-but-net score from the top of the key.

Notes

Introduction

1. I borrow the "fair and foul" term from an influential book by the sport sociologist Stan Eitzen (1999), who probed the multiple ways that our current social organization of sports delivers fun, pleasure, social belonging, and healthy exercise, along with crass commercialism, violence, injury, and divisiveness.
2. Sport studies scholar Daniel A. Nathan (2013) edited a thoughtful collection of essays that probe sport's role in "sharing and belonging," noting that "sport does not *just* bring us together *e pluribus unum*-like. Rather, the history of sports is also one of exclusion, of segregation, that has forced some people—African Americans and women, most obviously, but many others too—to play apart."
3. Teresa was elected by the readers of the local paper, *The Salinas Californian*. He is also in the Salinas Valley Sports Hall of Fame. "Inductees," Salinas Valley Sports Hall of Fame, accessed 2023, https://www.salinasvalleysportshalloffame.com/inductees.
4. Readers will meet world-class quarter-miler Eddie King in chapter 3.
5. The popular understanding that playing sports is good for girls is supported by a wealth of empirical research. See, for instance, Miller et al., 1999; Miller et al., 2005; and Sabo and Veliz, 2008.
6. Steinbeck, 1952, 3.
7. As I will note in chapter 1, a single volume of the *El Gabilan* survives from 1896, but I have found no others until 1903, the year the school started publishing the books regularly.
8. McKibben, 2022, 21.

9. There are varying accounts that date the origins of Salinas High School, and I suppose the varying dates depend on how one defines the date when the school and its building(s) were actually referred to as a high school. The 1896 *El Gabilan* includes a short history of the school and the city, detailing the following origin story: "The school was first opened in 1869 in a room rented for the purpose on Main Street . . . with Miss Harvey, no Mrs. Nathan Clark, as teacher. In 1870, a two-room building, now a part of the Lincoln Grammar School, was erected . . . In 1874 a bill for school and fire bonds was voted, raising $10,000 for school purposes and $5000 for the fire department. During this year and with this money the West End School and the engine house were built." The first school board was elected in 1875. 1896 *El Gabilan*, 5.
10. City demographics are from McKibben, 2022, 31, 73.
11. Many public buildings constructed in California in the 1890s and early 1900s, like Salinas High School, were built in the Spanish colonial revival style. Drawing from the work of Carey McWilliams, American literature scholar Susan Gillman argues that in California, Spanish colonial revival architecture, language, and stories helped to create a cultural "fantasy heritage," a "whitewashed colonial history that bypassed Mexico, with its racial heritage, in favor of Spain." And drawing from historian William Deverall, Gillman elaborates this point: "the Mexican history of the US that extended back before the founding of the missions and forward beyond the Mexican-American War was Americanized, sanitized for domestic consumption, by circulating through Spain. What was forgotten, or whitewashed, in the process was the racial violence of both the past and the present, against both Mexicans and Indians." Gillman, 2022, 61, 87. See Deverell, 2004, and McWilliams, (1948) 1968.
12. Salinas High School, 2022–2023.
13. The 2023 data from the city's other four high schools—Alisal, Everett Alvarez, North Salinas, and Rancho San Juan—indicate somewhat higher percentages of English learners and students qualifying for free and reduced-price meals, and somewhat lower graduation rates, lower rates of meeting CSU and UC course requirements, and lower average ACT scores than those of Salinas High School. Sourced from Education Data Partnership, accessed 2024, https://www.ed-data.org/school/Monterey/Salinas-Union-High/Salinas-High.
14. United States Census Bureau, "QuickFacts: Salinas city, California," 2023, accessed 2023, https://www.census.gov/quickfacts/salinascitycalifornia.
15. Zinn, 1995.
16. As quoted in Labaree, 1988, 13.
17. Dewey, 1915, 313–314. Dewey (1916, 1944) further elaborated on the need for public education as a counterforce against industrial capitalism's production of extreme wealth and income inequalities.
18. Bowles and Gintis, 1976, 8, 102.
19. Domina, Penner, and Penner, 2017
20. Even "good schools" operating with the best of intentions, researchers Lewis and Diamond (2015) have found, tend to informally deploy disciplinary practices and academic tracking that reproduce racial inequalities.
21. In this book I strive to create an intersectional analysis—that is, an understanding of how gender, race, and class are always present and always intertwined. Historical change and continuity in race and gender relations are far easier to "see" in high school yearbooks than is social class. This is partly due to the ubiquitous American beliefs in democracy and meritocracy, which together often render the nation's vast economic inequalities invisible.

I have addressed the obscurity of social class in school yearbooks by drawing on social and historical analyses that illuminate national and local political economy (economic booms and busts, war, labor strife, immigration, taxation policies, etc.).

22. McKibben, 247–248.
23. A navy pilot, Alvarez was shot down over Vietnam in 1964 and was held as a prisoner of war until early 1973.
24. McKibben, 250.
25. The ruling pigs in Orwell's (1945) novella declared, "All animals are equal, but some animals are more equal than others."
26. Indigenous peoples' populations and cultures were decimated by settler colonialism. But they continued to survive, resist, and today are reasserting their independence and traditions in many ways. See Estes, 2019.
27. The historian Peter Filene (1975) and sociologist Michael Kimmel (1987) described this historical moment as a period of "crisis of masculinity," especially for middle-class men. For a deeper historical analysis, see Bederman, 1996.
28. Miller, 1949; Steinbeck, 1961. I wrote about this topic in a short essay (Messner, 1994).
29. Kimmel, 1987.
30. Ibson, 2002, 45.
31. Robert Baden-Powell created the Boy Scouts in 1899 as a way to create men who would administer the British Empire, and thus Scouting was infused with a heavy dose of militarist masculinity. This was also true in the United States, but as historian Jeffrey Hantover (1978) discovered, the first wave of early twentieth-century Boy Scout leaders were mostly middle-class urban men who were most concerned with fears of the feminization of their sons and with the need to return to an imagined natural state of manhood.
32. Lefkowitz-Horowitz, 1986.
33. Messner, 1992.
34. Duberman, 1990; Hogan and Tygiel, 2006; Jacobs, 2023; Tygiel, 2008. There is a robust literature on the sociology and history of race and sport in the United States; much of the early work focuses almost entirely on men, but more recent work illuminates women's experiences. See, for instance, Carrington, 2010; Cooper, 2021; Edwards, (1968) 2018; Hartmann, 2004; King, 2001; Lansbury, 2014; Smith, 2007.
35. Cahn, 1994; Smith-Rosenberg 1986; Twin, 1979.
36. Thorne, 1993.
37. Thanks to Michela Musto for the picture window insight.
38. Tillie Olsen illuminated historical silences in literature, noting how the creative voices of women—especially married women and mothers—had been muted: "These are not *natural* silences," Olsen insisted. "The silences I speak of are unnatural" (1978, 6). She observed that where women's voices have "remained mute, or have never attained full capacity, it is because of circumstances, inner or outer, which oppose the needs of creation" (17).
39. Google searches for "movies about high school" and "popular music about high school" yielded lists that were even longer than I had imagined, including Rotten Tomatoes' "70 Best High School Movies of All Time" (accessed 2022, https://editorial.rottentomatoes.com/guide/best-high-school-movies/) and Music Industry How To's "45 Top Songs about School Life—For Those Days That'll Always Be in Your Memory" (December 27, 2023, https://www.musicindustryhowto.com/songs-about-school-life/).
40. High school themes have permeated popular film and music for decades; see Bulman, 2015. In her book about her own New Jersey high school class of 1958, anthropologist Sherry

Ortner asserts that "It is hard to overstate the significance of high school for the American cultural imagination" (2003, 95).

41. For a fascinating summary and analysis of national polls regarding peoples' perceptions of "the good old days" over the past hundred years, see Bowman and Goldstein, 2023.
42. This kind of nostalgia, especially for the imagined family, neighborhood, and community of the 1950s as a "simpler and happier" time, has helped to fuel a good deal of conservative backlash against changes brought about by feminism and LGBTQ+ advocacy in recent decades. The classic statement on the sources and dangers of this sort of nostalgia is Coontz, 2016.
43. Tanner, 2021, 34. During the American Civil War, the term "nostalgia" as a debilitating yearning for home was actually used to describe the emotional pain and psychological withdrawal that was common among soldiers. Later, this normal response to the traumas of war would be called "shell shock" in World War I and "battle fatigue" in World War II. Only at the end of the American war in Vietnam did the symptoms of internalized war trauma receive a medical designation as post-traumatic stress disorder (PTSD). See also Alpers, 2024.

Chapter 1 "All Prejudices Have Been Swept Away"

1. Benson, 1990, 24.
2. 1919 *El Gabilan*, 19.
3. Woolf, 1929.
4. As reported in the 1916 *El Gabilan's* history of Salinas High School, 41.
5. Unfortunately, the school does not have all four issues in each volume for the first several years. In 1902–3, I was only able to access one issue, and the school had only three of four issues for 1903–4, 1904–5, 1908–9, and 1909–10. In 1905–6, only three issues were published, as the 1906 earthquake made it impossible to complete and publish the final spring issue.
6. I can't be certain of this. To be sure, the 1904 spring issue does not have a photo of that year's graduating class, but since the school does not have a copy of spring issue of the 1903 *El Gabilan*, it's possible a senior class photo was in that issue.
7. "Throughout California and the western United States," historian Carol Lynn McKibben observed, "in almost every municipality and settlement, whites viciously attacked Chinese people and blamed them for everything from epidemics that were common in the nineteenth century (including bubonic plague, smallpox, influenza, and cholera) to economic downturns" (2022, 55).
8. "The Salinas Union District includes all territory in the Salinas Valley from Chualar on the south to Castroville on the north." 1916 *El Gabilan*, 29.
9. The 1916 yearbook noted that Cooper had taken first place in the pole vault and third place in the high jump in that year's CCAL meet. The 1919 *El Gabilan* listed Ulysses Cooper on its "In Memoriam" list. I wondered if he had been killed in the war, but he was not listed among the six Salinas High alums who died in combat. It is possible that Cooper was one of the many who succumbed to the worldwide flu pandemic that in 1918–19 killed 675,000 people in the United States, and between 50 million and 100 million in the world. Barry, 2005, 396–397.
10. Duncan and Murnane, 2011.
11. Lesko, 2012, 53.

12. Growing commercial forces were also key in creating teens as a cultural group. See Fass, 1977, and Lesko, 2012.
13. Salinas census numbers reported in McKibben, 2022, 85, 110.
14. McKibben (2022) states that the official 1920 count of 350 Asians in Salinas was "clearly underreported by early census takers" (95–96).
15. McKibben notes that between 1885 and 1910 roughly thirty thousand Japanese workers came to California. "As a result of their collective successes in agricultural production and marketing, Japanese immigrants and Japanese Americans were also deeply resented by Californians" (2002, 93–94).
16. Bederman, 1996, 10–11, 85–86.
17. Hall, 1905; Hall, 1914.
18. Bederman, 1996, 90, 97.
19. The early twentieth-century emphasis on muscular education for white middle-class boys paralleled similar efforts by the YMCA and the Boy Scouts of America, as well as Protestant religious sproutings of "Muscular Christianity." Lesko 2012, 47–48.
20. That stand-alone 1896 *El Gabilan* lauded the school's victorious football team, and it also applauded the baseball team's two wins over Watsonville High.
21. 1904 *El Gabilan* (March), 11.
22. 1904 *El Gabilan* (March), 12.
23. 1904 *El Gabilan* (June), 8.
24. 1905 *El Gabilan* (May), 16.
25. 1907 *El Gabilan*, 53.
26. 1909 *El Gabilan*, 16.
27. 1909 *El Gabilan*, 33.
28. For a detailed account of Cal and Stanford's shift from football to rugby and back, see Park, 1984.
29. 1911 *El Gabilan*, 20.
30. In his history of college football, sociologist Jeffrey Montez de Oca notes that there were "two crisis periods" in early days of the sport, the first from 1893 to 1897 and the second from 1905 to 1911. The latter crisis led to the establishment of the NCAA, and "a slew of reforms minimized the game's most obvious dangers, but as John Watterson argues, they may also have made the game more deadly given a surge of deaths in 1909" (2013, 9); see also Watterson, 2000.
31. 1918 *El Gabilan*, 16.
32. 1905 *El Gabilan* (September), 9, 12.
33. 1903 *El Gabilan*, 13.
34. DuBois, 1998; Stansell, 2011.
35. Twin, 1979.
36. Cahn, 1994; Hargreaves, 1994; Lenskyj, 1986.
37. 1910 *El Gabilan* (December), 15.
38. 1911 *El Gabilan* (March), 18.
39. 1915 *El Gabilan*, 42, 48.
40. The sources and consequences of asymmetrical gender marking in sports will be discussed more in later chapters. For an introduction to this topic, see Messner, Duncan, and Jensen, 1993.
41. 1918 *El Gabilan*, 72–73.

42. 1920 *El Gabilan*, 67, 76.
43. 1921 *El Gabilan*, 25.
44. 1921 *El Gabilan*, 47.
45. 1922 *El Gabilan*, 68.
46. 1923 *El Gabilan*, 70.
47. 1923 *El Gabilan*, 72.
48. 1923 *El Gabilan*, 15, 68.
49. 1924 *El Gabilan*, 60, 65.
50. 1925 *El Gabilan*, 74.
51. 1921 *El Gabilan*, 36.
52. 1921 *El Gabilan*, 23–24.
53. 1918 *El Gabilan*, 6.
54. 1918 *El Gabilan*, 35–36.
55. 1918 *El Gabilan*, 40–41.
56. Benson 1990, 23–24.
57. The historian Peter Filene (1975) observed that at the outset of the United States joining World War I many young men were enthused about the idea that participating in a war would offer them an opportunity to prove their manhood. This was likely a more profound feeling for middle- and upper-class college men, who faced what they feared was a feminizing world that was erasing men's opportunities to prove themselves.
58. 1919 *El Gabilan*, 53–54.
59. 1920 *El Gabilan*, 22–23.
60. 1919 *El Gabilan*, 18.
61. Verbrugge, 2012, 16.
62. Mrozek, 1983, 20.
63. Crosset, 1990, 53. This early twentieth-century belief was consistent with the rise of Freudian ideas at the time. Freud believed that individuals had a limited amount of libidinous energy, and that left to nature individuals would always choose to spend this energy in pursuit of the "pleasure principle." For civilization to be possible, society had to teach children to repress their pursuit of pleasure, diverting their energies toward the "reality principle." Advocates of sport saw this activity as a way to sublimate or divert boys' and men's libidinous energies toward socially acceptable goals. Freud summarized these ideas in one of his last books, *Civilization and its discontents*, first published in 1930. This idea lived well into the middle of the twentieth century. My basketball coach at Hartnell College in 1970–71 would implore the team at a pre-weekend practice to "stay away from the split-tails" (his term for women) and save ourselves for the upcoming game by avoiding "dissipation" of our energies through sex.
64. Pruter, 2013, 61.
65. Larned, 1909, as quoted in Pruter, 2013, 58.
66. Curtis, 1904, as quoted in Pruter, 2013, 58.
67. 1923 *El Gabilan*, 61–62.
68. 1907 *El Gabilan* (May), 30.
69. 1908 *El Gabilan* (March), 20.
70. 1908 *El Gabilan* (May), 35.
71. 1909 *El Gabilan* (December), 18.
72. 1910 *El Gabilan* (June), 43.
73. 1911 *El Gabilan* (June), 38.

74. 1911 *El Gabilan* (October), 16.
75. 1912 *El Gabilan* (March), 24.
76. 1917 *El Gabilan*, 29, 30.
77. 1917 *El Gabilan*, p. 31.
78. 1923 *El Gabilan*, p. 77.
79. Nathan, 2013.
80. 1906 *El Gabilan* (Fall), 20.
81. 1921 *El Gabilan*, 11.
82. 1919 *El Gabilan*, 73.

Chapter 2 Football Heroes and Girls with "Pep"

1. 1946 *El Gabilan*, 8.
2. 1935 *El Gabilan*, 36.
3. 1935 *El Gabilan*, 44.
4. 1940 *El Gabilan*, 104.
5. McKibben, 2022, 75.
6. McKibben (2022, 304) mentions in passing a Salinas City Council member from 1947 to 1951 named Ruth Wing. I assume this was the same Ruth Wing, who a year after retiring from her teaching job at the high school continued her public service with the city.
7. 1928 *El Gabilan*, 56.
8. In the late 1980s and early 1990s, as part of a study of gender in televised sports, my colleagues and I pointed to commentators' tendency to linguistically grant male athletes adult status as "men" while infantizing women athletes as "girls," in addition to regularly using the last names of men athletes while calling women athletes by their first names. We replicated this study every five years for three decades and found that the linguistic infantilization of women athletes in televised sports had nearly disappeared by the early 2000s, though other forms of trivialization and marginalization continued. Messner, Duncan, and, Jensen 1993.
9. Others who recorded "You Gotta Be a Football Hero" included Dick Robertson and His Orchestra (1933), Harry Reser and His Eskimos (1933), Thelma Watson and Her All-Girl Orchestra (sometime in the 1930s), and The Crew Cuts (in the 1950s). The song even appeared in 1970s TV shows *The Lawrence Welk Show* and *Petticoat Junction*. "You Gotta Be a Football Hero," Fleischer AllStars, accessed 2023, https://www.fleischerallstars.com/you-gotta-be-a-football-hero.html.
10. The 1928 *El Gabilan* spelled the trophy donor's name as "Scrachrd," and the 1929 book spelled it as "Scracherd." I use the latter spelling here, under the assumption that the 1928 spelling was a typo.
11. 1929 *El Gabilan*, 87.
12. The 1930 *El Gabilan* noted on page 84 that "Ray Duddy, of the California Theatre, donated a cup on which the winner of the punting champion each year is to have his name engraved."
13. 1931 *El Gabilan*, 91–92.
14. 1933 *El Gabilan*, 62.
15. Wikipedia, s.v. "Pop Warner," last modified April 2, 2024, 22:42, https://en.wikipedia.org/wiki/Pop_Warner.
16. 1936, *El Gabilan*, 78.

17. The building of the SHS football stadium echoed what had been happening across the nation in colleges and universities. The 1920s, the historian Paula S. Fass noted, "saw a veritable orgy of stadium-building [that] stand as symbols of a football mania never equaled in modern college history" (1977, 238).
18. 1931, *El Gabilan*, 89.
19. Adams and Bettis, 2003, 4.
20. "The role of competitive interscholastic sports for girls," according to historian Robert Pruter, "was one of the most contentious societal issues of the 1920s" (2013, 244).
21. Twin, 1979.
22. Pruter, 2013, 245.
23. Verbrugge, 2012, 33.
24. Verbrugge, 2012, 25.
25. 1926, *El Gabilan*, 79.
26. Verbrugge, 2012, 25.
27. Cahn, 1994, 74.
28. 1926 *El Gabilan*, 79.
29. 1927 *El Gabilan*, 79.
30. 1930 *El Gabilan*, 87.
31. 1931 *El Gabilan*, 39.
32. 1934 *El Gabilan*, 52.
33. 1940 *El Gabilan*, 108.
34. Cahn, 1994, 89.
35. 1926, *El Gabilan*, 80.
36. Cahn, 1994, 83, 87.
37. Cahn, 1994, 86.
38. Cahn, 1994, 88. Cahn notes that "student athletes sometimes expressed their dissatisfaction with the curbs administrators placed on competition" (101).
39. 1934 *El Gabilan*, 53.
40. 1935 *El Gabilan*, 41.
41. Theberge, 1989.
42. Vertinsky and McKay, 2003, 52. Vertinsky and McKay add, "Places are made through power relations which construct the rules, define the boundaries and create spaces with certain meanings in which some relationships are facilitated, other discouraged . . . these boundaries are both social and spatial. They mark belonging and exclusion—who belongs to a place and who may be excluded." (5). See also Ross and Bentley, 2003.
43. 1937 *El Gabilan*, 97.
44. Vertinsky, 2015, 542.
45. Cahn, 1994, 81–82.
46. Cahn notes how the containment of girls' sports reinforced trends in the larger culture: It "may have secured women physical educators some degree of respect and autonomy, but it had the additional effect of reinforcing the gendered organization of space in the wider culture. Under prevailing arrangements, bounded space, restricted movement, and a non-physical nature characterized femininity. Indeed, this description fit the reality for many women who were confined by dress styles, domestic duties, and lack of leisure time or access to sport" (1994, 101).
47. Verbrugge, 2012, 61.
48. 1941 *El Gabilan*, 107.

49. 1933 *El Gabilan*, 33.
50. Roughly the first half of the 1934 *El Gabilan* is printed on rough-stock paper that does not reproduce photos clearly. The second half of the book is printed on glossy paper akin to that used in previous and subsequent years, and photos are sharp and clearly reproduced. I do not know if this was a decision made for stylistic reasons, or one dictated by a tightened Depression-era budget.
51. McKibben, 2022, 120.
52. McKibben, 2022, 114.
53. *Salinas Index-Journal*, May 11, 1934, 1, quoted in McKibben, 2022, 150.
54. Quoted in McWilliams, (1939) 1999, 273.
55. McKibben, 2022, 131–132.
56. Steinbeck and Wallsten, 1975, 132.
57. McWilliams, (1939) 1999, 256. McWilliams's description of the 1936 Salinas lettuce packers lockout and strike is worth reading in its entirety (254–259), as is his classic book *Factories in the Field*.
58. John Steinbeck (1936) 1988, 20, 52. Partly as humanitarian social activism and partly as research for his novels, Steinbeck wrote a number of journalistic pieces on migrant agricultural workers in the 1930s. See also Steinbeck, 1936a, 302).
59. McKibben, 2022, 183.
60. McKibben, 2022, 126.
61. Steinbeck and Wallsten, 1975, 158.
62. From the introduction by Charles Wallerberg to Steinbeck, (1936) 1988, xiii.
63. Steinbeck, 1936b.
64. Steinbeck, (1939) 1978, 329.
65. By my count, there were 2 Black students of 320 graduating SUHS seniors in 1942, and 2 of 255 seniors in 1943. Between 1926 and 1946, every other graduating class included zero Black students. The racial numbers I report here are from my own count, based on carefully viewing photos and surnames of senior class members each year. This way of counting racial groups is of course imperfect, especially when compared with official counts based on students' own self-definitions, but these sorts of numbers do not exist from these earlier periods.
66. Poulson, 2021, 7. See also Poulson, McGee, and Wolfe, 2020.
67. In one of the very few exceptions in these years to the practice of all student leaders being white, Dorothy Sakasagawa served as freshman class secretary in 1941.
68. McKibben, 2022, 70.
69. McKibben, 2022, 70.
70. McKibben, 2022, 71.
71. Blanche Chin Ah Tye (2015), a 1937 SUHS graduate, penned a lovely memoir that gives insight into Salinas's Chinese American community during the first half of the twentieth century.
72. McKibben notes that the end of the Spanish-American War in 1898 resulted in the Philippines becoming a U.S. possession and Filipinos/as becoming "'insular subjects' of the United States, with free access to immigration in contrast to other excluded Asian groups." This "created a new stream of Filipino/a immigration to all parts of California" (2022, 93).
73. McKibben 2022, 139.
74. McKibben 2022, 95.
75. Kurashige, 2000. "See also Kurashige, 2002.

76. 1940 *El Gabilan*, 58.
77. Willms, 2017.
78. 1939 *El Gabilan*, 103.
79. 1942 *El Gabilan*, 5
80. 1943 *El Gabilan*, 6.
81. 1943 *El Gabilan*, 79.
82. 1943 *El Gabilan*, 97.
83. These numbers and dates are from Inada, 2000.
84. McWilliams, 1944.
85. McKibben, 2022, 191.
86. This conservative stance by Japanese Americans in Salinas was apparently not unusual. Lon Kurashige notes that in Southern California during the 1930s and early 1940s, "It was common among [Nisei] Japanese Americans to carry on the pro-business ideology of the Issei old guard and to portray labor organizers and other left-leaning activists as anathema to the group's social prestige and respectability" (2000, 1642).
87. McKibben, 2022, 193.
88. The 1983 *El Gabilan* featured a page (49) celebrating the centennial of Salinas Union High School, with two photos that included Gertrude Waterman, who had returned to the school along with some other former teachers, students, and administrators for the celebration.
89. McKibben, 2022, 191.
90. 1943 *El Gabilan*, 59.
91. McKibben 2022, 196.
92. 1946 *El Gabilan*, 117.
93. McKibben, 2012.
94. Feminist sport scholars Margaret Carlisle Duncan and Cynthia Hasbrook (1988) identified what they saw as an "ambivalent" framing of women athletes in sports media, a practice that seemed "respectful" on the surface but undermined women's empowerment with infantilizing language, emphasis on athletes' errors or failures, or descriptions that highlighted women athletes' heterosexual femininity (or perceived lack thereof).
95. 1944 *El Gabilan*, 106–107.

Chapter 3 Pageants of Gender

1. McKibben, 2022, 242.
2. McKibben, 2022, 199.
3. As quoted in McKibben, 2022, 199.
4. As quoted in McKibben, 2022, 199.
5. Steinbeck and Wallsten, 1975, 280.
6. McKibben describes in detail the protracted, complicated, and sometimes conflictual debates about the 1963 annexation of Alisal—debates that brought commercial interests, schools, neighborhood identity, and race into play. McKibben, 2022, see especially Chapter 6.
7. Flores, 2016, 108. Flores notes that the tension between Anglo and Mexican American students grew violent at King City High School at the southern end of the Salinas Valley, when "rival groups" of students fought off campus, resulting in injuries and one death.
8. "Name of school changed by recent action of the board," (Salinas High School) *Flashlight*, Monday, September 8, 1958.

9. Stephanie Coontz's influential book (2016) illustrates the pitfalls—especially for women—built into the glowing nostalgia that typically underlies cultural imagery of "the family" in the past.
10. Much of the postwar expansion of education, infrastructure, and public employment was a continuing legacy of what Gary Gerstle (2022) calls the "New Deal Order," a historic ordering of the political economy resting on a sort of truce between capital and labor and manifested in progressive taxation and expanding public sector spending.
11. 1949 *El Gabilan*, 2.
12. 1951 *El Gabilan*, 4–5.
13. In a 2019 book on U.S. war veterans, I chronicle the experiences of decorated World War II veteran Ernie Sanchez, who returned to the Los Angeles area only to find that the civilian work world was still hostile to dark-skinned Mexican American men like him. Sanchez did benefit from the GI Bill, but there are documented cases of Black veterans being denied these benefits.
14. Milkman, 1987.
15. Madison appeared last in the 1974 *El Gabilan*; Davis and MacKay's final year was 1978.
16. Verbrugge, 2012, p. 181; on postwar homophobia, 186–187.
17. Verbrugge 2012, 186.
18. 1958 *El Gabilan*, 148.
19. 1958 *El Gabilan*, 155.
20. Fletcher, 1984.
21. Cahn, 1994, 180.
22. 1959 *El Gabilan*, 138.
23. Cahn, 1994.
24. 1967 *El Gabilan*, 191.
25. Interview with Jo Ann (Langenhovel) Curtis, May 19, 2023.
26. The ordering of boys' sports in the yearbooks tended to follow the seasonal schedules of the sports, with football, a fall sport, coming first, the winter sport of basketball next, and spring sports like baseball and track and field near the end of the section. Spring sports got short shrift in the books in part because they were not popular spectator sports, but also because the yearbooks needed to be laid out and sent to printers well before the spring sports seasons ended.
27. In 1959, Audrey Boutte was vice president of the Girls' Sweater Society and also head pom pon girl.
28. That 1964 championship team was inducted into the Salinas Valley Sports Hall of Fame in 2024.
29. Montez de Oca, 2005, 149.
30. Montez de Oca, 2013.
31. In the late 1980s and early 1990s scholars began to map out histories of sport and masculinities. See, for instance, Crosset, 1990; Dunning, 1986; Messner, 1992; Whitson, 1990.
32. Ibson, 2007, 81, 71.
33. Ibson, 2019, 161, 163.
34. Sabo and Panepinto, 1990, 124.
35. It is hard to know, in retrospect, exactly what to make of this asymmetry. Clearly, boys wore their Block "S" sweaters and jackets a lot—I know I wore mine almost every day to school between 1967 and 1970—so photos of everyday student life and posed photos of boys in organizations reflected this. But the dearth of shots of girls wearing their white Block "S"

sweaters could mean that they rarely wore them publicly, or it could mean that when they did wear them, nobody took photos of them for the yearbooks.

36. The first year of their appearance in the *El Gabilan*, they were referred to as "pom pom girls," before the yearbooks settled on the designation "pom pon girls" (occasionally with a hyphen, i.e., "pom-pon girls").
37. Davis, 1990.
38. Adams and Bettis note that during World War II, more women moved into cheerleading as men went away to war. "When men returned from the war, they fought to regain their 'rightful' place in the worksite and on the cheerleading squads . . . Women prevailed, and following WWII, cheerleading squads became predominantly female, especially in elementary and secondary schools" (2003, 4).
39. Ortner, 2003, 117.
40. Adams and Bettis 2003, 109.
41. Adams and Bettis 2003, 71.
42. 1949 *El Gabilan*, 111.
43. 1950 *El Gabilan*, 116.
44. The escalation of the only boy in the 1965 Future Teachers club to the position of president anticipates an occupational pattern that sociologist Christine Williams named "the glass escalator." The rare man K–6 teacher in a predominantly female occupation, Williams found, was frequently assumed to be on a track to leadership and was often "escalated" to the principal position. This pattern was also evident for men—especially white men—in other occupations where women predominate, like social work and nursing. Williams, 1992.
45. Ibson, 2002, 9.
46. Ibson, 2002, 50.
47. 1961 *El Gabilan*, 113.
48. I write "the men from the girls" here purposefully. As I noted in chapter 2, football heroism has often elevated boys to adult status, as "men," while sport participation, cheering, or being homecoming queen does not similarly escalate girls symbolically to full adult status. The use of language to "adultify" athletic boys and men while infantilizing girls and women has been a key part of the gender asymmetries in sports media and culture. Messner, Duncan, and Jensen, 1993.
49. 1970 *El Gabilan*, 26.
50. For a foundational discussion of the role of degradation rituals in society, see Garfinkel, 1956. And for an analysis of degradation ceremonies in schools, see Chappell, Chappell, and Margolis, 2011.
51. Thorne, 1993.
52. My father had saved his Neptune Ceremony card he had earned after his first crossing of the equator on a U.S. Navy ship during World War II. I only came to understand what the card referred to when I read John Ibson's description of the Neptune Ceremony as an "intriguing combination of cruelty, eroticism, fellowship, cross-dressing, role reversal, and ritual rebirth" (2002, 90).
53. For an overview of the foundations of Sadie Hawkins day, see Wikipedia, s.v. "Sadie Hawkins Day," last modified June 12, 2024, 03:25, https://en.wikipedia.org/wiki/Sadie_Hawkins_Day.
54. 1966 *El Gabilan*, 96.
55. 1971 *El Gabilan*, 30–31.
56. Davis and Wiener, 2020.

57. McKibben notes that some Salinas residents resented Cesar Chavez for, in their minds, falsely conflating labor justice issues with racial justice issues. "Cesar Chavez hit the city like a sledgehammer in 1970," McKibben writes, "Chavez and other civil rights activists intended to disrupt the racial order that privileged whites at the expense of everyone else. That was the whole point of the movements of the 1970s" (2022, 260).
58. Flores, 2016.
59. Flores, 2016.
60. Strain, 2016.
61. Alice Echols, personal communication, November 7, 2021.
62. For analyses of the political, legal, and cultural foundations and impact of Title IX, see Brake, 2010; and Suggs, 2005.
63. 1972 *El Gabilan*, 192–193.
64. 1973 *El Gabilan*, 205.

Chapter 4 Boom, Bust, and Purple Pride

1. 1975 *El Gabilan*, 155.
2. 1979 *El Gabilan*, 214–215.
3. Although this is obviously anecdotal, it was still striking to me that several of the yearbooks I analyzed from the late 1970s and early 1980s (randomly purchased from eBay) included numerous inscriptions about "partying," getting high, smoking dope, and drinking. I never read any such open discussion of these matters in previous decades.
4. 1982 *El Gabilan*, 140, 196–197.
5. 1982 *El Gabilan*, 52–53.
6. Included in the 1989 *El Gabilan* "Mini-Magazine" insert, 5.
7. 1995 *El Gabilan*, 124.
8. McKibben 2022, 282.
9. 1984 *El Gabilan*, 86–87.
10. 1984 *El Gabilan*, 22.
11. 1984 *El Gabilan*, 135. The 1985 yearbook (118) noted that the elimination of *Flashlight* had opened space for two students to create "*The Advocate*, a renegade newspaper," and the 1986 book noted that the Journalism Club had succeeded in getting the "*Flashlight* back on the printing press" (84).
12. 1985 *El Gabilan*, 13–14.
13. From the 1980s through the first decade of the 2000s, the United States was governed by what Gary Gerstle (2022) calls "the neoliberal order," a dominant ideology inaugurated in the United States by Ronald Reagan and deepened by Democratic leaders like President Bill Clinton. Neoliberalism elevates the ideal of a "free market" that is untethered by government regulations, imposes lower taxes on corporations and the wealthy, and includes a belief that individual volunteerism or civic organizations—what President George H. W. Bush called "a thousand points of light"—can fill the gaps created when public services for the poor and previously generous funding of public schools were slashed.
14. The plant shutdowns in Salinas can be viewed as a microcosm of a national trend of deindustrialization that gained steam in the 1980s—the shuttering of long-standing industries that had formed the backbone of the U.S. economy through the mid-twentieth century. Deindustrialization hit the American Midwest especially hard. Corporate decisions to move

production to nations with low wages (and often with no unions), coupled with automation, eliminated tens of thousands of solid, often unionized, blue-collar jobs in the auto and related industries. In subsequent decades, the middle class was hollowed out, as newly created jobs benefited some highly educated and well-paid professionals while many more low-paid, non-union service sector jobs were created, expanding the ranks of the working poor. William Julius Wilson, 1990.

15. Demographic data on Salinas from McKibben 2022, 303.
16. These are my counts from the annual yearbooks, based on surnames and photos. The proportions of Spanish-surnamed students at the high school in these years is in reality substantially higher than these numbers suggest. Some years (but not all), the yearbooks included a list of "shutter shy" seniors whose individual studio portraits did not appear in the book. This list was always disproportionately made up of Spanish-surnamed students, who likely did not have a studio portrait taken for financial reasons or due to having recently arrived in Salinas. When I include the Spanish-surnamed "shutter shy" students, the proportion of Spanish-surnamed SHS seniors was 20 percent in 1985, 28 percent in 1987, and 49 percent in 1999.
17. My count of senior class photos revealed that from the mid-1970s through the 1990s, each senior class included an average of about a half-dozen Chinese American and somewhat fewer Japanese American students. A sprinkling of students with Vietnamese, South Asian, Arabic, or Pacific Islander surnames appeared in some of these senior classes. The number of African American students remained fairly constant during these years—about five in each senior class, on average, reaching a high of eleven in 1999.
18. 1988 *El Gabilan*, 195.
19. In a personal reflection on the organization that was founded in 1969, scholar Alvaro Huerta wrote that "MEChA, for someone like myself—a Chicano kid from the projects—represented a haven in a white-dominated space" (2019).
20. 1991 *El Gabilan*, 166–167.
21. Interview with Jennifer Rios, December 6, 2023.
22. 1993 *El Gabilan*, 238.
23. 1991 *El Gabilan*, 166–167. This strategy apparently achieved some success. The 1992 yearbook notes that the current ASB president, Juan Oliverez, had been president of MEChA.
24. McKibben, 2022, 316.
25. McKibben 2022, 321.
26. Fourteen of the eighty-seven inductees of the Salinas Valley Sports Hall of Fame are women, but as of 2022 only one of the twenty inductees from Salinas High School are women. "Inductees," Salinas Valley Sports Hall of Fame, accessed 2024, https://www.salinasvalleysportshalloffame.com/inductees.
27. To be fair, the two-page spread of the boys' track team that year also did not include captions under photos, nor were any individual accomplishments of the boys mentioned. But given the conventions of that era, it seems likely that a boy track and field athlete who amassed records and championships similar to Susan Springer's would have received some ink in the book.
28. Feminist sport scholar Jan Felshin introduced the concept of the female apologetic in 1974. In 1978, Emily Wughalter succinctly defined the basis of the concept: "The juxtaposition of social expectations of feminine behavior and the stereotyped masculine attributes of most sport participation generally cause conflict for the female athlete." Since then, many scholars have explored how or under what conditions female athletes might adhere to or

resist a female apologetic. Blinde and Taub, 1992; Broad, 2001; Davis-Delano, Pollock, and Vose, 2009; Musto and McGann, 2016.

29. Passed by Congress in 1972, Title IX was patterned after the language of Title VII of the Civil Rights Act of 1964, which prohibited discrimination of students on the basis of race, color, or national origin. Title IX reads, "No person in the United States shall, on the basis on sex, be excluded from participation in, be denied the benefits of, or be subjected to discrimination under any educational program or activity receiving federal financial assistance."
30. National participation numbers are from the NFHS survey of high school sports (2023), conducted annually from 1972 to the present.
31. A 2001 report from the National Women's Law Center revealed that vast gender inequities in school sports persisted: "We receive many calls from disgruntled parents, athletes, and coaches complaining of gender inequality in their school athletics program. Some of the more common problems raised are the failure to offer enough girls' sports; the scheduling of girls' sports in the 'off-season,' causing the girls to miss out on scholarship and recruiting opportunities; the authorization of paid coaching positions for boys' teams and volunteer coaching positions for girls' teams; and the provision of generally inferior equipment and facilities."
32. In 1998, in what some commentators called "the most important litigation to date on sex discrimination in intercollegiate athletics," a federal judge ruled against Brown University in clarifying the legal definition of "substantial proportionality." The ruling states that the proportion of female athletes at an institution should be within 3.5 percentage points of the proportion of female undergraduates. Jim Naughton, "Judge Approves Settlement of Brown U.'s Title IX Case," *Chronicle of Higher Education*, July 3, 1998. In 2000, the U.S. Department of Education's Office of Civil Rights (OCR) announced what would become known as "the One Percent Rule"—a policy that is hailed as a tremendously important clarification of Title IX. In 1997, the National Women's Law Center filed a Title IX complaint with the OCR, claiming that twenty-five universities failed to give female athletes their share of scholarship money. The outcome—the One Percent Rule—stipulates that a gap no wider than one percentage point should exist between the percentage of scholarship athletes of one sex and the percentage of total scholarship aid awarded to that sex. The National Women's Law Center hailed this new ruling as a great victory for sex equity in sports. "Education Dept. Resolves Last of 25 Bias Complaints Filed by Women's Group," *Chronicle of Higher Education*, January 21, 2000.
33. This is from my count of the total 521 boys and girls who appear in sports team photos from the 1990 book. Of course, some students play two or more sports, so this is a count of *athlete positions*, not of athletes.
34. In a study of gender and youth sports, I briefly summarize the history of Little League Baseball's legal struggle to exclude girls, its creation of a separate and different track for girls (Little League Softball), and the implications of those actions for gender relations in a community. Messner, 2009.
35. For strong arguments against separate and different sports for girls and boys, see McDonagh and Pappano, 2008. See also Young, 1980.
36. Ring, 2013.
37. 1985 *El Gabilan*, 66.
38. 1986 *El Gabilan*, 29.
39. For discussions of the legal debates, as well as the ideological battles surrounding Title IX, see Brake, 2010; Messner and Solomon, 2007; and Suggs, 2005.

40. Interview with Nancy Getris via Zoom, January 27, 2023.
41. 1995 *El Gabilan*, 21, 56.
42. 1984 *El Gabilan*, 177.
43. 1995 *El Gabilan*, 197.
44. These numbers are surely not precise, based as they are on my count of girls' photos and surnames in 1990 *El Gabilan* team photos, but I am confident that general point I am making here—that white girls were disproportionately represented in girls' sports teams in the 1970s and 1980s—is accurate.
45. 1998 *El Gabilan*, 112.
46. A simple Google search reveals that Starry Sprenkle did indeed become a scientist, in 2020 becoming Restoration Science Director at Conservation International, focusing on reforestation in Haiti and Costa Rica.
47. 1990 *El Gabilan*, 14.
48. It is difficult, simply from reading the yearbooks, to confidently claim a pattern here, but sport sociologists have long shown how boys from race- and class-marginalized backgrounds often come to view sport participation as a ticket out of poverty, to college, and to the pros. Sport sociologist Harry Edwards (1984) argued that visions of playing pro were, for the vast majority, a mirage that has been sold to them by a system that exploits them. In my first book (Messner, 1992), a study of the lives of men who were former athletes, I profiled men from poor and working-class families, many of them men of color with limited opportunities, who as youths almost single-mindedly pursued sports stardom. I contrasted these with stories of more privileged boys, including a star white middle-class high school athlete who saw sports stardom as "small potatoes" and skipped college sports to focus on becoming a dentist. I have also seen this play out in my college classes over the years, especially with talented African American young men in football and basketball who dream that their college scholarship will be their ticket to the NFL or NBA. By contrast, the African American women basketball players I have known in my classes tend to have a clear-eyed view of their athletic scholarships as tickets to a college education, to professional school, and to a (usually non-sporting) profession.
49. Women's Sports Foundation, 2022. Formed in 1974, the WSF has a long legacy of advocacy research for girls' and women's sports. "Our Research," Women's Sports Foundation, accessed 2023, https://www.womenssportsfoundation.org/what-we-do/wsf-research/
50. 1982 *El Gabilan*, 5.
51. 1995 *El Gabilan*, 210.
52. 1985 *El Gabilan*, 173.
53. 1996 *El Gabilan*, 38.
54. 1996 *El Gabilan*, 71.
55. It is not possible to assess, from viewing the yearbooks, whether or to what extent girl and boy cross-country or track and field athletes had a different experience from athletes in entirely sex-segregated sports. Research by sociologist Michela Musto on a youth swim team that engaged in sex-integrated practices (and sex-segregated competitions) showed that the daily experiences of practicing together created a context in which mutual respect was more likely to develop. Boys, Musto (2014) observed, especially had the opportunity to see the hard work and skill of their girl teammates, sometimes losing to them in the pool, and gaining respect for them as athletes.
56. 1995 *El Gabilan*, 241.

57. See Atencio et al., 2018; Poulson, 2016.
58. Sociologists have explored various aspects of youth immersion in consumer culture. See Best, 2006; Milner Jr., 2006; and Wilkins, 2008.
59. It is not possible to determine all the causes of this shift, but the broader cultural context was also shifting in these ways, with TV shows like *Beverly Hills 90210* and networks like MTV focusing on social issues facing youth.
60. 1977 *El Gabilan*, 37.
61. 1978 *El Gabilan*.
62. 1981 *El Gabilan*, 67.
63. 1982 *El Gabilan*, 32.
64. Anthropologist Douglas Foley (1990) contributed an insightful analysis of the asymmetrical gender meanings of powderpuff football in his analysis of a Texas high school.
65. One can only imagine what the boys of color who are depicted in the background of this photo might have been thinking during this "slave auction." 1975 *El Gabilan*, 89.
66. 1977 *El Gabilan*, 88.
67. 1993 *El Gabilan*, 28.
68. 1998 *El Gabilan*, 32.
69. 1999 *El Gabilan*, 21.
70. 1986 *El Gabilan*, 90–91.
71. 1988 *El Gabilan*, 92–93.
72. 1991 *El Gabilan*, 163.
73. The wildly popular *Revenge of the Nerds* came out in 1984 and was followed by several sequels (1987, 1992, 1994). These films reflected a cultural sensibility that positioned male jocks and female cheerleaders as jerks, bullies, and entitled kids. The "revenge" in these films knocks these previously entitled kids off center and opens cultural space for nonathletic, working-class, "alternative," perhaps queer youth and kids of color.
74. Kurman, 1986, 57.
75. 1991 *El Gabilan*, 190–191.
76. 1984 *El Gabilan*, 90–91.
77. 1989 *El Gabilan*, 74.
78. For a discussion of this debate, see Grindstaff and West, 2006.
79. Adams and Bettis, 2003.
80. 1993 *El Gabilan*, 90.
81. 1994 *El Gabilan*, 55, 72.
82. "Girl power" narratives connected with sport and cheering, as we will see in the next chapter, deepened in the early 2000s amid a context of growing neoliberalism. Cooky, 2010.
83. As quoted in Adams and Bettis, 2003, 10.
84. 1999 *El Gabilan*, 167.
85. Grindstaff and West, 2006, 500.
86. Interview with Jon Scattini via Zoom, December 3, 2022.
87. Acosta and Carpenter, 2000.
88. A similar dynamic occurred, but in the opposite direction, when the previously "male" (and higher-status) occupation of clerical work was rapidly de-skilled and "feminized" during an early twentieth-century period of rapid industrialization and bureaucratization. See Reskin and Roos, 1990.
89. Messner, 2009.

90. Interview with Gary Affonso via Zoom, December 4, 2022.
91. Chappell also won many championships and was eventually elected to the Salinas Valley Sports Hall of Fame. "Inductees," Salinas Valley Sports Hall of Fame, accessed 2023, https://www.salinasvalleysportshalloffame.com/inductees.
92. 1995 *El Gabilan*, 188.
93. 1987 *El Gabilan*, 52.
94. 1988 *El Gabilan*, 76.
95. Women AYSO coaches and LLB/S managers bemoaned critical scrutiny from parents, other coaches and managers, and even from umpires—but rarely, if ever, from the kids. Messner, 2009. My colleagues and I analyzed "gender marking" in early 1990s televised sports coverage. Messner, Duncan, and Jensen, 1993.
96. I looked at team pictures and text for all the school's interscholastic varsity, JV, and freshman teams, counting as best I could how many teams had men and/or women coaches.
97. 1999 *El Gabilan*, 1.
98. 1999 *El Gabilan*, 230.
99. 1999 *El Gabilan*, 27.

Chapter 5 "Who Runs This World?"

1. The 2010s and early 2020s were a time of escalating activism by professional women athletes in soccer, tennis, and basketball as they pressed for pay equity and equal respect for their work. Sport studies scholars Cheryl Cooky and Dunja Antunovic (2022) argue that this very public feminist activism has helped to grow public support for women's sports. It is likely that this has had some trickle-down effect in building equity and respect for girls and women's sports in college, high school, and youth sports.
2. I spoke alongside feminist attorney and women's sports advocate Nancy Solomon at the 2002 hearings in San Diego, California. We summarized our observations and analysis in our 2007 article, "Social Justice and Men's Interests: The Case of Title IX."
3. Cooky, 2009.
4. Track and field, cross-country, and sometimes swim and dive teams combined boys and girls for practices and posed them together for team photos; they averaged about six pages of yearbook space per year during this time.
5. Beyonce's 2011 song was titled "Run the World (Girls)."
6. 2004 *El Gabilan*, 305.
7. The yearbook's blurb on Nina Oropoza closes by predicting, probably only half-jokingly, that she "will likely be United States President" (2006 *El Gabilan*, 277). A 2023 Google search revealed that Oropoza has indeed been professionally successful: a bachelor's degree from UC Berkeley, a master's from Harvard, teaching jobs near the U.S.-Mexico border and elsewhere, and a current position as a school principal.
8. Pascoe, 2023, 110. Pascoe adds that girls who carry race and class privilege tend to have greater access to the individually empowering aspects of "boss-girl feminism."
9. Natasha Quadlin's research (2018), for instance, should give us pause in assuming that girls' higher GPAs—and perhaps even the leadership skills they develop as "girl-bosses" in high school—necessarily translate into higher-paying and leadership positions in workplaces.
10. See, for instance, Morris and Perry, 2017; Ray, 2022.

11. Recent research points to the conclusion that girls' academic and leadership accomplishments in school may not always translate into college or post-school positions of leadership but can instead be a training ground for the sorts of juggling of service and caretaking tasks that women are expected to do in workplaces and in the home. See Armstrong and Hamilton, 2013; Ispa-Landa and Oliver, 2020; and Musto, 2019.
12. 2000 *El Gabilan*, 5.
13. 2001 *El Gabilan*, 2.
14. Onufer, 2009.
15. McKibben, 2022, 324.
16. McKibben, 2022, 325.
17. McKibben, 2022, 334.
18. McKibben, 2022, 341.
19. McKibben, 2022, 342; In her study of a Southern California high school, Gilda Ochoa (2013) concluded that the school's AVID program had mixed results in achieving its goals.
20. Galvez-Arango et al., 2018, 5.
21. As with past yearbooks, I inferred the race/ethnicity of graduating seniors from their surnames and senior portraits. I assume that most Spanish-surnamed students are of Mexican origin, though a few of them are likely Filipino/a, Central American, or another race/ethnicity. This is, of course, an imprecise way to categorize people by race/ethnicity. Far better are numbers that result from self-identification. This sort of data for Salinas High School is available school-wide for the most recent years.
22. Salinas High School, 2022–2023.
23. 2019 *El Gabilan*, 96.
24. Devine, 2024a; 2024b.
25. See Hextrum, 2021.
26. Interview with Art Hunsdorfer, September 9, 2023.
27. Undoubtedly some students participate in more than one sport, so the 1,070 count here is the number of positions on teams, not the number of students who play on teams.
28. Hextrum (2020) observes that many white and African American high schoolers view sports as a possible avenue to upward mobility, but African American students also experience sports as "a refuge from racist schooling systems."
29. Hextrum, 2021, 105.
30. A 2020 national study of youth sports participation rates found huge differences correlated with family income. Fifty percent of boys and 57 percent of girls from families that earned $49,999 or less annually reported never having played youth sports. In middle-income families ($50,000 to $99,999 annually), 32 percent of boys and 45 percent of girls had never participated. And only 24 percent of boys and 30 percent of girls from higher-income families had never played youth sports. Zarrett, Veliz, and Sabo, 2020. A 2017 National Survey of Children's Health found similar participation gaps. Kids of color had somewhat lower rates of sports participation than white kids. But the largest gaps were correlated with social class, with youth from families at or near the poverty line showing sports participation rates roughly half of those from higher-income families. U.S. Department of Health and Human Services, 2019. See also Tompsett and Knoester, 2022.
31. Hispanic and Black girls have lower youth sports participation rates than white girls and also lower rates than Hispanic and Black boys. Zarrett, Veliz, and Sabo, 2020, 13. Girls of color also have lower rates of participation in school sports. National Women's Law

Center, 2015. See also Goldsmith, 2003; Hextrum, Knoester, and Tompsett, 2024; and Pericak and Martinez, 2022.

32. A multibillion-dollar "youth sports industrial complex" has blossomed in recent decades, and parents who want their kids to compete at high levels pay thousands of dollars a year for coaching and travel team expenses. Gregory, 2017; Goldsmith and Abel, 2022, 1.
33. 2003 *El Gabilan*, 204.
34. 2018 *El Gabilan*, 80.
35. 2019 *El Gabilan*, 13.
36. National Federation of State High School Associations, 2023.
37. It is difficult here to do justice to Hextrum's sophisticated analysis of how "alignment" across secondary and college sports tends to benefit athletes from race- and class-privileged families and schools. Hextrum, 2021, see especially pages 76–79.
38. 2015 *El Gabilan*, 117–118.
39. Interview with Art Hunsdorfer, September 9, 2023.
40. 2017 *El Gabilan*, 89.
41. The sociologist Natasha Warikoo's research (2022) shows that in response to their children's falling behind Asian American students in traditional markers of academic success such as GPA and entrance exams like the SAT, some upper middle-class white parents have pressed school administrators to shift the criteria for their kids' success away from academic achievement, homework, and test scores and toward emphasizing extracurriculars, "balance," and sports.
42. Snellman, Silva, and Putnam, 2015, 194.
43. Jayakumar, Mazyck, and Page, 2021.
44. 2001 *El Gabilan*, 218.
45. Bachman, 2022.
46. This estimate is from my rough count from team photos in the 2023 *El Gabilan*.
47. Allison, 2018.
48. Informal race/gender interactions can have an inhibiting impact on Latina girls' school sports experiences. Lopez, 2019, 2021, 2023; McGovern 2021.
49. McDonagh and Pappano, 2008; Travers, 2008.
50. Travers, 2016.
51. 2002 *El Gabilan*, 224.
52. Musto, 2014.
53. Epperson added that she intended to become "a cadet in West Point's Class of 2014 and going on to serve as an officer in the Army." A Google search revealed that she did just that. 2010 *El Gabilan*, 245.
54. Email exchange with Art Hunsdorfer, October 18, 2023.
55. The debate about transgender women playing in women's sports illuminates the inherent tension in the structural divide in sports between two supposedly binary categories, men and women. The political right's recent mobilization to oppose transgender athletes playing on girls' or women's teams might be viewed as ironic, given their limited attention to supporting women's sports in the past, but it has been a successful culture wars wedge issue. But even some long-time feminist women's sports advocates like Nancy Hogshead-Makar have sought to defend the boundaries of women's sports by suggesting that trans women should only be allowed to compete in women's sports if they had undergone medical transitions before puberty; see Lord, 2022. Other feminists disagree, supporting trans

athletes as a human rights issue and advocating the blurring or elimination of binary sex divisions in sports; see Cooky, 2022; Jones and Travers, 2023; and Pape, 2022.

56. 2001 *El Gabilan*, 222.
57. 2007 *El Gabilan*, 111. As discussed in the previous chapter, researchers in the 1970s and 1980s noted that some girl and women athletes overemphasized signs of femininity like makeup and hairstyles to counter fears or "accusations" of masculinization or lesbianism. This "female apologetic" in women's sports has faded in recent years, but research reveals its stubborn persistence in some contexts. Musto and McGann, 2016.
58. 2009 *El Gabilan*, 134.
59. 2015 *El Gabilan*, 101.
60. 2018 *El Gabilan*, 74.
61. Images of girl wrestlers in recent yearbooks echo similar themes of bodily empowerment that Jennifer Hargreaves pointed to in her 1997 article on women boxers.
62. Theberge, 2000.
63. Theberge, 1989.
64. National Federation of State High School Associations, 2023.
65. 2003 *El Gabilan*, 118.
66. 2019 *El Gabilan*, 12.
67. 2020 *El Gabilan*, 10–11.
68. 2023 *El Gabilan*, 23.
69. Nelson, 1994.
70. Messner, 1988, 206.
71. 2003 *El Gabilan*, 25.
72. Educational economist Marguerite Roza shows that despite the stated goals of public high schools, many allocated "a much greater per pupil investment in sports and electives than in core subjects" (2010, 6).
73. Messner, 1992. See also Sabo and Runfola, 1980 and Sabo, 1994.
74. This poll showed also that opposition to their sons playing football was much higher among professional-class parents than among poor or working-class parents. Linskey, 2014. See also Anderson and Kian, 2012 and Peters, 2023.
75. The data also show that boys in more liberal "blue states" or regions are more likely to be leaving the game of tackle football, while boys who live in more conservative communities and "red states" are still playing the game at rates similar to the past. Sheinin and Giambalvo, 2023.
76. 2010 *El Gabilan*, 196.
77. 2011 *El Gabilan*, 142.
78. 2015 *El Gabilan*, 70.
79. 2019 *El Gabilan*, 37.
80. 2002 *El Gabilan*, 88.
81. 2008 *El Gabilan*, 53.
82. 2000 *El Gabilan*, 209.
83. 2001 *El Gabilan*, 182.
84. 2002 *El Gabilan*, 234.
85. 2006 *El Gabilan*, 126.
86. 2007 *El Gabilan*, 77.
87. 2010 *El Gabilan*, 97.

88. 2012 *El Gabilan*, 176.
89. 2013 *El Gabilan*, 72.
90. 2019 *El Gabilan*, 59.
91. Tolentino, 2020.
92. Adams and Bettis, 2003, 129.
93. National Federation of State High School Associations, 2023.
94. 2014 *El Gabilan*, 49.
95. Because I rely so much on what is (or is not) in yearbooks, I am unable to speculate how, or if at all, a growing number of girls of color are impacting cheer in new ways. Research by sociologist Chelsea Johnson (2015) suggests cheer at a historically Black women's college is shaped by racial identity in ways that make it distinct in some ways from cheer at predominantly white colleges.
96. 2019 *El Gabilan*, 109.
97. Devine, 2023.
98. In some years the yearbooks did not include some of the coaches in some of the team photos (spring sports were especially idiosyncratic in this way). And frequently the books did not delineate the head coach from the rest of the coaching staff, so it was not possible to tally an accurate count of head coaches versus assistant coaches.
99. Yearbook team photos do not always include pictures or names of all coaches. In school data reported for the 2023 California Census of Coaching, Salinas High fares a bit better than the 15 percent women coaches I counted in the yearbook. That year, Salinas High reported that 24.8 percent of the school's coaches were women. This proportion of women coaches placed Salinas High just slightly below the state average of 26.5 percent, and within the range of other high schools in the district: Everett Alvarez High (22.2 percent), North Salinas High (26.6 percent); Alisal High (30.2 percent), and Rancho San Juan High (34.3 percent). California Interscholastic Federation, 2023.
100. At the college level, data on coaches existed for many years due to the longitudinal study conducted by Acosta and Carpenter from 1977 to 2014, which found that 43.4 percent of women's teams were coached by females and 3.5 percent of men's teams were coached by females. In 2024 the Tucker Center took the baton on data collection. Following "a decade of stagnation," they reported in 2023 that the proportion of Division I college women's teams with women head coaches had ticked up to 46.0 percent.
101. California Interscholastic Federation, 2023.
102. Messner, 2009. See also Goorevich and LaVoi, 2024.
103. Messner and Bozada-Deas, 2009.
104. Cooky and Antunovic, 2022.
105. Zirin, 2021.
106. 2001 *El Gabilan*, 253. While the Fellowship of Christian Athletes tends to present as a Christian support system for a school's athletes, the cumulative impact of Christianity (especially in its evangelical forms) as a movement in public schools has been reflected in judicial decisions that have eroded the constitutional distinctions between church and state, such as the 2022 Supreme Court ruling that supported a high school football coach who had been fired for having his team kneel and pray at the fifty-yard line of the field. Howe, 2022.
107. 2010 *El Gabilan*, 183.
108. "My Strength is Not for Hurting," a national campaign to involve boys and men in gender-based violence prevention, was organized in California schools by the California Coalition Against Sexual Assault (CALCASA). Messner, Greenberg, and Peretz, 2015.

109. In *Some Men*, for instance, my coauthors and I profile former football players Jackson Katz and Donald McPherson, who have been leaders and organization builders for decades in the national effort to engage boys and men in preventing gender-based violence.
110. Violence is a problem in white middle- and upper-class families but tends to be less visible because privileged families have the resources to insulate themselves legally and have greater access to therapeutic and other extralegal interventions.
111. Most likely the "gay-straight" in the club's original name no longer seemed to fit for a younger generation who increasingly views LGBTQ+ identities as a spectrum, rather than binary gay or straight categories.
112. A notable example of athletes being at the center of a high school GSA club is told in the memoir of gay Southern California cross-country coach Eric Anderson, whose athletes rallied to support him as well as gay and non-gay athletes who were being harassed and bullied, often by members of the football team. Anderson, 2009. See also Knott-Fayle, Kehler, and Gough, 2023.
113. These correlations between the existence of GSA clubs and positive campus climate seem to be robust. But researchers also point to evidence that suggests that GSA clubs bring greater benefits for white students and fewer to students of color. And some research has questioned whether the improved campus environment might benefit cisgender heterosexual students more than it does LGBTQ+ students. Fetner et al., 2012; Baams and Russell, 2020.
114. 2007 *El Gabilan*, 38.
115. 2010 *El Gabilan*, 24.
116. See Pascoe, 2023 and Gordon, 2023.
117. 2009 *El Gabilan*, 35.
118. 2009 *El Gabilan*.
119. 2018 *El Gabilan*, 46–47
120. 2002 *El Gabilan*, 2, 35.
121. 2021 *El Gabilan*, 210.
122. McKibben, 2022, 325.
123. 2015 *El Gabilan*, 36.
124. 2003 *El Gabilan*, 182.
125. For a more theoretical analysis of the ways that our views of girls and women have changed, versus our still relatively unreconstructed views of boys and men, see Messner, 2011.

Conclusion

1. My late sister Melinda Messner-Rios lobbied for years, including with letters to the editor in the *Salinas Californian* newspaper, for the gym to be named after our father, Russ Messner. Realizing the naming would go to Joe Chappell, she retreated to the idea that the floor of Joe Chappell Gym might be named Messner Court. Years ago, I joked with Joe Chappell that to me, a basketball gym is akin to house of worship, and perhaps the new gym could be called "Messner Chappell." The SHS Athletic Boosters Club also gives an annual "Joseph L. Chappell Award" to a community member who provides outstanding support to the athletics program.
2. It is interesting too that Springer's honorary plaque lists her as having participated in "Track and Cheerleading," but I could not find her among the cheerleaders in the 1977, 1978, or 1979 yearbooks.

3. This photo and the boys' names are reproduced here with permission from their parents.
4. Constraining stereotypes are often still imposed on Latina girls, views that see them through a "gendered cultural" lens as passive and subordinate. Sport participation, especially in a sport like wrestling, directly subverts these limiting stereotypes. Lopez, 2023.
5. Cooky and Messner, 2018.
6. Cahn, 2015, 283.
7. Based on its exhaustive 2022 empirical study of the uneven impact of Title IX after fifty years, a Women's Sports Foundation report concluded that "not all girls and women . . . have benefitted from the legislation or been well-served by it," underlining that Asian, Black, Indigenous, Latinx and other girls and women of color participate in sport at lower levels, face greater barriers to participation, and are historically excluded in sport leadership. The report also notes continuing challenges facing LGBTQ+ and female athletes with disabilities. Staurowsky et al., 2022. See also Hextrum and Sethi, 2022.

Appendix

1. 1926 *El Gabilan*, 23.
2. 1968 *El Gabilan*, 246.
3. 1938 *El Gabilan*, 1.
4. NSPA, accessed 2022, https://studentpress.org/nspa/.
5. National Scholastic Press Association, 2013.
6. Poulson, 2021, 17.
7. Margolis, 1999. See also Montez de Oca and Prado, 2013.
8. Olsen, 1978.
9. These are the "early bird" prices; the prices rise if purchased later. This info is from the online "Yearbook Announcement" in fall 2023 at https://yearbookordercenter.com (accessed 2023).
10. Poulson, 2021, 16–17.
11. Mulvey, 1975.
12. I have long been fascinated with the work of Frigga Haug (1987), who along with a collective of German feminist women engaged in a project of recalling, telling, and analyzing personal stories of their own experiences with embodiment. The general takeaway from their project was that even in patriarchal contexts that, a priori, objectify girls' and women's bodies, actual girls and women find ways to creatively (and sometimes resistantly) assert their bodily subjectivity.
13. Berger, 1972, 9–10.
14. Sontag, 1973, 3, 15, 28.
15. I make use of Ibson's (2002, 2019) work in several places in this book.
16. Chappell, Chappell, and Margolis 2011, 56–57.
17. Grosvenor, 1999, 94–95.
18. Sontag, 1973, 109, 154.
19. Cahn, 2007, 224.
20. My thinking on this issue is influenced by Grafton Tanner's (2021) insightful book on nostalgia. See Biklin, 2007.

References

Acosta, R. Vivien, and Linda Jean Carpenter. 2000. *Women in Intercollegiate Sport: A Longitudinal Study—Twenty-Three Year Update*. Brooklyn, NY: Brooklyn College.

Acosta, R. Vivien, and Linda Jean Carpenter. 2014. *Women in Intercollegiate Sport. A Longitudinal, National Study, Thirty-Seven Year Update. 1977–2014*. Brooklyn, NY: Brooklyn College. www.acostacarpenter.org.

Adams, Natalie Guice, and Pamela J. Bettis. 2003. *Cheerleader! An American Icon*. New York: Palgrave Macmillan.

Allison, Rachel. 2018. *Kicking Center: Gender and the Selling of Women's Professional Soccer*. New Brunswick, NJ: Rutgers University Press.

Alpers, Benjamin L. 2024. *Happy Days: Images of the Pre-Sixties Past in Seventies America*. New Brunswick, NJ: Rutgers University Press.

Anderson, Eric 2009. *Trailblazing: The True Story of America's First Openly Gay High School Coach*. Los Angeles: Alyson Books.

Anderson, Eric, and Edward M. Kian. 2012. "Examining Media Contestation of Masculinity and Head Trauma in the National Football League." *Men & Masculinities* 1, no. 2: 152–173.

Armstrong, Elizabeth A., and Laura T. Hamilton. 2013. *Paying for the Party: How College Maintains Inequality*. Cambridge, MA: Harvard University Press.

Atencio, Matthew, Becky Beal, E. Missy Wright, and ZaNelan McClain. 2018. *Moving Boarders: Skateboarding and the Changing Landscape of Urban Youth Sports*. Fayetteville: University of Arkansas Press.

Baams, Laura, and Stephen T. Russell. 2020. "Gay-Straight Alliances, School Functioning, and Mental Health: Associations for Students of Color and LGBTQ Students." *Youth & Society* 53, no. 2: 211–229.

Bachman, Rachel. 2022. "Girls Are Leaving High School Basketball, and Here's Why." *Wall Street Journal*, September 20, 2022.

Barry, John M. 2005. *The Great Influenza: The Epic Story of the Deadliest Plague in History*. New York: Penguin Books.

Beckerman, Marty. 2000. *Death to All Cheerleaders*. Flat Rock, NC: Infected Press.

Bederman, Gail. 1996. *Manliness and Civilization: A Cultural History of Gender and Race in the United States, 1880–1917*. Chicago: University of Chicago Press.

Benson, Jackson J. 1990. *John Steinbeck, Writer: A Biography*. New York: Penguin Books.

Berger, John. 1972. *Ways of Seeing*. New York: Penguin Books.

Best, Amy L. 2000. *Prom Night: Youth, Schools, and Popular Culture*. New York: Routledge.

Best, Amy L. 2006. *Fast Cars, Cool Rides: The Accelerating World of Youth and Their Cars*. New York: NYU Press.

Biklin, Sari Knopp. 2007. "Trouble on Memory Lane: Adults and Self-Retrospection in Researching Youth." In *Representing Youth: Methodological Issues in Critical Youth Studies*, edited by Amy L. Best, 251–268. New York: NYU Press.

Blinde, E. M., and Taub, D. E. 1992. "Women Athletes as Falsely Accused Deviants: Managing the Lesbian Stigma." *Sociological Quarterly* 33, no. 4: 521–533.

Bowles, Samuel, and Herbert Gintis. 1976. *Schooling in Capitalist America: Educational Reform and the Contradictions of Economic Life*. New York: Basic Books.

Bowman, Karlyn, and Samantha Goldstein. 2023. *The Nostalgia Impulse: How Americans View the Past*. Washington, DC: American Enterprise Institute for Policy Research.

Brake, Deborah L. 2010. *Getting in the Game: Title IX and the Women's Sports Revolution*. New York: New York University Press.

Broad, K. L. 2001. "The Gendered Unapologetic: Queer Resistance in Women's Sport." *Sociology of Sport Journal* 18, no. 2: 181–204.

Bulman, Robert C. 2015. *Hollywood Goes to High School: Cinema, Schools, and American Culture*. New York: Worth Publishers.

Cahn, Susan. 1994. *Coming on Strong: Gender and Sexuality in Twentieth-Century Women's Sport*. New York: Free Press.

Cahn, Susan K. 2007. *Sexual Reckonings: Southern Girls in a Troubling Age*. Cambridge, MA: Harvard University Press.

Cahn, Susan. 2015. *Coming on Strong: Gender and Sexuality in Women's Sport*. 2nd ed. Urbana: University of Illinois Press.

California Interscholastic Federation. 2023. "2022–23 CIF Census Coaching Data." Accessed 2023. CIFSTATE.org.

Carrington, Ben. 2010. *Race, Sport and Politics: The Sporting Black Diaspora*. Newbury Park, CA: Sage Publications.

Chappell, Dre, Sharon Chappell, and Eric Margolis. 2011. "School as Ceremony and Ritual: How Photography Illuminates Performances of Ideological Transfer." *Qualitative Inquiry* 17, no. 1: 56–73.

Cooky, Cheryl. 2009. "'Girls Just Aren't Interested: The Social Construction of Interest in Girls' Sport." *Sociological Perspectives* 52, no. 2: 259–284.

Cooky, Cheryl. 2010. "Do Girls Rule? Understanding Popular Culture Images of 'Girl Power!' and Sport." In *Learning Culture Through Sports: Perspectives on Society and Organized Sports*, edited by S. Spickard Prettyman and B. Lampman, 210–226. Lanham, MD: Rowman & Littlefield.

Cooky, Cheryl. 2022. "Lia Thomas' Championship Gives Women's Sports a Crucial Opportunity." Think, NBC News, March 21, 2022. https://www.nbcnews.com/think/opinion/we-should-be-celebrating-lia-thomas-we-did-jackie-robinson-ncna1292521.

Cooky, Cheryl, and Dunja Antunovic. 2022. *Serving Equality: Feminism, Media, and Women's Sports*. New York: Peter Lang.

Cooky, Cheryl, and Michael A. Messner. 2018. *No Slam Dunk: Gender, Sport, and the Unevenness of Social Change*. New Brunswick, NJ: Rutgers University Press.

Coontz, Stephanie. 2016. *The Way We Never Were: American Families and the Nostalgia Trap*. New York: Basic Books.

Cooper, Joseph. 2021. *A Legacy of African-American Resistance and Activism through Sport*. New York: Peter Lang.

Crosset, Todd. 1990. "Masculinity, Sexuality and the Development of Early Modern Sport." In *Sport, Men and the Gender Order: Critical Feminist Perspectives*, edited by Michael A. Messner and Donald F. Sabo, 45–54. Champaign, IL: Human Kinetics Press.

Curtis, Henry S. 1904. "A Football Education." *American Physical Education Review* 9, no. 4: 1–7.

Davis, Laurel R. 1990. "Male Cheerleaders and the Naturalization of Gender." In *Sport, Men and the Gender Order: Critical Feminist Perspectives*, edited by Michael A. Messner and Donald F. Sabo, 153–161 Champaign, IL: Human Kinetics.

Davis, Mike, and Jon Wiener. 2020. *Set the Night on Fire: L.A. in the Sixties*. London: Verso.

Davis-Delano, Laurel R., A. Pollock, and J. E. Vose. 2009. Apologetic Behavior among Female Athletes: A New Questionnaire and Initial Results. *International Review for the Sociology of Sport* 44, no. 2–3: 131–150.

Deverell, William. 2004. *Whitewashed Adobe: The Rise of Los Angeles and the Remaking of Its Mexican Past*. Berkeley: University of California Press.

Devine, John. 2023. "High School Football Tour: Zenk In Glorified Company as Salinas Head Coach." *Monterey Herald*, August 17, 2023.

Devine, John. 2024a. "High School Softball: Salinas High's Marley Panziera Commits to UC Davis," *Monterey Herald*, June 26, 2024.

Devine, John. 2024b. "High School Volleyball: Moore Looking for One More Magical Moment Indoors." *Monterey Herald*, June 26, 2024.

Dewey, John. 1915. *Schools of To-morrow*. New York: E. P. Dutton & Company.

Dewey, John. (1916) 1944. *Democracy and Education*. New York: Free Press

Domina, Thurston, Andrew Penner, and Emily Penner. 2017. "Categorical Inequality: Schools as Sorting Machines." *Annual Review of Sociology* 43 (July): 311–330.

Downey, Douglas B. 2020. *How Schools Really Matter: Why Our Assumption about Schools and Inequality Is Mostly Wrong*. Chicago: University of Chicago Press.

Duberman, Martin Bauml. 1990. *Paul Robeson: A Biography*. New York: Ballentine Books.

DuBois, Ellen Carol. 1998. *Woman Suffrage and Women's Rights*. New York: New York University Press.

Duncan, Greg J., and Richard J. Murnane. 2011. "Introduction: The American Dream, Then and Now." In *Whither Opportunity? Rising Inequality, Schools, and Children's Life Chances*, edited by Greg J. Duncan and Richard J. Murnane, 3–26. New York and Chicago: Russell Sage Foundation and Spencer Foundation.

Duncan, Margaret Carlisle, and Cynthia A. Hasbrook. 1988. "Denial of Power in Televised Women's Sports." *Sociology of Sport Journal* 5, no. 1: 1–21.

Dunning, Eric. 1986. "Sport as a Male Preserve: Notes on the Social Sources of Masculine Identity and Its Transformation." *Theory, Culture & Society* 3, no. 1: 79–90.

Edwards, Harry. (1968) 2018. *The Revolt of the Black Athlete*. Chicago: University of Illinois Press.

Edwards, Harry. 1984. "The Collegiate Athletic Arms Race: Origins and Implications of the 'Rule 48' Controversy." *Journal of Sport and Social Issues* 8, no. 1: 4–22.

Eitzen, D. Stanley. 1999. *Fair and Foul: Beyond the Myths and Paradoxes of Sport*. Lanham, MD: Rowman & Littlefield.

Estes, Nick. 2019. *Our History Is the Future: Standing Rock versus the Dakota Access Pipeline, and the Long Tradition of Indigenous Resistance*. London: Verso.

Fass, Paula S. 1977. *The Damned and the Beautiful: American Youth in the 1920s*. New York: Oxford University Press.

Felshin, Jan. 1974. "The Dialectics of Women in Sport." In *The American Woman in Sport*, edited by E. Gerber. Reading, MA: Addison Wesley.

Fetner, Tina, A. Elafros, S. Bortolin, and C. Dretchsler. 2012. "Safe Spaces: Gay-Straight Alliances in High Schools." *Canadian Review of Sociology* 49, no. 2: 188–207.

Filene, Peter. 1975. *Him/Her/Self: Sex Roles in Modern America*. New York: Harcourt Brace Jovanovich.

Fletcher, Sheila. 1984. *Women First: The Female Tradition in English Physical Education, 1880–1980*. London: Athlone Press.

Flores, Lori A. 2016. *Grounds for Dreaming: Mexican Americans, Mexican Immigrants, and the California Farmworker Movement*. New Haven, CT: Yale University Press.

Foley, Douglas. 1990. "The Great American Football Ritual: Reproducing Race, Class, and Gender Inequality." *Sociology of Sport Journal* 7, no. 2: 111–134.

Freud, Sigmund. (1930) 1961. *Civilization and Its Discontents*. New York: W. W. Norton.

Fried, Richard M. 1998. *The Russians Are Coming, The Russians Are Coming: Pageantry and Patriotism in Cold War America*. New York: Oxford University Press.

Galvez-Arango, Hanna, Anpo Jensen, Arriana Jones, and Jasmin Martinez. 2018. "A Multifaceted Examination of Salinas, California: Final Report." Urban Studies 164: Sustainable Cities, December 12, 2018. Salinas Public Library. https://salinaspubliclibrary.org/sites/default/files/media_browser/external_documents/a_multifaceted_examination_of_salinas.pdf.

Garfinkel, H. 1956. "Conditions of Successful Degradation Ceremonies." *American Journal of Sociology* 61, no. 5: 420–424.

Gerstle, Gary. 2022. *The Rise and Fall of the Neoliberal Order: America and the World in the Free Market Era*. New York: Oxford University Press.

Gillman, Susan. 2022. *American Mediterraneans: A Study in Geography, History, and Race*. Chicago: University of Chicago Press.

Goldsmith, Pat Antonio. 2003. "Race Relations and Racial Patterns in School Sports Participation." *Sociology of Sport Journal* 20, no. 2: 141–171.

Goldsmith, Rubio, and Richard Abel. 2022. "The Dice Are Loaded: Schools' Social Class Composition and Athletic Contests." *Socius: Sociological Research for a Dynamic World* 8: 1–15.

Goorevich, Anna, and Nicole L. LaVoi. 2024. "Essentially Different or Equally the Same: Uncovering Sport Coach Discourses about Coaching Girls." *Sports Coaching Review*. https://doi.org/10.1080/21640629.2024.2309786.

Gordon, Hava Rachel. 2023. "When Kids 'Play' Politics: Gender Play and Young People's Activism." In *Gender Replay: On Kids, Schools, and Feminism*, edited by Freeden Blume Oeur and C. J. Pascoe, 242–258. New York: New York University Press.

Gregory, Sean. 2017. "How Kids' Sports Became a $15 Billion Industry." *Time*, August 24, 2017.

Grindstaff, Laura, and Emily West. 2006. "Cheerleading and the Gendered Politics of Sport." *Social Problems*, 53, no. 4: 500–518.

Grosvenor, Ian. 1999. "On Visualising Past Classrooms." In *Silence and Images: The Social History of the Classroom*, edited by Ian Grosvenor, Martin Lawn, and Kate Rousmaniere, 83–104. New York: Peter Lang.

Hagerman, Margaret A. 2018. *White Kids: Growing Up with Privilege in a Racially Divided America*. New York: New York University Press.

Hall, G. Stanley. 1905. *Adolescence: Its Psychology and Its Relations to Physiology, Anthropology, Sociology, Sex, Crime, Religion, and Education*. New York: Appleton.

Hall, G. Stanley. 1914. "Education and the Social Hygiene Movement." *Social Hygiene* 1: 29–35.

Hantover, Jeffrey. 1978. "The Boy Scouts and the Validation of Masculinity." *Journal of Social Issues* 34, no. 1: 184–195.

Hargreaves, Jennifer. 1994. *Sporting Females: Critical Issues in the History and Sociology of Women's Sports*. London: Routledge.

Hargreaves, Jennifer. 1997. "Women's Boxing and Related Activities: Introducing Images and Meanings." In *Boxer: An Anthology of Writings on Boxing and Visual Culture*, edited by David Chandler, John Gill, Tania Guha, and Gilane Tawadros, 212–231. London: Institute of International Visual Arts.

Hartmann, Douglas. 2004. *Race, Culture, and the Revolt of the Black Athlete: The 1968 Olympic Protests and Their Aftermath*. Chicago: University of Chicago Press.

Haug, Frigga 1987. *Female Sexualization: A Collective Work of Memory*. Verso Books.

Hextrum, Kirsten. 2020. "Socializing Sport: How Academic Exclusion and Athletic Inclusion Draw Black Youth to Sport." *Journal of Contemporary Athletics* 14, no. 4: 281–305.

Hextrum, Kirsten. 2021. *Special Admission: How College Sports Recruitment Favors White Suburban Athletes*. New Brunswick, NJ: Rutgers University Press.

Hextrum, Kirsten, Chris Knoester, and James Tompsett. 2024. "Inequalities in Girls' High School Sports Participation: How Social Class Race/Ethnicity, and Gender Route Opportunities to Play and Persist in Athletics." *Sociological Focus* 57, no. 2: 63–93. https://doi.org/10.1080/00380237.2024.2317480.

Hextrum, Kirsten, and Simran Sethi. 2022. "Title IX at 50: Legitimizing State Domination of Women's Sport." *International Review for the Sociology of Sport* 57, no. 5: 655–672.

Hoffman, Lynn M. 2002. "Why High Schools Don't Change: What Students and Their Yearbooks Tell Us." *High School Journal* 86, no. 2: 22–37.

Hogan, Laurence D., and Jules Tygiel. 2006. *Shades of Glory: The Negro Leagues and the Story of African-American Baseball*. Washington, DC: National Geographic.

Hout, Michael, and Alexander Janus. 2011. "Educational Mobility in the United States since the 1930s." In *Whither Opportunity? Rising Inequality, Schools, and Children's Life Chances*, edited by Greg J. Duncan and Richard J. Murnane, 165–186. New York and Chicago: Russell Sage Foundation and Spencer Foundation.

Howe, Amy. 2022. "Justices Side with High School Football Coach Who Prayed on the Field with Students." *ScotusBlog*, June 27, 2022. https://www.scotusblog.com/2022/06/justices-side-with-high-school-football-coach-who-prayed-on-the-field-with-students/#:~:text=The%20Supreme%20Court%20on%20Monday,protected%20by%20the%20First%20Amendment.

Huerta, Alvaro. 2019. "Reflections of a MEChista by a Chicano Scholar Activist." Latino Rebels, April 5, 2019. https://www.latinorebels.com/2019/04/05/reflectionsofamechista.

Ibson, John. 2002. *Picturing Men: A Century of Male Relationships in Everyday American Photography*. Washington, DC: Smithsonian Institution Press.

Ibson, John. 2007. "Picturing Boys: Found Photographs and the Transformation of Boyhood in the 1950s." *Thymos: Journal of Boyhood Studies* 1, no. 1: 68–83.

Ibson, John 2019. *The Mourning After: Loss and Longing Among Midcentury American Men*. Chicago: University of Chicago Press.

Inada, Lawson Fuseo. 2000. *Only What We Could Carry: The Japanese American Internment Experience*. Berkeley, CA: Heyday Books.

Ispa-Landa, Simone, and Mariana Oliver. 2020. "Hybrid Femininities: Sorority Rankings and Reputation." *Gender & Society* 34, no. 6: 893–921.

Jacobs, Sally H. 2023. *Althea: The Life of Tennis Champion Althea Gibson*. New York: St. Martin's Press.

Jayakumar, Uma Mazyck, and Scott E. Page. 2021. "Cultural Capital and Opportunities for Exceptionalism: Bias in University Admissions." *Journal of Higher Education* 92, no. 7: 1109–1139. https://www.tandfonline.com/doi/full/10.1080/00221546.2021.1912554.

Johnson, Chelsea Mary Elise. 2015. "'Just Because I Dance Like a Ho I'm Not a Ho': Cheerleading at the Intersection of Race, Class and Gender." *Sociology of Sport Journal* 32, no. 4: 377–394.

Jones, CJ, and Travers. 2023. "The Sports Issue: An Introduction." *Transgender Studies Quarterly* 10, no. 2: 93–99.

Kane, Mary Jo. 1995. "Resistance/Transformation of the Oppositional Binary: Exposing Sport as a Continuum." *Journal of Sport and Social Issues* 19, no. 2: 191–218.

Kidd, Bruce. 1990. "The Men's Cultural Centre: Sports and the Dynamic of Women's Oppression/Men's Repression." In *Sport, Men and The Gender Order: Critical Feminist Perspectives*, edited by Michael A. Messner and Donald F. Sabo, 31–44. Champaign, IL: Human Kinetics.

Kimmel, Michael S. 1987. "Men's Responses to Feminism at the Turn of the Century." *Gender & Society* 1, no. 3: 517–530.

King, C. Richard 2001. *Beyond the Cheers: Race as Spectacle in College Sport*. New York: State University of New York Press.

Knott-Fayle, Gabriel, Michael Kehler, and Brendan Gough. 2023. "Navigating Allyship: Straight and Queer Male Athletes' Accounts of Building Alliances." *NORMA: International Journal for Masculinity Studies* 19, no. 2: 80–95. https://doi.org/10.1080/18902138.2023.2277087.

Kurashige, Lon. 2000. "The Problem of Biculturalism: Japanese American Identity and Festival before World War II." *Journal of American History* 86, no. 4: 1632–1654.

Kurashige, Lon. 2002. *Japanese American Celebration and Conflict: A History of Ethnic Identity and Festival in Los Angeles, 1934–1990*. Berkeley: University of California Press.

Kurman, George. 1986. "What Does Girls' Cheerleading Communicate?" *Journal of Popular Culture* 20, no. 2: 57–64.

Labaree, David F. 1988. *The Making of an American High School: The Credentials Market and the Central High School of Philadelphia, 1838–1939*. New Haven, CT: Yale University Press.

Lansbury, Jennifer H. 2014. *A Spectacular Leap: Black Women Athletes in Twentieth-Century America*. Fayetteville: University of Arkansas Press.

Larned, Charles W. 1909. "Athletics from a Historical and Educational Standpoint." *American Physical Education Review* 14, no. 1: 1–9.

Lefkowitz-Horowitz, Helen. 1986. *Campus Life: Undergraduate Cultures from the End of the Eighteenth Century to the Present*. New York: Alfred A. Knopf.

Lenskyj, Helen. 1986. *Out of Bounds: Women, Sport, and Sexuality*. Toronto: Women's Press.

Lesko, Nancy. 2012. *Act Your Age! A Cultural Construction of Adolescence*. New York: Routledge.

Lewis, Amanda E., and John B. Diamond. 2015. *Despite the Best Intentions: How Racial Inequality Thrives in Good Schools*. New York: Oxford University Press.

Linskey, Annie 2014. "Half of Americans Don't Want Their Sons Playing Football, Poll Shows." *Bloomberg Politics*, December 10, 2014.

Lopez, Vera. 2019. "No Latina Girls Allowed: Gender-Based Teasing within School Sports and Physical Activity Contexts." *Youth & Society* 51, no. 3: 377–393.

Lopez, Vera. 2021. "The 'Othering' of Latina Girls in School Sports Contexts." *Journal of Adolescent Research*, 33, no. 1: 303–331.

Lopez, Vera. 2023. "Latina Teens and Sports Participation: Moving Beyond Gendered Cultural Explanations." In *Family and Sport*, edited by Steven M. Ortiz, 75–86. Vol. 19 of *Research in the Sociology of Sport*. Bingley, UK: Emerald Insight.

Lord, Craig. 2022. "Nancy Hogshead-Makar to Trans Champion Lia Thomas: 'Sports Not Based on Identity but Biology . . . Advantages of Male Puberty Cannot Be Rolled Back.'" *SOS: News and Views on the State of Swimming*, June 6, 2022.

Manno, Michelle J. 2023. *Denied: Women, Sports, and the Contradictions of Identity*. New York: New York University Press.

Margolis, Eric. 1999. "Class Pictures: Representations of Race, Gender and Ability in a Century of School Photography." *Visual Sociology* 14, no. 1: 1, 7–38.

McDonagh, Eileen, and Laura Pappano. 2008. *Playing with the Boys: Why Separate Is Not Equal in Sports*. New York: Oxford University Press.

McGovern, Jen. 2021. "The Intersection of Class, Race, Gender and Generation in Shaping Latinas' Sport Experiences." *Sociological Spectrum* 41, no. 1: 96–114.

McKibben, Carol Lynn. 2012. *Racial Beachhead: Diversity and Democracy in a Military Town*. Stanford, CA: Stanford University Press.

McKibben, Carol Lynn. 2022. *Salinas: A History of Race and Resilience in an Agricultural City*. Stanford, CA: Stanford University Press.

McWilliams, Carey. (1939) 1999. *Factories in the Field: The Story of Migratory Farm Labor in California*. Berkeley: University of California Press.

McWilliams, Carey. 1944. *Prejudice: Japanese-Americans, Symbol of Racial Intolerance*. Boston: Little, Brown.

McWilliams, Carey. (1948) 1968. *North from Mexico: The Spanish-Speaking People of the United States*. New York: Greenwood Press.

Messner, Michael. 1988. "Sports and Male Domination: The Female Athlete as Contested Ideological Terrain." *Sociology of Sport Journal* 5, no. 3: 197–211.

Messner, Michael A. 1992. *Power at Play: Sports and the Problem of Masculinity*. Boston: Beacon Press.

Messner, Michael A. 1994. "The Fall of Patriarchy in *The Winter of Our Discontent*." *Masculinities* 2: 1–9.

Messner, Michael A. 2002. *Taking the Field: Women, Men, and Sports*. Minneapolis: University of Minnesota Press.

Messner, Michael A. 2009. *It's All for the Kids: Gender, Families and Youth Sports*. Berkeley: University of California Press.

Messner, Michael A. 2011. "Gender Ideologies, Youth Sports, and the Production of Soft Essentialism." *Sociology of Sport Journal* 28: 151–170.

Messner, Michael A. 2019. *Guys Like Me: Five Wars, Five Veterans for Peace*. New Brunswick, NJ: Rutgers University Press.

Messner, Michael A., and Suzel Bozada-Deas. 2009. "Separating the Men from the Moms: The Making of Adult Sex Segregation in Youth Sports." *Gender & Society* 23, no. 1: 49–71.

Messner, Michael A., Margaret Carlisle Duncan, and Kerry Jensen. 1993. "Separating the Men from the Girls: The Gendered Language of Televised Sports." *Gender & Society* 7, no. 1: 121–137.

Messner, Michael A., Max A. Greenberg, and Tal Peretz. 2015. *Some Men: Feminist Allies and the Movement to End Violence against Women*. New York: Oxford University Press.

Messner, Michael A., and Nancy M. Solomon. 2007. "Social Justice and Men's Interests: The Case of Title IX." *Journal of Sport and Social Issues* 31, no. 2: 162–178.

Milkman, Ruth. 1987. *Gender at Work: The Dynamics of Job Segregation by Sex during World War II*. Champaign: University of Illinois Press.

Miller, Arthur. 1949. *Death of a Salesman*. New York: Viking Press.

Miller, Kathleen, Merrill Melnick, Grace Barnes, Michael Farrell, and Don Sabo. 2005. "Untangling the Links among Athletic Involvement, Gender, Race, and Adolescent Academic Outcomes." *Sociology of Sport Journal* 22, no. 2: 178–193.

Miller, Kathleen, Don Sabo, Michael Farrell, Grace Barnes, and Merrill Melnick. 1999. "Sports, Sexual Activity, Contraceptive Use, and Pregnancy among Female and Male High School Students: Testing Cultural Resource Theory." *Sociology of Sport Journal* 16, no. 4: 366–387.

Milner, Murray, Jr. 2006. *Freaks, Geeks, and Cool Kids: Teenagers in an Era of Consumerism, Standardized Tests, and Social Media*. 2nd ed. London: Routledge.

Montez de Oca, Jeffrey. 2005. "As Our Muscles Get Softer, Our Missile Race Becomes Harder": Cultural Citizenship and the 'Muscle Gap.'" *Journal of Historical Sociology* 18, no. 3: 145–171.

Montez de Oca, Jeffrey. 2013. *Discipline and Indulgence: College Football, Media, and the American Way of Life during the Cold War*. New Brunswick, NJ: Rutgers University Press.

Montez de Oca, Jeffrey, and Jose Prado. 2013. "Visualizing Humanitarian Colonialism: Photographs from the Thomas Indian School." *American Behavioral Scientist* 58, no. 1: 145–170.

Morris, E. W., and B. L. Perry. 2017. "Girls Behaving Badly? Race, Gender, and Subjective Evaluation in the Discipline of African American Girls." *Sociology of Education* 90, no. 2: 127–148.

Mrozek, D. J. 1983. *Sport and the American Mentality, 1880–1910*. Knoxville: University of Tennessee Press.

Mulvey, Laura. 1975. "Visual Pleasure and Narrative Cinema." *Screen* 16, no. 3: 6–18.

Musto, Michela. 2014. "Athletes in the Pool, Girls and Boys on Deck: The Contextual Construction of Gender in Co-ed Youth Swimming." *Gender & Society* 28, no. 3: 359–380.

Musto, Michela. 2019. "Brilliant or Bad: The Gendered Social Construction of Exceptionalism in Early Adolescence." *American Sociological Review* 84, no. 3: 369–393.

Musto, Michela, and P. J. McGann 2016. "Strike a Pose: The Femininity Effect in Collegiate Women's Sport." *Sociology of Sport Journal* 33, no. 2: 101–112.

Nathan, Daniel A., ed. 2013. *Rooting for the Home Team: Sport, Community, and Identity*. Urbana, IL: University of Chicago Press.

National Federation of State High School Associations. 2023. *High School Athletics Participation Survey*. Accessed 2023. https://www.nfhs.org/media/7212351/2022-23_participation_survey.pdf.

National Scholastic Press Association. 2013. *NSPA Yearbook Guidebook*. Minneapolis, MN: NSPA.

National Women's Law Center. 2001. "The Battle for Gender Equity in Athletics in Elementary and Secondary Schools." http://www.nwlc.org.

National Women's Law Center. 2015. *Finishing Last: Girls of Color and School Sports Opportunities.* Washington, DC: National Women's Law Center.

Nelson, Mariah Burton. 1994. *The Stronger Women Get, the More Men Love Football.* New York: Harcourt, Brace & Co.

Ochoa, Gilda. 2013. *Academic Profiling: Latinos, Asian Americans, and the Achievement Gap.* Minneapolis: University of Minnesota Press.

Olsen, Tillie. 1978. *Silences.* New York: Feminist Press.

Onufer, Tracy L. 2009. "Understanding Environmental Factors That Affect Violence in Salinas, California." Master's thesis, Naval Postgraduate School, https://hdl.handle.net/10945/4466.

Ortner, Sherry B. 2003. *New Jersey Dreaming: Capital, Culture, and the Class of '58.* Durham, NC: Duke University Press.

Orwell, George. 1945. *Animal Farm, A Fairy Story.* London: Secker & Warburg.

Pape, Madeleine. 2022. "Something Old, Something New: Biofeminist Resistance to Trans Inclusion in Sport." In *Justice for Trans Athletes: Challenges and Struggles,* edited by Helen Lenskyj and Ali Durham Greey, 95–108. Bingley, UK: Emerald.

Park, Roberta J. 1984. "From Football to Rugby—and Back, 1906–1919: The University of California-Stanford Response to the 'Football Crisis of 1905.'" *Journal of Sport History* 11, no. 3: 5–40.

Pascoe, C. J. 2023. *Nice Is Not Enough: Inequality and the Limits of Kindness at American High.* Oakland: University of California Press.

Pericak, Kaitlin, and Brandon P. Martinez. 2022. "How Systemic Racism Shapes Access to Interscholastic Sports and Why It Matters." *Sociological Focus* 55, no. 3: 271–284.

Peters, Sam. 2023. *Concussed: Sport's Uncomfortable Truth.* London: Atlantic Books.

Poulson, Stephen C. 2016. *Why Would Anyone Do That? Lifestyle Sport in the Twenty-First Century.* New Brunswick, NJ: Rutgers University Press.

Poulson, Stephen C. 2021. *Racism on Campus: A Visual History of Prominent Virginia Colleges and Howard University.* London: Routledge.

Poulson, Stephen C., Hailey S. McGee, and Tyler J. Wolfe. 2020. "Racism on Campus: Yearbook Pictures from Prominent Virginia Colleges (1890–1930)." *Contexts* 19, no. 4: 56–61.

Pruter, Robert. 2013. *The Rise of American High School Sports and the Search for Control.* Syracuse, NY: Syracuse University Press.

Quadlin, Natasha. 2018. "The Mark of a Woman's Record: Gender and Academic Performance in Hiring." *American Sociological Review* 83, no. 2: 331–360.

Rancano, Vanessa. 2018. "How Proposition 13 Transformed Neighborhood Public Schools throughout California." KQED.org, October 25, 2018. https://www.kqed.org/news/11701044/how-proposition-13-transformed-neighborhood-public-schools-throughout-california.

Ray, Ranita. 2022. "School as a Hostile Institution: How Black and Immigrant Girls of Color Experience the Classroom." *Gender & Society* 36, no. 1: 88–111.

Reskin, Barbara F., and Patricia A. Roos. 1990. *Job Queues, Gender Queues: Explaining Women's Inroads into Male Occupations.* Philadelphia: Temple University Press.

Ring, Jennifer. 2013. *Stolen Bases: Why American Girls Don't Play Baseball.* Champaign: University of Illinois Press.

Ross, Becki L., and Erin Bentley. 2003. "Gold-Plated Footballs and Orchids for Girls, A 'Palace of Sweat' for Men." In *Bodies in the Gymnasium: Memory, Monument and Modernism,* edited by Patricia A. Vertinsky and Sherry McKay, 99–116. London: Routledge.

Roza, Marguerite. 2010. *Educational Economics: Where Do School Funds Go?* Washington, DC: The Urban Institute Press.

Sabo, Don. 1994. "Pigskin, Patriarchy, and Pain." In *Sex, Violence and Power in Sports: Rethinking Masculinity*, edited by Michael A. Messner and Donald F. Sabo, 82–88. Freedom, CA: Crossing Press.

Sabo, Donald F., and Joe Panepinto. 1990. "Football Ritual and the Social Reproduction of Masculinity." In *Sport, Men and the Gender Order: Critical Feminist Perspectives*, edited by Michael A. Messner and Donald F. Sabo, 115–126. Champaign, IL: Human Kinetics Press.

Sabo, Donald F., and Ross Runfola. 1980. *Jock: Sports and Male Identity*. Englewood Cliffs, NJ: Prentice Hall.

Sabo, Donald F., and Phil Veliz. 2008. *Youth Sport in America*. East Meadow, NY: Women's Sports Foundation.

Salinas High School. 2022–2023. *School Plan for Student Achievement (SPSA) Template*. Salinas Union High School District, accessed 2024. https://www.salinasuhsd.org/Page/669.

Sheinin, Dave, and Emily Giambalvo. 2023. "The Changing Face of American's Favorite Sport." *Washington Post*, December 18, 2023.

Smith, Earl. 2007. *Race, Sport and the American Dream*. Durham, NC: Carolina Academic Press.

Smith-Rosenberg, Carroll. 1986. *Disorderly Conduct: Visions of Gender in Victorian America*. New York: Oxford University Press.

Snellman, Kaisa, Jennifer M. Silva, and Robert D. Putnam. 2015. "The Engagement Gap: Social Mobility and Extracurricular Participation among American Youth." *Annals of the American Academy of Political and Social Science* 657, no. 1: 194–207.

Sontag, Susan. 1973. *On Photography*. New York: Doubleday.

Stansell, Christine. 2011. *The Feminist Promise: From 1792 to the Present*. New York: Random House.

Staurowsky, E. J., C. L. Flowers, E. Busuvis, L. Darvin, and N. Welch. 2022. *50 Years of Title IX: We're Not Done Yet*. New York: Women's Sports Foundation.

Steinbeck, Elaine, and Robert Wallsten, eds. 1975. *Steinbeck: A Life in Letters*. New York: Penguin.

Steinbeck, John. 1936a. "Dubious Battle in California." *The Nation*, September 12, 1936, 302.

Steinbeck, John. 1936b. *In Dubious Battle*. New York: P.F. Collier & Son.

Steinbeck, John. (1936) 1988. *The Harvest of Gypsies: On the Road to Grapes of Wrath*. Berkeley, CA: Heyday.

Steinbeck, John. (1939) 1978. *The Grapes of Wrath*. New York: Penguin.

Steinbeck, John. 1952. *East of Eden*. New York: Viking Press.

Steinbeck, John. 1961. *The Winter of Our Discontent*. New York: Viking Press.

Strain, Christopher B. 2016. *The Long Sixties: America, 1955–1973*. Hoboken, NJ: Wiley-Blackwell.

Suggs, Welch. 2005. *A Place on the Team: The Triumph and Tragedy of Title IX*. Princeton, NJ: Princeton University Press.

Tanner, Grafton. 2021. *The Hours Have Lost Their Clock: The Politics of Nostalgia*. New York: Random House.

Theberge, Nancy. 1989. "Women Athletes and the Myth of Female Frailty." In *Women: A Feminist Perspective*, 4th ed., edited by Jo Freeman, 507–522. Mountain View, CA: Mayfield.

Theberge, Nancy. 1993. "The Construction of Gender in Sport: Women, Coaching, and the Naturalization of Difference." *Social Problems* 40, no. 3: 301–313.

Theberge, Nancy. 2000. *Higher Goals: Women's Ice Hockey and the Politics of Gender*. Albany: State University of New York Press.

Thorne, Barrie. 1993. *Gender Play: Girls and Boys in School*. New Brunswick, NJ: Rutgers University Press.

Tolentino, Jia. 2020. "The Pathos of 'Cheer' and Wild Deceptions of Cheerleading," *New Yorker*, January 16, 2020.

Tompsett, James, and Christ Knoester. 2022. "The Making of a College Athlete: High School Experiences, Socioeconomic Advantages, and the Likelihood of Playing College Sports." *Sociology of Sport Journal* 39, no. 2: 129–140.

Travers. 2008. "The Sport Nexus and Gender Injustice." *Studies in Social Justice Journal* 2, no. 1: 79–101.

Travers. 2016. "Transgender and Gender-Nonconforming Kids and the Binary Requirements of Sport Participation in North America." In *Child's Play: Sport in Kids' Worlds*, edited by Michael A. Messner and Michela Musto, 179–201. New Brunswick, NJ: Rutgers University Press.

Travers. 2018. *The Trans Generation: How Trans Kids (and Their Parents) Are Creating a Gender Revolution*. New York: New York University Press.

Tucker Center for Research on Girls and Women in Sport. 2023. "A New Era: The Women in College Coaching Report Card: Year 11." Minneapolis: University of Minnesota Press.

Twin, Stephanie. 1979. *Out of the Bleachers: Writings on Women and Sport*. Old Westbury, NY: Feminist Press.

Tyack, David B. 1974. *The One Best System: A History of American Urban Education*. Cambridge, MA: Harvard University Press.

Tye, Blanche Chin Ah. 2015. *Full of Gold: Growing Up in Salinas Chinatown Living in Post War America*. North Charleston, SC: CreateSpace Independent Publishing Platform.

Tygiel, Jules. 2008. *Baseball's Great Experiment: Jackie Robinson and His Legacy*. New York: Oxford University Press.

U.S. Department of Health and Human Services. 2019. *National Youth Sports Strategy*. Washington, DC: U.S. Department of Health and Human Services.

Verbrugge, Martha B. 2012. *Active Bodies: A History of Women's Physical Education in 20th-Century America*. Oxford: Oxford University Press.

Vertinsky, Patricia A. 2015. "Reconsidering the Female Tradition in British Physical Education: The Impact of Transnational Exchanges in Modern Dance." *International Journal of the History of Sport* 32, no. 4: 535–550.

Vertinsky, Patricia A. 2018. "Requiem for the College Women's Gymnasium: Disciplining the Female Body in Educational and Architectural Space." *International Journal of the History of Sport* 34, no. 14: 1453–1467.

Vertinsky, Patricia A., and Sherry McKay, eds. 2003. *Bodies in the Gymnasium: Memory, Monument and Modernism*. London: Routledge.

Warikoo, Natashia. 2022. *Race at the Top: Asian Americans and Whites in Pursuit of the American Dream in Suburban Schools*. Chicago: University of Chicago Press.

Watterson, John S. 2000. *College Football: History-Spectacle-Controversy*. Baltimore: Johns Hopkins University Press.

Whitson, David. 1990. "Sport in the Social Construction of Masculinity." In *Sport, Men and the Gender Order: Critical Feminist Perspectives*, edited by Michael A. Messner and Donald F. Sabo, 19–30. Champaign, IL: Human Kinetics Press.

Wilkins, Amy C. 2008. *Wannabes, Goths and Christians: The Boundaries of Sex, Style, and Status*. Chicago: University of Chicago Press.

Williams, Christine L. 1992. "The Glass Escalator: Hidden Advantages for Men in 'Female' Professions." *Social Problems* 39, no. 3: 253–267.

Willms, Nicole. 2017. *When Women Rule the Court: Gender, Race and Japanese-American Basketball*. New Brunswick, NJ: Rutgers University Press.

Wilson, William Julius. 1990. *The Truly Disadvantaged: The Inner City, the Underclass, and Public Policy*. Chicago: University of Chicago Press.

Women's Sports Foundation 2022. "Benefits—Why Sports Participation for Girls and Women." Accessed 2022. https://www.womenssportsfoundation.org/wp-content/uploads/2016/08/benefits-why-sports-participation-for-girls-and-women-the-foundation-position.pdf.

Woolf, Virginia. 1929. *A Room of One's Own*. London: Hogarth Press.

Wughalter, Emily. 1978. "Ruffles and Flounces: The Apologetic in Women's Sports." *Frontiers: A Journal of Women's Studies* 3, no. 1: 11–13.

Young, Iris M. 1980. "Throwing Like a Girl: A Phenomenology of Feminine Body Comportment, Motility, and Spatiality." *Human Studies* 3: 137–156.

Zarrett, N., P. T. Veliz, and D. Sabo. 2020. *Keeping Girls in the Game: Factors That Influence Sport Participation*. New York: Women's Sports Foundation.

Zinn, Howard. 1995. *People's History of the United States, 1492–Present*. New York: HarpPeren.

Zirin, Dave. 2021. *The Kaepernick Effect: Taking a Knee, Changing the World*. New York: New Press.

Index

About the Author

MICHAEL A. MESSNER, born and raised in Salinas, California, is professor emeritus of sociology and gender studies at the University of Southern California. His work spans the topics of gender and sport, men and feminism, gender-based violence, and war and peace. *The High School* is his twentieth book. Messner has been honored with the Jessie Bernard Award from the American Sociological Association and the Pursuit of Justice Award from the California Women's Law Center for his advocacy for girls and women in sports. He lives with his wife, Pierrette Hondagneu-Sotelo, in Santa Fe, New Mexico. http://www.michaelmessner.org/.

AVAILABLE TITLES IN THE CRITICAL ISSUES IN SPORT AND SOCIETY SERIES:

Rachel Allison, *Kicking Center: Gender and the Selling of Women's Professional Soccer*
Jules Boykoff, *Activism and the Olympics: Dissent at the Games in Vancouver and London*
Diana Tracy Cohen, *Iron Dads: Managing Family, Work, and Endurance Sport Identities*
Cheryl Cooky and Michael A. Messner, *No Slam Dunk: Gender, Sport, and the Unevenness of Social Change*
Joseph N. Cooper, *Black Sporting Resistance: Diaspora, Transnationalism, and Internationalism*
Andrew M. Guest, *Soccer in Mind: A Thinking Fan's Guide to the Global Game*
Jennifer Guiliano, *Indian Spectacle: College Mascots and the Anxiety of Modern America*
Kathryn E. Henne, *Testing for Athlete Citizenship: Regulating Doping and Sex in Sport*
Jeffrey L. Kidder, *Parkour and the City: Risk, Masculinity, and Meaning in a Postmodern Sport*
Alan Klein, *Lakota Hoops: Life and Basketball on Pine Ridge Indian Reservation*
Michael A. Messner, *The High School: Sports, Spirit, and Citizens, 1903–2024*
Michael A. Messner and Michela Musto, eds., *Child's Play: Sport in Kids' Worlds*
Jeffrey Montez de Oca, *Discipline and Indulgence: College Football, Media, and the American Way of Life during the Cold War*
Joshua I. Newman, Holly Thorpe, and David L. Andrews, eds., *Sport, Physical Culture, and the Moving Body: Materialisms, Technologies, Ecologies*
Stephen C. Poulson, *Why Would Anyone Do That? Lifestyle Sport in the Twenty-First Century*
Aarti Ratna, *A Nation of Family and Friends? Sport and the Leisure Cultures of British Asian Girls and Women*
Courtney Szto, *Changing on the Fly: Hockey through the Voices of South Asian Canadians*
Nicole Willms, *When Women Rule the Court: Gender, Race, and Japanese American Basketball*